W9-BAD-703

JIMMY STEWART
BOMBER PILOT

Colonel Jimmy Stewart

JIMMY STEWART
BOMBER PILOT

STARR SMITH
FOREWORD BY WALTER CRONKITE

Original hardcover Zenith Press edition published in 2005. Softcover edition published in 2006 by Zenith Press, an imprint of MBI Publishing Company, Galtier Plaza, Suite 200, 380 Jackson Street, St. Paul, MN 55101-3885 USA

© Starr Smith, 2005

All rights reserved. With the exception of quoting brief passages for the purposes of review, no part of this publication may be reproduced without prior written permission from the Publisher.

Zenith Press titles are also available at discounts in bulk quantity for industrial or sales-promotional use. For details write to Special Sales Manager at MBI Publishing Company, Galtier Plaza, Suite 200, 380 Jackson Street, St. Paul, MN 55101-3885 USA.

Library of Congress Cataloging-in-Publication Data

Smith, Starr
    Jimmy Stewart, Bomber Pilot / by Starr Smith
    p. cm.
    Includes bibliographical references.
    ISBN-13: 978-0-7603-2824-8
    ISBN-10: 0-7603- 2824-2
        1. Stewart James, 1908—2. United States. Army Air Forces. Air Force, 8th—Biography. 3. World War, 1939–1945—Aerial operations, American. 4. World War, 1939–1945—Campaigns—Western Front. 5. Bomber pilots—United States—Biography. 6. Motion picture actors and actresses—United States—Biography. I. Title

    D790.228th .S65 2005
    940.54'4973'092—dc22
    [B]

Designed by Mandy Iverson

Printed in the United States of America

In memory of two members of my family, now deceased, who served as flying officers in the Army Air Corps/United States Air Force in World War II and beyond: My brother, Colonel James W. Smith, who was on active duty for more than thirty years, and my brother-in-law, First Lieutenant Chandler "Chuck" Clover, who flew B-24 Liberators in the Pacific in World War II. And to my colleagues—the Liberator combat crewmen of the Eighth Air Force in the ETO in World War II.

ᏚᏙᏚ

"Jimmy Stewart was that rare public man who performed his duty without calling attention to himself. Stewart has found his biographer in Starr Smith, a man who knew Stewart, who knew the World War II Army Air Corps, and who surely knows how to write."

—Wayne Flynt, professor of history, Auburn University

"This is an excellent biography of a distinguished airman and fine human being, not a Hollywood star in uniform but a dedicated officer whose primary interest was the campaign of the Eighth Air Force. It is the work of a very accomplished writer, one who really knows his craft. When you turn the last page, you cannot but have a clear understanding of Jimmy Stewart's character."

—Roger A. Freeman, air power historian and author, *The Mighty Eighth*

"Several senior-officer mentors, recognizing Stewart's competence as more than merely respectable, secured him combat assignments when Hollywood and the air force would probably rather have kept him making training films . . . Smith dishes no dirt, possibly because, like other Stewart limners before him, he found none to dish."

—American Library Association, *Booklist*

CONTENTS

FOREWORD

We met—Jimmy Stewart and I—in an atmosphere as far removed from Hollywood's make-believe as it was possible to imagine. It was in Britain during World War II on an American Liberator bomber base. Both of us were there on business. I was a war correspondent. Jimmy was a squadron commander in the 445th Bombardment Group, assigned—as were the rest of the U.S. Eighth Air Force and Royal Air Force's entire heavy bomber fleet—to bomb Nazi Germany to its knees.

Captain Stewart had been on duty in England for a few weeks before the word leaked out that this famous movie star was in such perilous action as flying bombers against the enemy. The word was probably spilled in one of the G.I. bars, perhaps a Red Cross club, by one of Stewart's enlisted men on weekend leave in London.

When I applied to visit Stewart's group, Eighth Air Force Headquarters pretended no knowledge that he was in the British Isles, let alone flying missions and commanding aircrews.

The denial stories didn't hold up for long—but an instantly imposed ban against any press visits to Stewart's base proved harder to break. We correspondents covering the air war finally broke the ban by appealing to the same modest, unselfish motivation that had caused Stewart to impose the press blackout in the first place. We simply pointed out that the courage under fire, heroics, and daring exploits of bringing crippled bombers back to base by his combat crews were not making their hometown newspapers as was the case with all the rest of the Eighth Air Force.

I heard later that Stewart was crushed when he was made to realize how his closed gates had denied the press access to his own aircrews.

But Stewart's modesty remained undaunted. He opened his base to the press, and ordered that he was not available to meet the press in an interview. He yielded just a little bit on this with one or two of us, not to submit to an interview but for an occasional informal chat with a stern warning that his remarks were not for publication.

I have met a few movie stars and I've found many of them in real life not to be so different as themselves in reel life, but of them all, I think that Jimmy Stewart was most like those modest heroes he portrayed. The occasional times after the war when we met at small parties, he seemed to enjoy our short chats, and the war was mentioned only when he or I inquired of mutual friends with whom one or the other of us had lost touch.

Now journalist Starr Smith—wartime Eighth Air Force intelligence officer who worked with Jimmy Stewart briefing the combat crews for their daring daylight raids on German targets—has raised the curtain on Stewart's gallant service as a bomber pilot and air combat commander in World War II. It's a true story of personal knowledge, with sharp insight, and told with skill, respect, and admiration.

—Walter Cronkite
New York City
November 2004

Walter Cronkite in his war correspondent uniform in England in World War II while covering the Eighth Air Force.

A DAUGHTER'S TRIBUTE

Left to right, Judy, Kelly, Jimmy, and Gloria Stewart in 1988.

My father's experiences during World War II affected him more deeply and permanently than anything else in his life. Yet his children grew up knowing almost nothing about those years. Dad never talked about the war. My siblings and I knew only that he had been a pilot, and that he had won some medals, but that he didn't see himself as a hero. He saw only that he had done his duty.

Starr Smith's book has opened a door for me into this part of my father's life. Mr. Smith conveys with great skill what it meant to fly in the Eighth Air Force during the war; to be Operations Officer of a Bomb Group; what was involved, for example, in the planning and execution of missions. Above all, Mr. Smith, who worked with my father during that time, shows us what he was like as an individual in this role of pilot and leader. I know the war held terrible memories for my father, as it must for anyone who lived through the combat. But he was also deeply proud to have served his country. He would feel honored by this book.

—Kelly Stewart Harcourt
University of California, Davis

INTRODUCTION

On a bright, crisp day in early fall 1945, the majestic *Queen Elizabeth* arrived at Pier 50 in New York City after a danger-free voyage from Europe. Aboard was Colonel Jimmy Stewart, the renowned Hollywood movie star, and, now, the commander of the Second Combat Wing of the famous Eighth Air Force. Along with Stewart and his troops on the *Queen Elizabeth* that day were soldiers, sailors, and airmen returning to America after their victorious battles in the European Theater of Operations (ETO). Although they had no way of knowing it—and no inclination to think about it on that joyful day in New York—for millions of Americans who served their country, World War II would be the primal point, the defining years of their lives. Time would be measured, friendships and dates remembered, events and experiences recalled—all based on "before the war," "during the war," "after the war," and "the war years." Jimmy Stewart was no different. Jonathan Coe, author of *Jimmy Stewart: A Wonderful Life*, wrote: "Almost fifty years later, he would tell an interviewer that his military experience was something he thought about every day and said it was one of the great experiences of his life. In response to the question, 'Greater than being in the movies?' Stewart answered without hesitation, 'Much greater.'"

But this September 1945 day was homecoming. In true American style, the big bands of Sammy Kaye and Cab Calloway gave the veterans a musical welcome as they disembarked from the *Queen Elizabeth*.

Leland Hayward, Stewart's longtime friend and business associate, managed to be the first to greet him. Stewart later told Hayward's daughter, Brooke, now the wife of bandleader Peter Duchin, that he had always admired her father's ingenuity but never more than when he got through the military security and was the first to welcome him home. Friends of mine who made the Atlantic crossing with Stewart have said that he shook the hand of every person in his wing as they stepped off the *Queen Elizabeth* that day.

When Colonel Stewart said goodbye to his men he had been in uniform for more than four years. He wore the ribbons of the Distinguished Flying Cross, with Oak Leaf Cluster, presented by General Jimmy Doolittle; the Air Medal with three clusters; the French Croix de Guerre with palm; and the commendations of his superiors. Although he would be the last person to admit it, and, truly, the first to shy away from any suggestion of such an idea, the simple fact was that Jimmy Stewart was returning to America as a wartime hero, a decorated bomber pilot and combat leader—not just a movie star in uniform.

Stewart was on combat duty with the Eighth Air Force in England for almost two years, at an essential time, flying combat missions in enemy skies, and commanding bomber crews. He flew twenty missions, including a pivotal raid on Berlin.

My wartime service with Stewart was in 1943–1944 on a

Captain Starr Smith, Intelligence Officer, Eighth Air Force, England, 1943–44.

cold and windswept American B-24 Liberator bomber base of the Eighth Air Force called Old Buckingham (Buckenham), or Old Buc, near the little train-station village of Attleboro near the North Sea between Cambridge and Norwich in England's East Anglia. The commanding officer of our outfit, the 453rd Bomb Group, was Colonel Ramsay Potts, a battle-tested Liberator warrior who had been a flight leader on the historic Ploesti mission a year earlier. Jimmy Stewart, then a major, was the group's operation officer and I was an intelligence officer, a captain, and together we handled many of the briefings for the combat crews prior to their bombing missions to German targets. It was in these times that I worked with Stewart, night after night, preparing the details of the mission. He briefed on the operations aspect of the mission, and I did the intelligence side.

I remember our first meeting after Stewart's arrival at Old Buc from another base after his promotion to operations officer. He brought with him a formidable reputation as a bomber pilot of the first rank and an air commander highly respected by the combat crews. Tall and very slim, he was wearing a worn leather flying jacket, baggy pants, hightop shoes, and his overseas cap did not fit exactly straight on his head. Stewart was older than me and the combat crews as well. He didn't talk much.

Well over a year before Pearl Harbor, while still in Hollywood, Stewart felt that America would soon be at war. At that time, Jimmy Stewart dug deep into his own heritage. His grandfather on his mother's side, Samuel M. Jackson, had served with distinction in the Civil War, and his father, Alex, fought in the Spanish-American War and World War I. Patriotism was a way of life in his background and Stewart knew that if war came, he wanted to be in uniform. And he wanted to be overseas with a combat job fighting the enemy.

So, on December 7, 1941, Pearl Harbor day, Stewart was pulling guard duty as a corporal in the Army Air Corps at Moffett Field, California. And by January, 1944, he was flying combat missions from wartime England against Nazi Germany.

In March of 1941, James Maitland Stewart, at 33—movie star, Academy Award–winning actor, American folk hero, Princeton graduate, aviator, bachelor, and prime favorite with the Hollywood ladies—entered the army as a private. At the end of World War II, Stewart was a full colonel and commander of a combat bomber wing of the Eighth Air Force. He was said to be the highest ranking of Hollywood stars and directors who went off to war, and among the very few officers in American military history to rise from private to colonel in slightly over four years. Moreover, Stewart was actually in combat situations all the time he was overseas, performing demanding and exposed duties—lead pilot, squadron operations officer, squadron commander, group operations officer, wing operations officer, and later, at the end, wing commander—all the while flying combat missions as a B-24 Liberator pilot and command pilot. As stated in the magazine *Osprey Combat Aircraft*, "few stories linked Stewart to Hollywood stars who wore uniforms but did not have serious military duties. . . . The truth was that Stewart flew B-24s, and he was more than a 'celebrity in uniform.' Stewart was very much a combat pilot, officer and leader." The article continued, "One veteran of the 445th Bomb Group remembers that, 'we couldn't keep him out of the cockpit, and, the brass worried about what might happen to such a well-known figure.'"

Perhaps the ultimate compliment about Jimmy Stewart's military service in World War II came from General Jimmy Doolittle, commander of the Eighth Air Force in the ETO. He said, "If the war had gone on another month Jimmy would have become a group commander, which was the most important job in the Air Force, in my opinion, much like a regimental commander in the Army or a ship's captain in the navy. . . . I have always thought him a very special individual."

Jimmy Stewart never made a World War II movie and was quoted as saying that Hollywood war pictures never seemed to show things the way they happened. In this book I want to tell his story the way it really happened, to show things the way they really were. I've tried to be inclusive while giving primary regard to the wartime service of a famous American who volunteered for military duty before the U.S. entered the war. While Stewart did not have to join the service, once in uniform he worked doggedly for months on end, flying night and day in all kinds of weather—in spite of efforts by the U.S. government to deny him an overseas combat assignment. Yet, once in uniform, in a perilous wartime situation, Stewart handled himself with dedication, fortitude, honor, and distinction.

Here too is the story, as I saw it and lived it, of the combat crews— the real heroes of the air war—going through their spartan and severe Nissen hut–existence; flying disciplined, dangerous, and constant missions, with an occasional three-day pass for a quick visit to London; bailing out of damaged and falling bombers; ditching in high seas; enduring the horrors of German POW camps; facing the cold and lonely nights and loss of friends who did not come back. In this book you'll meet the Wright crew and observe their combat life—day after day, mission after mission—and you'll meet the air force officers who guided Jimmy Stewart's wartime career and became his friends. It's also possible that you'll discover another Jimmy Stewart.

Late in the summer of 1945, as Stewart was getting his Wing ready for departure from the ETO and the return trip to America, his commanding general gave a victory party at his headquarters. It was a distinguished gathering of ranking people from the Eighth Air Force, the Royal Air Force, and other fighting units of the ETO—combat survivors, planners, veterans of a winning conflict, victorious warriors of the air who had defeated the Luftwaffe and cleared the enemy skies over Normandy. There were generals, air marshals, colonels, group captains, commanders, a sprinkling of women, some civilians, VIPs all, who had won a great victory. Now there was a celebration. Colonel Jimmy Stewart mingled quietly and unobtrusively with the crowd—at ease and poised, not as a Hollywood icon or a famous actor, not as a celebrity or a well-known face, but as an air combat colleague and leader who was tested in battle, and who had earned a place with his wartime peers.

After Stewart returned to America in the fall of 1945, he accepted a commission as a full colonel in the Air Force Reserve. He was later promoted by President Eisenhower to brigadier general and held that rank until retirement, at 60, in 1968. Stewart donated his retirement pay to the Falcon Foundation to fund the James Stewart Scholarships at the Air Force Academy.

With the myriad honors of a celebrated and eclectic career—including the highest in his profession, the Academy Award—and the decorations and promotions in the military service of his country, it is still not too much to believe that Jimmy Stewart reached the blue lawn of his life in those eventful and uncertain years of World War II. He was a smalltown boy who grew up with strong family values and a bedrock foundation in honesty and integrity, intertwined with a fervent patriotism. Stewart fought for his country without doubt or hesitation. He served with unbending determination, subtle style, and a quiet mystique.

I have never known a more intelligent, knowledgeable, hardworking, conscientious, and dedicated officer. Jimmy Stewart was a combat bomber pilot and commander—a man who was famous in another world and volunteered for wartime duty directly from civilian life, a man who trained hard and served well, a man who from the beginning wanted desperately to join the hunt in the cause of freedom. He was a man who led and inspired his fellow airmen in battle, won the respect and admiration of his superiors, and, in the end, was like many another—a good man who fought the good fight.

This is his story.

—Starr Smith
Montgomery, Alabama
December 2004

CHAPTER 1

HOME IN PENNSYLVANIA

"It's true there is something special about the place
where you were raised—your hometown."

—Jimmy Stewart

James Maitland "Jimmy" Stewart was born on May 20, 1908, in Indiana, Pennsylvania, in his parents' home at 965 Philadelphia Street, the only son of Alexander and Elizabeth Stewart. (An historic plaque now marks the site of his birthplace.) After Jimmy's arrival the family expanded to include daughters Virginia and Mary. The Stewarts had lived in Indiana for generations, and the family business, the J. M. Stewart Hardware Store, was located in a building, also on Philadelphia Street, constructed in 1853. It was Alex Stewart's fervent wish that Jimmy would return to Indiana after college, take over the store, and round out three generations of the family enterprise.

When Jimmy was five years old, the Stewart's moved to a house at 107 North Seventh Street, on top of Vinegar Hill, with a view overlooking downtown Indiana, which was generally considered to be the best residential section in town. The Stewart family was gentry in Indiana.

In Jimmy's early life and boyhood in Indiana, the little town of 8,000 people was ethnocentric, a little smug, and somewhat isolated. Located on the Appalachian plateau in western Pennsylvania about fifty miles slightly northeast of Pittsburgh, Indiana is best known as the home-town of Jimmy Stewart. But not just a hometown. Indiana was Stewart's taproot, his capstone, and his clarion call. Long after he had left Indiana, he returned for his fiftieth birthday dinner in 1958 and said to the guests: "Through the years Indiana has been something of tremendous importance in my life. It's true there is something special about the place where you were raised—your hometown. My father has been almost fanatical in his determination to keep our family together and he has done it. Time and distance haven't seemed to have affected this."

In his growing-up days in Indiana, lanky, shy, good-humored Jimmy made the scene—working at the hardware store, being a pro-jectionist at the Strand Theater, loading bricks, painting white stripes on the roads for the highway department in the summertime, doing odd jobs. Well liked. Not exactly a typical smalltown boy, but close.

There were other outlets for an innovative and well-placed young fellow in a slow-moving and insular community. Jimmy stayed busy. He performed magic tricks in an act with friend Bill Neff and made model airplanes with best friend Hall Blair. Soon, the venturesome entrepreneurs branched out into making small crystal radios that could pick up America's pioneer station KDKA in Pittsburgh. These twenty-dollar radios were an instant hit with townspeople and farmers. And there was the First United Presbyterian Church and life with a close-knit family. Thanks both to the family's anchor, Mother Bessie, and Princeton-educated Alex, the Stewart family lived in a refined, mannered, and religious atmosphere.

Hall Blair was closer to Jimmy and his family than anyone else in Indiana. He once told the *Tribune-Democrat*, a Pennsylvania newspaper:

> Jimmy had an interesting family life. They were
> very close. At every meal they all took hands and said
> Grace. On Sunday they all went to church. [Alex] was
> in the choir and [Bessie] was the organist. . . . At
> home they all sang hymns and had musical Sunday

evenings. They always had the *New York Times* and magazines like *Atlantic Monthly* and *Scribner's*. They followed theater and opera.

The musical Sunday evenings involved the entire Stewart family, who gathered around the Steinway grand in the drawing room of the Dutch colonial house on Vinegar Hill. Both Bessie and Virginia Kelly "Ginny" played piano, Mary Wilson "Doddie" played violin, with Alex as the impresario and singer. Jimmy played accordion, which began a musical career that, later enhanced by the piano, became a Jimmy Stewart signature for the rest of his life. His piano playing was never more enjoyed, even cherished, than the times, years later, when he sat at an old upright piano on an Eighth Air Force bomber base near the North Sea on dark and foggy nights in wartime England.

Airplanes and flying had been a passion for Jimmy since he was 10 or 12. Then in high school, Jimmy Stewart got his first airplane ride. Cost: A dollar a minute. The word had gotten around that a barnstorming pilot named Jack Law with a war surplus Curtiss biplane would be taking passengers for a ride from a big pasture on the outskirts of town. Naturally, his father was part of this experience, as Jimmy recalled much later in an interview with Pete Martin of the *Saturday Evening Post*:

> I had been saving every cent I could for a long time—mostly money I had picked up working around the hardware store. Both my parents, Dad as much as my mother, were against it. But I had made up my mind, and I think I knew I would always be able to persuade Dad at the last minute. When the big day finally came, and Law had landed in this pasture outside of town, Dad came around. But on the way out to the pasture, he insisted on stopping

to pick up the family doctor! And even that wasn't enough for him. The whole time I was up in the air, he stayed in the car with the engine running, just in case a wing or something fell off and he had to rush to the crash site!

So, Jimmy Stewart, who later logged thousands of flying hours, many in combat, and wore the wings of an air force pilot, had his first airplane ride—for fifteen minutes.

As the airplane-ride incident indicated, Alex Stewart was very much a concerned father. Rugged, muscular, strongly built, and commanding, he stood well over six feet. As son Jimmy was growing up, some of his friends thought his father was even bigger. A volunteer fireman, he had served in the Spanish-American War, had seen action in France in the Great War, sang in the choir at the First United Presbyterian Church, and was the sole proprietor of the hardware store founded by his father, who died at 93. Known as Alex, he was forceful, domineering, worldly, and highly opinionated.

Jimmy has said that his father was directly and constantly involved in all aspects of his life from the time he was born until Alex died at 89 on December 28, 1961. Through it all, Alex Stewart had a lasting and profound influence on Jimmy's life.

His mother, Bessie, was well-born, cultured, and intelligent. She died in August of 1953. Jimmy later told an interviewer: "My mother was the most tolerant and understanding of women. She forgave faults in everybody, including me. I can honestly say that she never did anything to embarrass me as a boy, although small boys embarrass easily. No one doubted that she was going to get into heaven."

At 16, Jimmy Stewart observed one of life's essential rites of passage for a young man—leaving home for the first time. He entered Mercersburg Academy, which bore the name of its location—Mercersburg, a small town near the Pennsylvania-Maryland border, about one hundred miles from Indiana. With his baggage, accordion, model airplane, and one of his own crystal radios in tow, Alex and

Bessie drove Jimmy down to Mercersburg. He maintained a high academic standing, whetted his interest in airplanes, and got his first taste of performing onstage before a live audience.

During the years since its founding, Mercersburg has turned out quite a number of distinguished graduates. One of these was Benjamin Franklin Mahoney, from the class of 1918, who designed and built *The Spirit of St. Louis*, Charles Lindbergh's famous airplane that now hangs in the Smithsonian's National Air and Space Museum in Washington.

In his junior year at Mercersburg, Jimmy ran into some health problems and spent several weeks at home in Indiana. During this time, one of the world's most momentous events took place, an event that had a lifelong effect on Jimmy Stewart. He told Peter Martin about it in the *Saturday Evening Post*:

> I was still at home on May 20, 1927, when Lindbergh made his now-historic flight from New York to Paris. . . .
>
> One of my jobs during my convalescence was trimming the windows in the Stewart Hardware Store. When Lindy was ready for his flight, I made ready for a simulated flight of my own. First I put together a model of his plane, the *Spirit of St. Louis*. Then I built my idea of New York's Woolworth Building on one side of the window, and the Eiffel Tower on the other side. In between I spotted Newfoundland and Ireland. Then Lindbergh took off, and the next the world heard of him he was sighted over Newfoundland. I knew about that sighting at once because I kept running across the street from the hardware store to watch the teletype in the office of the *Indiana Evening Gazette*.
>
> Every time I got a flash that a fishing boat or a steamer had sighted Lindy's plane, I rushed to the

store window and moved my model plane closer to France. Then came the moment when Lindy landed. It was like New Year's Eve in our town. Church bells rang. Everybody quit work. The town busted loose. It gave the whole country an emotional lift when it needed one. For a time we could forget about the weaknesses of our society in the amoral Roaring Twenties—the gin flask, the flapper, the parking and petting, the bribery of big-city cops by prohibition's gangsters. Lindbergh's feat reminded everyone that a man could still find the courage, the determination and the desire to face a seemingly insurmountable challenge and win.

In his senior year at Mercersburg, Jimmy made his first appearance as an actor. He had a leading role in the drama club's stage production of *The Wolves*, a French play set in the years following the French Revolution. In his review of the play, the school's drama critic rated Stewart's performance as "excellent."

Before and during Mercersburg, Jimmy had entertained the idea of attending the Naval Academy at Annapolis. Certainly, with his family's gilt-edged connections in high places, an appointment could have been arranged. And, with Jimmy's excellent academic record at Mercersburg, he could have passed the entrance requirements. But, true to his style, subtle and otherwise, Alex had other plans for his son: In the fall of 1928, Jimmy Stewart was enrolled in the Princeton University class of 1932.

The biggest and most influential single element of Stewart's time at Princeton was his involvement with the Triangle Club. While he graduated in architecture in 1932 with honors, it was the activities of Triangle, Princeton's celebrated drama club, that initially drew and later sustained his interest in performing. The accordion was Jimmy's entry card, but he soon moved on to speaking parts and singing.

Josh Logan, an upperclassman and Triangle composer and producer, said later, "He was good. . . . I knew deep down he loved acting but was too embarrassed to admit it."

There can be little doubt that Jimmy Stewart got the acting bug at Princeton. He also made a friend who would open a career avenue that eventually led to Hollywood. That friend was Josh Logan. Soon after leaving Princeton, a year ahead of Stewart, Logan became a director for a group called the University Players in Falmouth, Massachusetts. It was here that Logan hired Stewart, just out of Princeton, as an accordion player for the Players tearoom. Later, Logan gave him a small part in a play called *Goodbye Again*.

Working with the University Players, Stewart met a fellow player who would become his close friend for life—Henry Fonda. New York was the next stop. The two budding actors shared an apartment in New York and a mutual interest in building model airplanes. Both had moderate success on Broadway and in due course passed Hollywood screen tests.

With an MGM contract in hand, Jimmy Stewart arrived in Hollywood in June of 1935. Fonda was already there and was waiting for him when Stewart stepped off the train at the Pasadena station. Stewart carried with him a model of the Martin Bomber the two of them had been working on back in New York.

After moving into Fonda's house in Brentwood and checking in at MGM, Jimmy Stewart began making plans for a lifelong ambition— taking flying lessons. His first stop was Minesfield.

Stewart was not the only Hollywood type who flew at Minesfield (and, later, Clover Field) in the middle-to-late 1930s. He was consistently seeing Joan Fontaine, the singer Frances Langford, Robert Taylor, and Tyrone Power. Leland Hayward, the flamboyant and enterprising theatrical agent, and Stewart's friend from New York, was also a pilot. Hayward owned a Waco and entered it in a national air race between Los Angeles and Cleveland with himself as pilot. He invited Stewart to be his copilot for the race. The year was 1937. Stewart never turned down an opportunity to fly and thought the experience would be worthwhile.

The Waco led the race for much of the way, but engine trouble kept the Hayward-Stewart flying team out of the money. Later, in 1939, Hayward, ever the entrepreneur, got the actor-pilot involved in a commercial aviation venture in Phoenix, Arizona. This later became Thunderbird Field, which turned out thousands of pilots during the war. Still, Jimmy Stewart's heartthrob memories always returned to those early flying days at Minesfield, now the site of the Los Angeles International Airport.

CHAPTER 2

A FAREWELL
TO HOLLYWOOD

*"It may sound corny, but what's wrong with wanting
to fight for your country. Why are people reluctant to
use the word* patriotism?*"*

—Jimmy Stewart

At the beginning of 1941, Jimmy Stewart was near the top of his
form as a movie actor and international star. His 1939 picture,
Mr. Smith Goes to Washington, had made him a folk hero throughout America, and he was destined for an Academy Award for his
role as the reporter in *Philadelphia Story*. His life was blissful,
romantic, flawless, and ahead was the golden promise of infinite
stardom as one of the premier movie players of all time. And there
were the ladies. Stewart was, at this time in his life, the quintessential
eligible man about town, the perfect bachelor—handsome,
famous, successful, charismatic, and furthermore, he could play the
piano. So it followed that his girlfriends would be of a like pattern
and beauties all—Ginger Rogers, Olivia de Havilland, Norma
Shearer, Marlene Dietrich, Loretta Young, Yvonne de Carlo, Shirley
Ross, and even more.

All the glorious hues of a rainbow glowed in profusion in Jimmy
Stewart's Hollywood life. But glamorous nights and romantic music
with beautiful ladies at Ciro's, the Trocadero, Chasen's, and the

Coconut Grove could not overshadow the unrelenting realism of the sinister headlines or pierce the baleful, dark clouds of war that were gathering day-by-day. England had been fighting Hitler since September of 1939, and night after night, Edward R. Murrow reported that grim and gallant story in his "This . . . Is London" CBS broadcasts. Stewart had many English friends in Hollywood—Cary Grant, Laurence Olivier, David Niven, Cedric Hardwick. And Leslie Howard, who later died when his Clipper was shot down by German fighters as he returned home to help defend his country.

These were stirring times in America. The country's most famous airman, Jimmy Doolittle, who had been called to active duty as a major in the air corps, was quoted as saying, "the United States involvement in the war [is] . . . foreordained. The rest of the world seems to be on fire. It would take only a spark to involve us." Fortunately, the air corps was expanding. President Roosevelt had already alerted Congress that American air strength was "utterly inadequate" and must be increased.

For years, Stewart had been not only a strong aviation advocate but was now an experienced and enthusiastic pilot. In early 1941, he had both a private and commercial license, owned a sporty Stinson 105 two-seater, and had logged more than 300 hours of personal flying time in his logbook. Moreover, his passion for flying bordered on euphoria. Stewart was quoted as saying: "You're like a bird up there. It's almost as if you're not part of society anymore. All you can think about is what you're doing and you have a complete escape from your worldly problems. You have a feeling of real power up there—that we human beings aren't really altogether helpless, that we can be completely in command of an amazing machine, that we do have some control over our destiny. And, of course, it's the only place where one can really be alone."

In spite of the wave of isolationism that was so much a part of those threatening times, Stewart was a strong advocate of preparing for war and building superiority in the air. And the Stewart family had a long history of fighting America's wars. Considering all the factors—his own strong beliefs, his family, the mild but haunting influence of his English friends, and, far more important, the bleak radio reports and black headlines— Jimmy Stewart decided to join the fight. Later, in giving his reasons for his decision to enlist, Stewart said, quite simply, "It may sound corny, but what's wrong with wanting to fight for your country. Why are people reluctant to use the word *patriotism*?"

But, as patriotic and unselfish as Stewart's decision was, he faced two major roadblocks. One was from his boss, the other from his country. Louis B. Mayer, the forceful and dictatorial head of MGM, Stewart's studio, used every persuasive tactic at his command— choice roles, contract revisions, free time to help with the war effort as a civilian. Stewart could have all of these as long as he stayed out of uniform and continued to make pictures for MGM. The other matter was different.

He was drafted. The Selective Service Act was the law. Men between the ages of 21 and 36 were required to register. Being 32, Stewart registered and was quoted later as saying, "The only lottery I ever came close to winning was the drawing for the first draft before Pearl Harbor." Then, in late 1940, he was called in for a physical examination. Perhaps in anticipation of the examination, Stewart had for months been involved in a rigorous exercise program. But it didn't work. The army doctors found that he was ten pounds underweight for his height-weight ratio. That could have ended the whole affair with the draft and the army. And as Louis B. Mayer rather forcefully pointed out: He was ready to go and the army had turned him down. So that was that. But not exactly.

Thinking perhaps of his family's involvement in wartime service and his own fervent love of country, Stewart then went the volunteer route. Now, too, there was another factor, although certainly not a decisive one. In all of his professional life, Jimmy Stewart had been a darling of the press, a golden boy, not only with the Hollywood columnists like Louella Parsons, but with the mainstream press as well. After the army's rejection for being underweight, he was faced with an unfair press and headlines like: "Movie Hero Heavy Enough to Knock Out Villain—But Too Light for Uncle Sam." While he was firmly and absolutely rejected by the army at the time, there was a possibility that, later, the physical standards would be lowered and he could make the weight requirements. But that possibility had little appeal, and the waiting even less.

Forthwith, Jimmy Stewart appealed the army's decision.

There seem to be two versions of Stewart's eventual entry into military service. Was he drafted or did he volunteer? It has been said and written that he volunteered for service ahead of the draft. Not so. In early 1943, I was in Combat Intelligence School at Harrisburg, Pennsylvania, with Burgess "Buzz" Meredith, Stewart's former Hollywood housemate. Meredith told me that essentially both versions are true. He was drafted. He was turned down. Then, he did volunteer to appeal the army's decision. And he made the weight requirements the second go-around. Stewart once told me, with a slight grin, that he had a friend operating the scales for the second weigh-in. Stewart reported for induction on March 22, 1941, wearing a tweed-like brownish suit and tie, at Fort MacArthur, California. Meredith drove him to the induction center. The simple fact is that, although he did not have to go and others in Hollywood were seeking to avoid service, Stewart defied his own boss and took every possible step to get into uniform. And he finally made it.

CHAPTER 3

BAD NEWS
AT SALT LAKE CITY

"Static personnel" *with a hold order.*
—Stewart's classification at Gowen Field,
Boise, Idaho (meaning no transfer and
no combat crew assignment)

A t the induction and processing center at Fort MacArthur, Stewart, because of his experience as a pilot and interest in flying, was assigned to the Army Air Corps* and sent to Moffett Field near San Francisco. Too old for regular flying-cadet status and based on his flying experience and educational background, Stewart applied for training directly as an Army Air Corps pilot. He was accepted and immediately began an extensive schedule of flight training and ground school class work leading to a commission and pilot's wings.

Toward the end of his flight training, Stewart was given a "check ride" by Captain Bobby Heilpern, a veteran flying instructor and now a retired Montgomery, Alabama, businessman. Heilpern remembers Stewart as, "shy, intense, not much of a talker, and a very competent pilot." He shared life with his fellow enlisted soldiers and did his share of KP, close order drill, and guard duty.

There were other duties as well. Taking advantage of his famous name, the air corps scheduled limited public appearances. Stewart appeared several times on network radio with Edgar Bergen and Charlie

*The flight arm of the army was called the Air Corps, Army Air Corps, and Army Air Force; after the war, in 1947, it became a separate branch, the United States Air Force.

McCarthy. Shortly after Pearl Harbor, he performed with Orson Welles, Edward G. Robinson, Walter Huston, and Lionel Barrymore in an all-network radio program called "We Hold These Truths," dedicated to the 150th anniversary of the Bill of Rights. But mostly Stewart's days and nights were spent preparing for his upcoming flight tests, ground school, and academic examinations for his commission. He was successful, and his commission came through on January 19, 1942. By this time, Stewart had been promoted to corporal. Colonel Beirne Lay, himself an Eighth Air Force combat pilot and commander, said, "Corporal Stewart had won his commission not by pulling a string in Washington nor on the strength of civilian prominence, but by the unspectacular method of meeting the official requirements."

Newly commissioned as a second lieutenant, Stewart was stationed initially at Moffett Field. In his new Army Air Force uniform and wearing his pilot wings, he felt that now the first hurdle was passed; the next was getting a combat assignment overseas. Shortly thereafter, in March, 1942, Stewart was invited to attend President Franklin D. Roosevelt's birthday gala on behalf of the March of Dimes in Washington, D.C. His flight from California was weathered in for a day at Maxwell Field, near Montgomery. The *Montgomery Advertiser*'s society writer, Esther Mahoney, wrote: "a tall, handsome second lieutenant strolling down the corridor of Austin Hall, headquarters of the Southeast Air Corps Training Center . . . typewriters operated by girls ceased to clack—dictation was left in mid-air. No uniform could conceal those characteristics so well known to the moviegoer—that walk, that peculiar lower lip, those honest, though at times evasive, eyes." The *Advertiser* reported that Stewart spent the day at Maxwell, "studying the training program." The next day the weather cleared, and he flew on to Washington.

It is worthy of note that on this 1942 California–Washington flight with Lieutenant Stewart were Lieutenant Colonel Thomas Power and Lieutenant Colonel David Schlatter, who were going to Washington for wartime conferences. Both officers, like Stewart, went on to notable World War II careers. And, after the war, Power headed the Strategic Air

Command and retired as a four-star general. Schlatter became deputy commander of the new Air University as a major general.

Lieutenant Jimmy Stewart was a great success at the March of Dimes gala, a series of balls held in Washington hotels in honor of President Roosevelt's birthday. The gala celebrated a nationwide campaign to raise funds for the fight against infantile paralysis. Naturally, all eyes were on the charismatic president, now in his third term and rapidly emerging as a popular and forceful wartime leader. War had been declared on Germany and Japan, and the president's "Day of Infamy" speech had already become a rallying cry for all Americans. President Roosevelt received young Lieutenant Stewart at the White House, and he was also a special guest at the hotel balls. It was Stewart's first public appearance as an officer, and newspapers reported that the trim actor-flyer cut quite a dashing figure in his dark-green air corps uniform with crushed hat and silver wings.

Upon his return to California, Stewart immediately sought a position to train for combat duty. Although he had only just returned from a triumphant trip to Washington, it was not in his nature to pull strings. He had received his commission and air corps pilot's wings by merit, hard work, and devotion to duty; he would seek combat duty the same way. Still, he had three major goals in mind: he wanted to get all the experience he could out of the training schedule; he wanted a combat slot as pilot or copilot; and he hoped that his assignment, if it ever came through, would be in the Eighth Air Force, which was rapidly becoming a first-line American heavy bombardment organization and was already flying daylight missions against the Germans.

At first, the air force seemed to be cooperating. Things were going well, and the cards fell the right way. A training pattern took shape that Stewart hoped would lead to a combat crew slot. He remained at Moffett for instrument instruction and night and formation flying. Soon he was dispatched to the instructor's class at the advanced flying school at Mather Field, California, where, upon completion, Stewart became a twin-engine instructor. Another air force career-building opportunity came when he was transferred to Kirtland Field in

Albuquerque, New Mexico. At Kirkland, he flew bombardier students and was introduced for the first time to the Norden bomb sight, which, would later become a big part of his combat life.

Moving from one training base to another in the early months of his wartime career, Stewart had little time for social life in the towns of Northern California, Utah, and New Mexico, where he was stationed. On his short leaves and three-day passes, he usually headed for his old haunts in Hollywood, getting a hop in an air force plane or flying commercial.

On one of his Hollywood visits, Stewart had a reunion with his old friend, Clark Gable, who was now a newly commissioned air force officer, having just graduated from the Air Force Officer Training School (OTS) at Miami Beach, Florida. Gable's wife, the vivacious Carole Lombard, had recently lost her life in an airliner crash while on a war-bond fundraising trip for the government. The Gable-Lombard marriage had been viewed in Hollywood as a deep and emotional love match, and her sudden death had a profound effect on the rugged *Gone with the Wind*

Lieutenant Jimmy Stewart and Captain Clark Gable on leave in Hollywood in late 1942.

star. It has been said that the numbing grief of his wife's passing, and the simple fact that at the time of her death she was in wartime service, propelled Gable to seek an active role in uniform—even at 41. Over lunch at Chasen's restaurant, the two famous actors shared "war stories," and Gable told Stewart about some of his classmates at Miami: fellow Hollywood luminaries William Holden, Gilbert Roland, John Carroll, Robert Preston, Bruce Cabot; and sports figures: tennis great Donald Budge, golfer Ben Hogan, and baseball star Hank Greenberg.

At Chasen's that day, Gable told Stewart that he already had orders for combat gunnery school and was on track for an overseas assignment. Stewart was now more determined than ever to somehow join the fighting. As fall was ending and the New Year of 1943 approached, Stewart got lucky, and the future now held the promise of combat duty. Stewart was assigned to the B-17 transition school for four-engine pilots at Hobbs Field, New Mexico. This was his first step to fighting in the war.

At long last, he was on his way—or so it seemed. Stewart wanted big airplanes, and the B-17 Flying Fortress and its sister plane, the B-24 Liberator, were the prime bombers in the air force. He fell in love with the powerful and graceful B-17 and checked out easily on the majestic bomber. The 100-hour course at Hobbs would qualify him as a four-engine pilot and aircraft commander, which could be his ticket to combat. Stewart was older and more experienced than his classmates, who were mostly fresh out of advanced flying schools. He loved the big bomber, flew it well, and graduated near the top of his thirty-student B-17 class. Graduation was in February, 1943. Now Stewart could no longer be viewed as an actor in uniform, a celluloid hero. He was a four-engine bomber pilot, certified by the U.S. government. Along with his classmates, Stewart departed for the Air Force Combat Crew Procession Center at Salt Lake City, Utah. There they would be assigned to newly activated bomber groups and, after three months of crew training, be deployed to overseas action.

Alas, for Stewart, a combat crew assignment was not to be. Twenty-nine graduates of the Hobbs four-engine pilot transition class of February, 1943, were immediately given combat crew assignments. The lone exception was Stewart. Instead, he was assigned to the 29th Training Group at Gowen Field, Boise, Idaho. At Gowen, he was classified as "static personnel" with a hold order in his file, which meant that he was not to be transferred from Boise. His job: B-17 instructor pilot in first-phase training for combat crews headed overseas.

CHAPTER 4

COLONEL DWIGHT D. "IKE" EISENHOWER IN LOUISIANA: LOOKING FOR A COMBAT JOB

"The Chief says for you to hop a plane
and get up here right away."
—orders for Colonel Eisenhower
to report to Washington

In 1940 and 1941, I was working as a radio news reporter in central Louisiana. I had gone there as a young journalist to cover the aftermath of the Huey and Earl Long political regime. But I was soon filing more stories on the huge military buildup and maneuvers in that area of the South. War seemed inevitable. England had been fighting Germany since September of 1939. A few months later, in May of 1940, Hitler's Panzer divisions smashed France's Maginot Line, and in a matter of days Paris fell to the Nazis on June 14. Four days earlier, at Charlottesville, Virginia, President Roosevelt warned that America could not become "an island in a world dominated by . . . force."

In making this focal and warning speech, President Roosevelt knew that—with Hitler overrunning Europe, and England standing as the lone bastion between America and total Nazi domination—neutrality seemed impossible. Yet there were strong demands in high places for America to remain neutral. So as England fought on, the debate in this country reached fever heat between the interventionists and the isolationists. The president sensed that the American people wanted to stop Hitler. Throughout America there was mounting support for that belief. William Allen White, the highly respected editor of the Emporia, Kansas, *Gazette*, and founder of the Committee to Defend America by Aiding the Allies, wrote to the president, "As an old friend, let me tell you that you may not be able to lead the American people unless you catch up with them."

In that dark and seminal month of May, 1940, there were rays of hope—Winston Churchill became prime minister of Great Britain, and President Roosevelt asked Congress for money to build 50,000 warplanes a year. By late summer, the Battle of Britain raged over the skies of England and the English Channel, and the world was introduced to a new kind of fighting man, a different breed of warrior—the RAF Spitfire pilot.

Inspired by the hour-by-hour deeds in the sky of Churchill's "few" and buoyed by its own indomitable spirit, England fought on, and America seemed to be losing its taste for neutrality. In October of 1940, President Roosevelt asked Congress to pass the Lend-Lease Act to aid Britain. It became law in March of 1941. That same month, Jimmy Stewart was inducted into the U.S. Army in California.

In those dramatic and galvanic times, there was another American who was just beginning to emerge from U.S. Army ranks and, within the space of three years, would become one of the most famous men in the world. His name: Dwight D. "Ike" Eisenhower. A West Pointer, class of 1915, Eisenhower had served for many years as a major and lieutenant colonel. In that eventful month of March, 1941, he was promoted to full colonel.

Before the draft was enacted, the U.S. Army was restricted to 375,000 officers and men. Along with the draft there was a call-up of National Guard and reserve units. So in a very short time, the army had to set up training camps and bases for the tremendous infusion of civilian draftees, guardsmen, and reservists, augmented by regular army troops. A major location for these training camps was the flat countryside of central Louisiana near Alexandria. Almost overnight, Camp Livingston, Camp Claiborne, and, later, Camp

Polk (now Fort Polk) sprang up, and soldiers by the thousands poured into the area. Nearby was old-line Camp Beauregard, home of the Louisiana National Guard. The adjutant general of Louisiana in 1940–1941 was Major General Raymond Fleming. Many thought that General Fleming's monumental national reputation in military circles contributed to locating the training camps in Louisiana.

The army, with funds now available for men and equipment, began to stage the largest peacetime maneuvers in its history. North Louisiana was the centerpoint—an area sliced by the Red River and dotted with pines, open spaces, scrub oaks, and small towns. The battle pitted Lieutenant General Walter Krueger's Third Army against the Second Army, commanded by the formidable Lieutenant General Ben Lear. Colonel Dwight Eisenhower was Lieutenant General Krueger's chief of staff. At this point, the U.S. Army was comprised of approximately 1,500,000 officers and men.

I covered these war games, and almost from the beginning it was obvious that Eisenhower stood far above his fellow senior officers. He had recently returned from the Philippines, where he saw service as General Douglas MacArthur's right-hand man. Now in Louisiana, with troops and an important job and war clouds looming in Europe, he was knowledgeable, confident, articulate, personable, and approachable. When the maneuvers were over and reports, critiques, and evaluations were in—shortly before Pearl Harbor—most historians have agreed that Eisenhower's reputation gained discernible luster, and his peerless leadership contributed immeasurably to the Third Army's victory in the war games. After the war, Eisenhower wrote in his book, *Crusade in Europe,* of the Louisiana maneuvers:

> The beneficial results of that great maneuver were incalculable. It accustomed the troops to mass teamwork; it speeded up the process of eliminating the unfit; it brought to the special attention of seniors certain of the younger men who were prepared to carry out the most difficult assignments in staff and

command; and it developed among responsible leaders skill in the handling of large forces in the field. . . . The maneuvers provided me with lessons and experience that I appreciated more and more as subsequent months rolled by.

Then-Colonel Dwight D. Eisenhower in the field during Louisiana's 1940–1941 maneuvers.

Early observations and viewpoints of Eisenhower's obvious capabilities were made in the field by his boss, General Krueger, and by reporters, maneuver umpires, and senior officers on both sides of the mock conflict. But the most important and decisive observer of all, from Eisenhower's standpoint, was Army Chief of Staff George C. Marshall. Both in Washington and Louisiana, Marshall had kept a watchful and knowing eye on the progress, personnel, and direction of the maneuvers, the largest and toughest ever undertaken by American forces in peacetime. The brilliant, far-seeing, and perceptive Marshall was also looking for commanders, and he kept a little black book to keep track of the most promising candidates.

After the war, General Eisenhower's naval aide—my friend, Captain Harry Butcher—observed in his best-selling book *My Three Years with Eisenhower*: "In the fall of 1941, I read a glowing account of Colonel Eisenhower's work as Chief of Staff of the Third Army which had just finished maneuvers in Louisiana."

I had not been long out of military school and figured, correctly as it turned out, that I would soon be in uniform. I must say that I found the whole army scene engrossing and fascinating. I had an old Dodge coupe and kept the roads hot between Camps Livingston and Claiborne and the maneuver areas. I was constantly in the field, filing reports and doing interviews for my radio station, KALB in Alexandria, Louisiana.

Many of my interviews with high-ranking officers were conducted at the Bentley Hotel in downtown Alexandria, a large and stately hotel that served as an informal headquarters and R&R retreat for ranking officers. It's been said that many decisions dealing with the war games in the surrounding countryside were made at the

General George Marshall.

Bentley, specifically in the Mirror Room Bar on the ground level. My station had a remote line in the hotel, and I can now recall interviews with Eisenhower, Bradley, Stilwell, Lawton Collins, and other young and rising officers. All were colonels at the time, but they were destined to become three- and four-star generals; Eisenhower and Bradley were five-star generals at war's end. The Bentley Hotel has also gained a measure of fame and historical notice because of its indelible association with those momentous times and vivid personalities—joining the ranks of celebrated wartime places like the War Room in London, the Scribe Hotel in Paris (Allied press headquarters), and the schoolhouse in Rheims, France, where the German surrender was signed.

One night at the Blue Moon nightclub in Alexandria, I met an army captain, a West Pointer and career military officer. We became friends and talked often of the future, and the coming war. He was

Hotel Bentley, Alexandria, Louisiana, was the rest and relaxation headquarters of the high-ranking army officers, including Colonel Eisenhower, during the Louisiana maneuvers. A commemorative plaque (next page) hangs there today.

LOUISIANA MANEUVERS

In 1940 Lt. Gen. Stanley D. Embrick of the U.S. Army Fourth Corps Area, Atlanta, Ga., selected central Louisiana as site of training maneuvers to prepare American forces for possible involvement in war in Europe. Louisiana's 1941 maneuvers were the Army's largest peacetime training exercise. Approximately 400,000 troops were divided into armies of two imaginary countries: "Kotmk" (Kansas, Oklahoma, Texas, Missouri and Kentucky) and "Almat" (Arkansas, Louisiana, Mississippi, Alabama and Tennessee), supposedly at war over Mississippi River navigation rights. These maneuvers allowed Army strategists to test conventional defenses attacked by armored vehicles. Maj. Gen. George Patton's tanks pushed back conventionally-armed defenders but failed to achieve a spectacular victory. Army commanders also encountered reconnaissance and troop supply problems expected in battlefield conditions and thus had several months to formulate solutions before the U.S. entered World War II. The Army conducted smaller scale maneuvers in 1942 and 1943 in the same area, but cancelled 1944 exercises to allow troops to participate in the D-Day invasion of Europe. In addition to Patton, military leaders who visited central Louisiana during the maneuvers included Joseph Stilwell, Dwight Eisenhower, Omar Bradley, Mark Clark and J. Lawton Collins. Many of these headquartered at the Hotel Bentley.

JOHNSON BROWN POST 1730 – VETERANS OF FOREIGN WARS

already a breveted battalion commander, and he desperately hoped for a combat assignment if war came. He told me, "I have worked and trained all of my life to fight a war. If war comes, I must be in combat with troops. I have to be in the action wherever it is. If I am left behind in the States, like an instructor, and miss combat duty overseas—I'll feel that my whole career was a failure."

At that time and at that place, there in Louisiana, as the maneuvers were winding down—my captain friend was not the only career army officer who was looking ahead and hoping for a combat job. Less than a week after Pearl Harbor, Colonel Eisenhower was ordered to Washington from Third Army headquarters at Fort Sam Houston in San Antonio, Texas. His bravura performance in the maneuvers had not escaped the attention of General Marshall. The call was terse and to the point. "The Chief says for you to hop a plane and get up here right away." But he was not being called to Washington to command troops. Eisenhower tells of his disappointment in *Crusade in Europe*:

> The message was a hard blow. During the first World War every one of my frantic efforts to get to the scene of action had been defeated—for reasons which had no validity to me except that they all boiled down to "War Department orders." I hoped in any new war to stay with troops. Being ordered to a city where I had already served a total of eight years would mean, I thought, a virtual repetition of my experience in World War I. Heavyhearted . . . within the hour I was headed for the War Department.

CHAPTER 5

A WINTER IN BOISE

"Barbara [Stanwyck] is quite a chick . . .
and a good bowler, too."
—a fellow flight instructor of Stewart's
after a night out with Stanwyck,
her husband Robert Taylor, and
Stewart in Boise

At Gowen Field in Boise, Idaho, in the winter of 1943, First Lieutenant Jimmy Stewart began the somber process of going through the same disappointment, frustration, and soul-searching that Colonel Eisenhower had experienced when he arrived for a Washington assignment eighteen months earlier. Like the man who was destined to command all Allied forces in Europe and direct the D-day landing in France little more than a year later, and like the West Point captain on the Louisiana maneuvers, combat duty remained Stewart's driving goal and unconditional ambition; it was almost an obsession. But he had personally resolved that he would not ask for special consideration or favors; as far as the military was concerned, he would play it as it lay.

So in the dead of a cold and dreary Idaho winter, perhaps the most strenuous, oppressive, and confounding time of Jimmy Stewart's life began. It seemed obvious that somebody up the chain of command had placed a hold order in his personnel file. In short, apparently nobody wanted to take the responsibility of sending a famous movie star into combat when, if shot down, he could become a valuable hostage for the enemy. Of course, this was never written or said, but it was obvious. This was a bitter blow, disappointing, heartbreaking, and patently unfair. But true to his nature, Stewart complained to no one. Later, he told a friend it was the most disconcerting thing he had ever dealt with. Still, he made no calls, pulled no strings.

Setting his disappointment and heartbreak aside, he threw himself full force into the all-consuming task at hand. He flew around-the-clock as a B-17 instructor pilot and was soon promoted to captain and given more responsibility as squadron commander. The war was on, and—from the Joint Chiefs of Staff in Washington through the chain of command to the generals, colonels, majors, and on to instructor pilot Captain Jimmy Stewart—the order was to get the crews ready for combat, whatever the cost.

The snow, ice, fog, and almost unflyable weather of 1943 was treacherous, the nearby mountains foreboding and extremely dangerous, the flying schedule demanding and exhausting. Stewart lost friends, a roommate, and several of his own students. At one point, Stewart himself almost bought the farm (air force parlance for losing one's life in a fatal crash). Author and command pilot Colonel Beirne Lay wrote that:

> One night Jimmy was checking a new airplane commander. He had given his co-pilot's seat temporarily to the navigator, who wanted to see how things functioned in the cockpit. The navigator got an eyeful a moment later, when a blinding flash of light came from the No. 1 engine on the pilot's side, accompanied by a loud explosion. Somehow, Jimmy got the navigator out of the co-pilot's seat, so that he could reach the No. 1 fire extinguisher selector valve. He regained control, and he set the bomber down safely.

Stewart soldiered on. Like his instructor colleagues there at Gowen that winter, it was all-consuming duty, a dismal and grim routine—night and day, day and night. Stewart had an old Ford V-8 with a banged-up door that he and his friends drove to the flight line, the BOQ (Bachelor Officers Quarters), and the post office.

But every now and then there were diversions, off nights when the weather was even worse than usual and flying was impossible. On one of these nights when everything was stood down, Stewart gathered two or three fellow instructors, and they piled into the old Ford and drove to Boise. They were having a drink at a bar when Robert Taylor and his wife, Barbara Stanwyck, walked in. They quickly joined Stewart's group. Later, they all went bowling, and the next day one of Stewart's friends told him, "Barbara is quite a chick. And a good bowler, too."

There in the mountains of Idaho, radio was Stewart's main link to the outside world—and to the war. He listened in his BOQ, the Ford, the officer's club, the mess hall, wherever he could find a radio. He listened to H. V. Kaltenborn, Lowell Thomas, H. R. Baukage, Cedric Foster, Fulton Lewis Jr., Walter Winchell, and other stateside commentators. Friends sent the Sunday *New York Times*. He pored over overseas maps. From Charles Collingwood, the CBS correspondent in North Africa, he learned of the progress of the Torch landing there, and, from Edward R. Murrow reporting for CBS from London, he learned of the first Eighth Air Force mission to Germany.

Commanding Officer of the 29th Training Group at Boise's Gowen Field was Lieutenant Colonel Walter "Pop" Arnold, a University of Arizona ROTC graduate and Army Air Corps career officer. A native of El Paso, Texas, Arnold had earned his pilot's wings in the mid-1930s at Randolph and Kelly Fields in San Antonio, and was already known as a top military flyer and commander. At 28, Arnold was one of the youngest air corps group commanders. He had known Stewart and his reputation as a hard worker who asked no favors before he was assigned as a B-17 instructor pilot to the 29th. He knew of Stewart's ability as a superior pilot, instructor, and leader, and of his strong desire for combat duty. He also knew about the "static personnel" hold order in Stewart's file. From the beginning, Arnold kept a close eye on Stewart. After the war, Arnold related this story to his daughter, Kathleen, who later told it to me.

Pop got a call alerting him that a plane had crashed and there were fatalities. Jimmy's co-pilot, Bob (something,) Pop couldn't recall his last name, was killed in the crash and it was Pop's job to go up and inspect the crash site and oversee the retrieval of the bodies. Jimmy and his co-pilot were good friends and knowing this, Pop called Jimmy, told him what happened and said he was going to come get him. Jimmy was pretty shaken about his friend's death, but appreciated Pop calling him personally. They hiked up the mountain, retrieved the bodies and on the way down, Jimmy slipped or fell, and hurt his back pretty bad. The rest of the team descended and Pop stayed behind with Jimmy pondering what to do. Concerned that walking would cause Jimmy further injury, he decided to carry Jimmy the rest of the way down. Now imagine a little, 5 foot 6 inch man carrying a man well over 6 feet! He put Jimmy over his shoulders in the "fireman's

Colonel Walter "Pop" Arnold, Boise, Idaho, 1943. Arnold made a crucial phone call on Stewart's behalf.

carry" and slowly made his way down the mountain with Jimmy in tow. After carrying him down, a truck had been left for them, so Pop put Jimmy in the back of it, started it up and barreled down a dirt road, plowing right through a fence, leaving the main road over rough terrain to find the quickest route to the hospital. Pop said the guys at the hospital were pretty surprised when the truck screeches up and out jumps their commanding officer with an injured Jimmy Stewart in the back! Jimmy stayed in the hospital while his back healed and he eventually went back on active flight status. When he told me this story, Pop chuckled and said, "That wild truck ride probably damn near killed him, or caused him more pain, but he never said a word!" He said later, they reminisced about this story and Jimmy laughed and said, he still can't believe a little guy like Pop was able to get him down that mountain!

There is no record anywhere—after the traumatic episode on the mountainside, the loss of a close friend, his own injury, and a lengthy stay in the hospital—that Stewart backed away from his fervent but calm, passionate but controlled, eager but not testy goal, leading to an overseas combat assignment. Still, with spring coming to the mountains and bringing better flying weather, perhaps Stewart had a subtle feeling of stoicism. His fortitude was certainly there. His excitement was there. But perhaps his passion was tempered. On the plus side, he could see the results of his grim and bone-weary task. His students were passing their final check rides, getting orders, and moving on to assignments on combat crews with bomber groups going overseas. Still, the war was moving on. For the thirty-six-year-old Stewart, combat duty seemed far away and unreachable, and he had no clear plans for the future.

But then a rumor that Stewart would be taken off flying status and assigned to making training films or selling bonds called for his immediate and decisive action, because what he dreaded most was the hope-shattering specter of a dead end.

Casting aside all reservations and resolutions, he went in to see Colonel Arnold in his office. After the fatal airplane crash when the Colonel had carried him bodily down the mountainside and the wild truck ride to the hospital, Stewart and his commanding officer had developed an informal captain-colonel relationship. Moreover, the colonel, wearing his worn leather A-2 jacket, was easy to talk with. Captain Stewart laid it out to Colonel Arnold pure and simple, man-to-man: He desperately wanted a combat job, he had worked hard and was now afraid of being relieved of flying duty and assigned to making films, he had instructor and formation experience in four-engine aircraft, and he deserved a shot at combat duty.

Taking decisive action to determine his fate in the military, and knowing fully that he was violating his own resolution, Stewart had carefully planned and rehearsed what he would say. And perhaps his meeting with Colonel Arnold would set into motion a chain of events that would determine the course of his World War II service and lead to his coveted combat assignment.

Stewart could not have come to a better man to plead his case. Colonel Arnold had started his army career in the cavalry and had also desperately sought flight training. He now had over 3,000 hours pilot time and had been checked out on most of the planes in the air corps inventory. He was a realist, known for independence, good judgment, and superb flying ability. Moreover, as a pilot, he fully understood Stewart's fear of being taken off flying duty. Arnold had been carefully vetted as commander of the 29th Training Group. His job was to supervise and train heavy bombardment combat crews slated for assignment to B-17 and B-24 groups headed overseas. In this capacity, he was constantly aware of the staffing needs of the various training groups before they shipped out. He knew that Colonel Bob Terrill had his 445th Group of B-24 Liberators in third-phase training at Sioux City, Iowa. He also knew Colonel Terrill needed a squadron operations officer. He picked up the phone. Before the call was over, Colonel Terrill had hired a squadron operations officer. Within hours, Captain Jimmy Stewart was on his way to Sioux City.

Colonel Arnold later said: "I knew Stewart well, promoted him to captain and squadron commander. I knew he was mature, experienced, and dependable. He was an excellent pilot and instructor, extremely capable. I felt he would be an asset to any group commander. Of course, I knew he wanted to get overseas. And, I felt that if he wanted combat duty, to fight the war, that badly, I'd help him."

Arnold did not mention then, or later, the static personnel hold order. Did he defy the order, challenge it, disobey it, or simply ignore it? Insofar as anyone knows, or air force records indicate, it was never discussed and was never an issue. Colonel Arnold's only statement on the subject was his first: "if he wanted combat duty, to fight the war, that badly—I'd help him." Colonel Arnold's widow, Catherine, who lives in Colorado Springs, also has no recollection of the matter ever being mentioned. And his daughter, Kathleen, of Denver, his confidante and biographer, told me that her father never mentioned the static personnel hold order and that there was no trace of it in any of his papers.

In taking this pivotal action on Stewart's behalf at a critical point in his career, Colonel Arnold became the first of five Army Air Corps/Army Air Force officers to shape and mold Stewart's wartime service, and counsel, advise, and guide him

Lieutenant Beirne Lay, Jr., seated in the cockpit of a Martin B-10 bomber prior to World War II.

in the fields of battle and airlanes of war. Perhaps the brilliant airman and writer Colonel Beirne Lay said it best: "Only a tiny nucleus of officers who had grown up with the Air Corps carried within them the sound air doctrine and military know-how with which the violently expanding AAF had to be inoculated in 1942. Stewart listened to these men and his attitude was humble."

Stewart would be shaped by his other four mentors as his wartime days progressed, but he always remembered Colonel "Pop" Arnold—the man who went to bat for him at a crucial time and perhaps placed his own career on the line. As it turned out, they were to meet after the war at a very joyous time and remain friends for life. Shortly after his call on Stewart's behalf, Colonel Arnold got his own overseas command, taking the 485th Bomb Group of B-24 Liberators to Italy. He had an illustrious combat record and was shot down over Germany on his eighteenth mission and spent several months in a German prison camp. Colonel Arnold retired from the air force after the war with the rank of major general.

CHAPTER 6

A SUMMER IN SIOUX CITY

"When Captain Jimmy Stewart came to the Group, we didn't know what to think about this movie star in our midst. But he turned out to be a regular guy."
—Item in 445th History about Stewart's arrival in Sioux City

In the summer of 1943, a bright-eyed seven-year-old girl had found the perfect niche for meditation and daydreaming—in a haystack on her father's farm in the countryside near Sioux City, Iowa. Her name was Pat Juneman. Now, more than sixty years later, she is Mrs. Pat Mustain, a Sioux City businesswoman. She told me that, "mostly in the afternoon and sometimes at night, there in the haystack, I'd look up at the sky and all I could see were those big planes." Those planes were the four-engine B-24 Liberators of the 445th Bomb Group, Jimmy Stewart's new outfit, flying training missions over Iowa's farmland. That young girl in a haystack dreaming her summer dreams had no way of knowing that in scant months the crews of those big planes with the two tails would be flying combat missions against Hitler in the war skies of Germany.

Pat went on to tell me, "They were flying out of our airbase at Sergeant Bluff, a few miles from Sioux City. Sometimes I could see them take off and land. But mostly they seemed to be flying over my head, like a hundred of them."

Sioux City is a port city on the Missouri River, in western Iowa. Its wartime population was around 75,000, and at that time most of the country had heard of it from a jazzy dance tune called "Sioux City Sue." The city later became famous as the birthplace of the late newspaper columnist Ann Landers, who was known in her hometown as Esther "Eppie" Friedman, where she was born, along with a twin sister, on the Fourth of July, 1918.

Stewart's departure from Boise was anything but ceremonial. The old Ford V-8 was passed on to his fellow instructor pilots with the proviso that it be used on stand-down nights for bar hops into town and as a communal vehicle for daily trips to the flight line and post office. Packing was easy. The War Department had decreed after Pearl Harbor that the military wear only uniforms. No civilian clothes. So Stewart packed his B-4 bag and a small carry-on and was ready for his new assignment with the 445th. Colonel Arnold had set up a "hop" for him on a B-17 training flight. All the way across Idaho, Wyoming, and parts of Nebraska, he flew as copilot for one of his own students, arriving at Sergeant Bluff late in the afternoon. The airbase was seven miles from Sioux City, and Stewart hit the ground running, learning the ropes of his new job.

It didn't take the community long to discover that a movie star was at the airbase. When I talked to Pat Mustain a few months ago, she told me this story about her mother, Mrs. Kathryn Juneman: "Mother came home one afternoon all excited. She had heard that one of the department stores had just gotten in a shipment of nylon stockings. She went downtown immediately. After buying the nylons, she was walking back to her car. While waiting for the light to change, she glanced around, and there stood Jimmy Stewart. They stood side by side, waiting for the light to change, then walked across the street, still not saying a word. On the other side, each went in different directions." Pat said she heard her mother on the phone that night. "She was talking to a friend, telling of the encounter: He was slim and tall and very handsome in his uniform. Just like he looked in the movies."

*   *   *

Perhaps no writer in American history has written about military air power—specifically the Army Air Corps/Army Air Force and the U.S. Air Force—with more skill, perception, authority, affection, and personal feeling—than the late Colonel Beirne Lay. He wore the wreathed star over his silver pilot's wings that signified his status as a command pilot with thousands of hours as a military flyer. He came to England in early 1942 with General Ira Eaker, father of the Eighth Air Force, as one of Eaker's key officers. He flew, along with General Eaker, on the first Eighth Air Force mission to Rouen, France, on August 17, 1942.

Earlier in his writer/pilot career, Beirne Lay wrote *I Wanted Wings*—a highly successful movie starring Veronica Lake that stirred the spirits of thousands of young American men with the desire to learn to fly high-powered air corps warplanes. After his first mission with General Eaker, Lay went on to a signal and decorated Eighth Air Force career as a combat pilot and commander. The Yale-educated pilot-writer commanded the 487th bomb group, and in December, 1944, led the largest Eight Air Force mission of the war against Nazi Germany. Lay was later shot down over occupied France but eluded capture and returned to England. After the war, Lay wrote the movie *Twelve O'clock High* starring Gregory Peck, which is generally regarded as the seminal and definitive story of the wartime Eighth Air Force. Immediately after the war ended, Colonel Lay wrote a two-part series for the *Saturday Evening Post* about the wartime career of his friend, colleague, and Eighth Air Force compatriot Jimmy Stewart. Here are his comments about Stewart's arrival in Sioux City, after Colonel Arnold's telephone call to Colonel Terrill, setting up Stewart's assignment to Terrill's 445th Bomb Group:

> When Captain Stewart reported to Col. Bob Terrill at Sioux City, he felt like a new man. Soon he would be out of the country, in combat, and beyond the reach of those who might try to cast him in a picture. Here with the 445th there was a terrible

immediate purpose to everything a man learned. . . . In exactly nineteen days, Colonel Terrill appointed the newcomer a squadron commander. Perhaps this assignment was more significant than any Stewart has received, when it is considered that no group commander, faced with departure for combat, would have promoted an officer to such a key position without cold-blooded appraisal.

Captain Howard "Doc" Kreidler, of Tilden, Nebraska, was commander of the 701st Squadron of the 445th Bomb Group when Stewart arrived at Sergeant Bluff as the operations officer of the 703rd Squadron. The two small-town boys hit it off immediately and

Liberators take shape on the production line at Fort Worth, Texas, where 3,034 were built.

remained friends throughout the war. Now a retired brigadier general living in Hilton Head, South Carolina, Kreidler told me, "We knew that Jim was a real good pilot before he arrived, and had a lot of hours in the B-17. But we were on a tough, tight schedule in third-phase training and needed to get him checked out on 24s right away. This was no problem. One of the lead pilots in the 703rd checked him out and it was no sweat."

The B-24 Liberator was a bigger, faster, and newer combat bomber than its glamorous four-engine stablemate, the B-17 Flying Fortress. The first Liberator was airborne from Lindbergh Field in San Diego, California, in late December of 1939. It was designed by Consolidated Aircraft, and by the end of World War II, more than 18,000 Liberators had been produced in five different American plants, and the plane had been in combat in all war theaters around the globe. The Liberator was powered by four Pratt & Whitney fourteen-cylinder 1,200-horsepower radial engines. The Davis Laminar wing housed eighteen tanks holding 2,750 gallons of fuel, and the large deep fuselage sitting atop a tricycle landing gear carried a bomb load of 8,800 pounds. This payload was almost two tons more than the B-17 Flying Fortress that Stewart had been flying at Hobbs and Boise.

A fully loaded Liberator carried a crew of ten. For firepower it had a total of ten 50-caliber machine guns, two each in four moveable turrets and two individual guns in the waist. The bomber had a range of 2,850 miles, a ceiling of 32,000 feet, and an air speed exceeding 300 miles per hour. In combat, many B-24 missions were round trips of 1,500 miles, with some nearly 2,000 miles. It was a big plane with a 110-foot wing span, 66 feet long, 18 feet high, set off with its signature wide twin tails. A few days before Stewart was checked out on the Liberator there at Sergeant Bluff, the plane received extensive press notice throughout the world: On August 1, 1943, a huge armada of 178 Liberators took off from the desert sands of Libya for a long low-level raid on the synthetic oil plants at Ploesti, Romania. One of the leaders of this historic and dramatic mission was a man destined to be Jimmy Stewart's friend, mentor, and commanding officer, Ramsay Potts.

Right from the start at the air base in Sioux City, the B-24 Liberator became Jimmy Stewart's airplane. He flew the Liberator overseas to the Eighth Air Force, and he flew it on all of his combat missions.

In those last months at Sioux City, as Doc Kreidler had said, the 445th was on a fast, tough, and unrelenting third-phase training track leading to a successful POM (preparation for overseas movement) inspection, after which they would be deployed to a combat zone that everyone hoped would be the Eighth Air Force in England. Heavy bombardment groups (the Forts and Liberators) were trained in three phases in the U.S. prior to overseas assignment. The 445th was formed in Wendover, Utah, and had taken first- and second-phase training there before coming to Sioux City early that summer. Now, as summer waned, and the impending POM loomed, the little farm girl in the haystack saw a lot of twin-tailed bombers in the skies over western Iowa. The heat and pressure were on.

Colonel Terrill lost no time in getting his new operations officer of the 703rd up to speed. Stewart—who was happy, dedicated, and flying around the clock—blended well, studied, and responded keenly to Terrill's vigorous, spirited, and highly informative training schedule for the group. They trained in heavy bombardment tactics; cross-country missions; tight formation, instrument and night flying; navigation, bombing and aerial gunnery exercises; intelligence briefings; interrogations; weather report briefings; and the exhilarating experience of learning to fly the B-24, first with three engines, then with two. There was some ground school instruction, but the real matter at hand was learning all facets and flying characteristics of the big bomber.

The officers and men of a heavy bombardment group in those times were divided into two sections, the air echelon and the ground echelon. The air echelon was composed of personnel directly involved with flying the mission. Shortly after the group was formed at Wendover, Colonel Terrill and his top air echelon staff were ordered to Orlando, Florida, to attend the Air Force School of Applied Tactics (AFSAT). With prime officers of other groups in training for combat duty, Colonel Terrill and his staff had undergone a six-week crash course of simulated heavy bombardment tactics and techniques under actual mission conditions. The Orlando school utilized reports from overseas on bombing missions and instructors who had just returned from combat duty.

From 1930 to 1940, as Jimmy Stewart was honing his acting skills and adding cockpit time to his pilot's logbook in California, the Air Corps Tactical School had been operating at Maxwell Field in Alabama. In Air Corps/Air Force circles it became known simply as the Tac School, and its mission was to teach air corps officers the use and potential of air power and precision bombing technique. Colonel Terrill was a graduate of the Tac School, which closed in 1941. Shortly thereafter, AFSAT in Orlando was established for senior officers like Terrill and their staffs who were headed to combat.

At Sergeant Bluff, Colonel Terrill and his staff put the 445th crews through a sharp and direct schedule of training modeled as closely as possible on the real thing as taught at Orlando. It was showdown time. And in less than three weeks, Colonel Terrill promoted Jimmy Stewart from operations officer to commander of the 703rd Squadron, according to Beirne Lay.

Stewart always felt that he was extremely lucky to be with the 445th at the start of his combat career and to come under the influence of a commander of Terrill's caliber and experience. Early in the war, Terrill had commanded a bomber group operating out of Cairo, Egypt, and, back in the states, had headed the 382nd bombardment group prior to taking over the 445th. Almost from his early boyhood in Faneuil, Massachusetts, where he was born in 1910, it seemed that Terrill was destined to become one of America's most gifted combat commanders of World War II—a cool, influential, and inspiring leader, and an expert on the B-24 Liberator.

After graduating from West Point in 1932, Terrill got his wings at Kelly Field in Texas and immediately set out on tours of duty, mostly in pursuit aircraft in the mid- to late-1930s. This was the nomadic life of a young air corps pilot, learning his trade, constantly flying in places like Wheeler Field in Hawaii and at March and Hamilton Fields in California. He was a new major at March Field in Riverside, California on December 7, 1941, and had just pinned on the eagles of a full colonel when he responded to the phone call from "Pop" Arnold and hired Jimmy Stewart as an operations officer in a new group headed for the ETO. At that time, Terrill was two years younger than his new operations officer and would become the second air corps officer, after Arnold, to guide and direct Stewart's World War II career.

Here are notable entries in the official history of the 445th Bomb Group covering the summer of 1943 in Sioux City:

> Probably our most publicized personnel addition, which occurred in the early days of August, was the assignment of Captain Jimmy Stewart as 703rd Bomb Squadron Operations officer. The novelty of having this movie star in our midst soon wore off, especially since he proved himself to be a hardworking, sincere, "regular" fellow. . . .
>
> On August 13 we received by teletype authorization to increase our combat crew strength to seventy crews. This meant an increase in personnel of 88 officers and 132 enlisted men.
>
> August 26, 1943, ushered in a period of disaster for the Group. It was a grim foretaste of things to come. One of our ships on a night training flight crashed, and the nine men aboard were killed. On Thursday, September 2, a few minutes before midnight, another ship went down in flames, killing all ten crew members. The plane crashed just a short distance from the Base, and many persons saw it go down in flames. We had hardly recovered from the shock of this tragedy when about noon on Saturday,

September 4, we received news of a third crash, which claimed eight victims. It was no wonder that we were beginning to feel jinxed, and a bit jumpy. Fortunately, this proved to be the last accident of our Operational Training days in the States.

September came. And October. The good weather held. The intense training regimen continued for the 445th. The POM inspection had been successful. Days were getting shorter. The new Liberators were arriving and being outfitted for overseas flights. Wives and girlfriends were visiting Sioux City, and three-day passes were granted when training permitted. Excitement was everywhere, in town and at Sergeant Bluff. Orders would be coming down any day.

As the training schedule reached these final hectic stages, Stewart had never felt more alive, more involved, more a part of a rapidly emerging and noble undertaking that he truly believed in. The learning experiences of Moffett, Mather, Kirkland, Hobbs—and the snow, mountains, and frustration of Boise—were in the past. That was yesterday. The future was now. He was happy. He was ready.

As the training had progressed over a period of almost three dynamic months, Stewart could see every day the results of Colonel Terrill's masterful and productive leadership. Early on, from the time Terrill had picked him to lead the 703rd Squadron, Stewart had viewed the tall, soft-spoken West Point–educated fighter-pilot-turned-bomber-commander as a role model. From the beginning, Stewart had developed an easy, friendly, approachable rapport with both officers and men of his squadron. He had seen Terrill's leadership move the group into a fine-tuned, well-trained, cohesive unit with a clear sense of purpose and dedication. He sought this same goal in his own command and worked very hard to achieve it. He had direct responsibility for over four-hundred men and twenty-four bombers. With both officers and other ranks, Stewart was friendly, approachable, and, above all, professional. They all knew of his other life in Hollywood, and they also knew he was a crack pilot and leader, and the word had been passed down about his undaunted and sure-handed skill in the weather and mountains of Boise.

While his primary interest involved the flying crews, Stewart had a special affection for the often unheralded ground crewmen who maintained the complicated Liberators. It was at Sergeant Bluff that Stewart began his personal custom of always remaining at the control tower until his last crew had returned. This hands-on interest became Stewart's signature during his World War II career. And many of his men always mentioned it to me in times of combat.

CHAPTER 7

THE WRIGHT CREW

"Of course. That's Captain Stewart."
—Lieutentant George Wright to
Sergeant Robbie Robinson

Captain Stewart met the Wright crew early in the morning of September 22, 1943. The newcomers reported to the commanding officer of the 703rd Squadron as replacements for the unlucky crew that had crashed a few days previously at Sergeant Bluff. The Wright crew became a constant presence in Stewart's combat experience in England in the crucial, perilous months ahead and, indeed, in the years to come. Looking back, it would not be too much to say that the Wright crew, if not his favorites, certainly were faithful, loyal, and enduring—traits that were returned in kind by Stewart. Perhaps this was because of the professional esteem, respect, and personal fondness he had for John Harold "Robbie" Robinson, an insightful and sensitive Tennessean, a flight engineer-gunner who had emerged as something of an advisor, philosopher, and role model for the Wright crew. Robinson—innovative, thoughtful, mature, although about the same age as his colleagues (22–23)—had been an engineer for a Memphis hotel before being drafted and leaving his new wife, Elizabeth, for wartime service in the Army Air Corps.

The Wright Crew's Liberator—"Tennessee Dottie."

Almost half a century later, in 1988, Robinson—with his diaries; his boundless and unique memories; encouragement from friends, family, and wartime colleagues, including Jimmy Stewart; and his compassion and unveiled emotions—wrote the book *A Reason to Live: Moments of Love, Happiness, and Sorrow,** which he dedicated to Elizabeth.

A Reason to Live has become an important chronicle of combat life in the Eighth Air Force and recounts in poignant and gripping terms the cold and dangerous lives of heavy bombardment crews in their missions against Nazi Germany. In my judgment, Robinson has recorded these grim encounters of the combat airmen with the same impassive eye, knowing heart, and trenchant words that Ernie Pyle and Sergeant Bill Mauldin used in their perceptive stories of the heroic deeds of other American warriors who fought in other places, in other ways, in World War II.

Jimmy Stewart was a leader of these dauntless combat crews. Perhaps the single most appealing and lasting factor in his military career was the devotion and faith that his men had for him, and the influence that followed. Robinson knew of this trait early on. His observations, little by-the-way tales, vignettes, and striking and graphic accounts of combat missions and other times embraced the tender moments of harsh times. Robbie's aim is true—right to the heart and close to the bone.

The B-24 Liberator went to war in the Eighth Air Force with a crew of ten men, four officers and six enlisted men. For the most part, the crews were put together in the military manner, by the numbers, after individual specialized training. Usually, the crews evolved into finely

*Published by Castle Books, PO Box 17262, Memphis, TN 38187.

tuned teams or crews—professionally and personally. A crew is always named after the pilot's last name, such as the Elebash crew, the Miller crew, the Milam crew, the Thompson crew, the Clover crew, and the Newton crew. So it was with the Wright crew.

After being inducted into the army in the fall of 1942, John Harold Robinson was trained as an aircraft mechanic and flight engineer-gunner. In the summer of 1943, after stints at Salt Lake City and Boise, Robinson was posted to the Pocatello Army Air Base at Pocatello, Idaho. There, he was assigned as a flight engineer to the crew of a B-24 Liberator bomber in second-phase training. The pilot was Second Lieutenant George Wright of Baltimore, Maryland. From Pocatello, the Wright crew was transferred to Jimmy Stewart's squadron at Sioux City, Iowa.

The Wright Crew: (top row, left to right) George Wright, Bob Alexander, Buckey Kroll, and William Witman; (bottom row, left to right) William Cook, Harold "Robbie" Robinson, Kenneth Dabbs, John Van Bogelman, E. O. Cross, and Marvin Tyler.

In that summer of 1943 at Pocatello, the Wright crew logged more than 72 hours of flying time, in addition to intensive ground-school work. In mid-September, the transfer came: The Wright crew was going to Sioux City to join the 445th Bomb Group, which was in third-phase training. The Wright crew had been selected for the assignment because it had an excellent bombing record and had more flying time than the other crews at Pocatello.

The combat crew of Lieutenant George Wright of Maryland was a typical all-American group: Lieutenant Bob "Buckey" Kroll of New Jersey was copilot; E.O. Cross (Texas) was ball-turret gunner; Marvin Tyler of Texas was waist gunner and second engineer; John Van Bogelman from Michigan was the radio man; first engineer William Cook was a New Yorker; armorer-gunner Kenneth Dabbs was also from Texas; Lieutenant William Wittman of Mississippi was the bombardier; the navigator was Lieutenant Bob Alexander of New York; and Harold Robinson of Tennessee was flight engineer-gunner.

During stateside training, and later in England, officers and enlisted men lived in separate quarters. Living conditions were usually about the same in both countries. On training bases in the States, two officers sometimes shared a room. In England, both ranks lived in Nissen huts. Combat crews in England had their own mess halls. The officers were usually college men, and as the draft began to send men into the air corps training program, many of the lower ranks were college trained as well. All crew members were highly intelligent, quick, technically inclined, and skillfully trained for the job.

The Nissen hut, with its distinctive corrugated metal roof and sides, was smaller than its Pacific War offspring, the Quonset hut.

Rank among the combat crews, especially overseas, was observed, but practiced in a casual we're-all-in-

Right, Robbie Robinson at
battle station in the ETO.

this-thing-together attitude.
Friendships among crew
members formed quickly
and often endured throughout the war and into many
years of civilian life. Crew
members met as young men.
They trained together, lived
together, fought together, cried
together, drank together—died together. Perhaps at no time in the
history of warfare has there been such a relationship among fighting
men as existed with the combat crews of heavy bombardment aircraft, notably in the Eighth Air Force in World War II. As a combat
intelligence officer—training, flying, living with and working with
these daring men night and day—I can only say that their dangerous
lives and triumphant deeds were thrilling and memorable to behold.

Robbie Robinson told me about his first meeting with Jimmy
Stewart after the train ride from Pocatello:

> In Sioux City, we were taken immediately to the
> air base, to an empty barracks, and then to the mess
> hall. We were to report to the operations headquarters
> on the flight line the next morning at about 7. We all
> met at headquarters on the flight line at 7 a.m. the
> next day. Our officers were already there when we
> arrived. Wright went into a small office and we all
> followed him in. The small office was full, with all of
> us crowded in it.
>
> The lanky captain sitting at the desk looked
> familiar, for some reason. He said, "Well, fellows, we
> are sure glad to see you guys. Glad you're here with

us." Rubbing one side and his chin, he said, "You know—You fellows are—uh—replacing one of our fine crews that hit a water tank on landing approach last week." He looked at us and thought for a minute and said, "You fellows will just have to be more careful, you know."

The captain stood up and thought a minute. Then he said, "Have you fellows been home lately? To see your folks, I mean?"

Everyone said, at one time, a loud, "NO."

"Well, now," said the captain, "How about going on a furlough? Say, for five days or so. Starting about right now." He scratched his chin. "The sergeant, here, will get you your papers. That's all, and you fellows have a good time."

We stepped outside.

Seemed like a nice guy, I thought, wondering where I had seen him before, or was it just my imagination?

We stood outside the captain's office, waiting for his sergeant to get our furlough papers ready. We were happy as we could be about getting to go home. We could hardly believe our new captain.

I said to Wright, "That guy sure does look familiar."

Wright smiled. "Of course. That's Captain Stewart."

The Wright crew returned from furlough to find Captain Stewart's 703rd Squadron and the entire 445th Bomb Group heavy into the final days of third-phase training. It wouldn't be long before the ship-out date came. The rumors were that it would be the Eighth Air Force. Tension mounted. And the pressure on the crews—up at five every morning, shower, shave, bunk make-up, mess hall, flight line, Captain Stewart's briefing, aircraft preflight, gear on board, ammunition loading—and, flying, flying, flying—every day for hours at a stretch.

Because of the extensive specialized training of the combat crews, and the day-to-day danger of the missions, General "Hap" Arnold, the air corps' top commander back in Washington, decreed that all enlisted crews on heavy bombardment combat aircraft would have the rank of staff sergeant. Robbie told me how the Wright crew heard the news of their promotions:

"Jimmy Stewart walked into our barracks. We were all fooling around. Cross, Tyler, and I saw him coming, and we jumped out of our cots and acted like we were trying to clean up the barracks.

"Stewart said, 'Fellows, we have got to leave this barracks good and clean when we leave here this time.' He picked up a broom and started helping us sweep the barracks floor. He said, 'You see how dirty it is. You know we have got to get all that brown stuff off the commodes, too. Be sure we clean them good.'

"He stood the broom against a bunk. 'It's got to be clean in here. You know what I mean.' We told him it would really be clean when we left," Robinson related

"He looked at each one of us and smiled and walked out of the barracks.

"After he left, we did clean up the place a bit. I gathered most of my personal belongings, and we all walked together to our aircraft and put our gear on board. We looked the airplane over good and everything was in good shape.

"We walked on back to the barracks together. As we entered the barracks, there stood Lieutenant Wright and Captain Stewart. I was sure we were in for a chewing about the barracks not being clean. We really had done very little except sweep the floor and pick up our personal gear.

"As soon as we entered our barracks we all gave Wright and Stewart a snappy salute because we were sure we were in for a chewing. Stewart and Wright returned our salute." said Robinson.

"'Well, I see you fellows did a pretty good job of cleaning up the barracks,' Stewart said. 'Make sure you don't get it dirty tonight. We gotta leave things clean for the next guys coming in.' He studied us a minute and said, 'Oh, yes. You know, fellows, you are all staff sergeants now. Congratulations.'

"He smiled and strode out of the barracks with Wright staying behind with us.

"We looked at each other, grinning.

"'Staff sergeants?' Tyler said.

"'Us?' I said.

"'Can you beat that?' said Cross.

"Wright congratulated us. 'Captain Stewart came by here earlier today to tell you about the promotions,' Wright said. 'He said you looked like you were cleaning up the place. He decided not to say anything until I could come along with him.'

"Now we knew the real reason that Stewart came by the barracks that morning—and it wasn't to tell us to clean up the place."

"We really liked this guy. There was more to him than just a Hollywood celebrity—a lot more."

Then the news came: Colonel Terrill and Captain Stewart called a briefing. The 445th had a ship-out date. Robinson told me about the last few hours:

"All the flight crews of the 703rd were given a pass to go to town. We all dressed up in our Sunday-best uniform, put on our fifty mission crush hats, and thought we really looked like sharp air force crewmen.

"We all went to town together. When we got to town we broke up in groups. No one knew what he wanted to do. We felt a bit uncertain. So guys went their own ways. Cross, Tyler, and I walked around and found the Rathskeller, a restaurant and bar in the basement of a building on Main Street. We went in, and about half of the crews of the 703rd Squadron were there," Robinson related.

"People were singing and having a good time. Someone got up on the bar and recited a happy but sentimental farewell to the 703rd Squadron, to all 'the brave lads going overseas in a couple of days.'

"Everyone was in a real noisy state of mind. It was almost a military stag party. The officers and enlisted men of the 703rd had taken over the place. It wasn't long before someone made up a song about Jimmy Stewart being the best squadron commander in the world. Then there was another noisy toast, made to the brave men of the 703rd Squadron who were 'leaving for overseas with Jimmy Stewart, the best damned squadron commander in the world.' Several others gave a toast to Stewart," said Robinson.

Stewart had often flown back home from California in his little Stinson to see his parents. And Alex and Bessie visited Hollywood a number of times to see their only son. It now seemed obvious that the 445th would soon be shipping out, so Jimmy invited his parents to Sioux City for a farewell visit. They came immediately and stayed at Sioux City's Hotel Warrior where Jimmy had made reservations. As a squadron commander, he had a Jeep and met his parents for dinner as often as time and duties would allow. One night they taxied out to the officers club for dinner and met Colonel Terrill and his wife.

Alex and Bessie stayed until the day of Jimmy's departure, and they were at the Sergeant Bluff Terminal as the air echelon departed. The ground echelon had already left by train for New York, continuing by ship to England. The group's new Liberators were parked on hard-stands out on the field, and the combat crews were ready to leave. As Jimmy and his crew boarded a truck for the short ride to the plane, his father handed him a sealed envelope. He asked his son to open it after the plane was airborne. Jimmy was flying copilot on takeoff. As the pilot set a heading, Captain Stewart opened the envelope and read his father's letter.

> My dear Jim boy, Soon after you read this letter, you will be on your way to the worst sort of danger. I have had this in mind for a long time and I am very much concerned. . . . But Jim, I am banking on the enclosed copy of the 91st Psalm. The thing that takes the place of fear and worry is the

promise in these words. I am staking my faith in these words. I feel sure that God will lead you through this mad experience. . . . I can say no more. I continue only to pray. Goodbye, my dear. God bless you and keep you. I love you more than I can tell you. Dad.

He then read the enclosed 91st Psalm:

I will say of the Lord, He is my refuge and my fortress. . . .

His truth shall be thy shield and buckler.

Thou shalt not be afraid for the terror by night; nor for the arrow that flieth by day;

For He shall give his angels charge over thee, to keep thee in all thy ways.

They shall bear thee up in their hands, lest thou dash thy foot against a stone.

The date was November 11, 1943.

CHAPTER 8

COMBAT LIFE AT TIBENHAM

"There are 39,000 antiaircraft guns on the Western Front. . . . When you get a burst from one of these guns near you, it will make a strange noise and then you will hear small pieces of steel hitting your plane."
—Briefing of veteran RAF bomber pilot to new American combat flight crews

Captain Jimmy Stewart, at the controls of a B-24 Liberator bomber, arrived in England on the afternoon of November 25, 1943. The overseas flight had taken a little more than two weeks, counting weather delays along the way. Each plane in the group flew individually, handling its own navigation. This was the standard operating procedure (SOP) of combat groups on their way to England, including my own, the 453rd, which followed Stewart's 445th, two weeks later. The flight path was known as the "warm weather" route, which avoided the North Atlantic in wintertime. From take-off in Sioux City, planes of the 445th flew to Lincoln, Nebraska; Morrison Field near Palm Beach, Florida; San Juan, Puerto Rico; Georgetown, British Guiana; Belem and Natal, Brazil; Dakar in Senegal, North Africa; Marrakech, French Morocco; and finally on to England. And Tibenham.

Stewart and First Lieutenant Lloyd Sharrard, chief of the Sharrard crew, shared the pilot's left seat all the way over in their aircraft (Tenofus 41-29132). Sharrard was a crack pilot of the 703rd

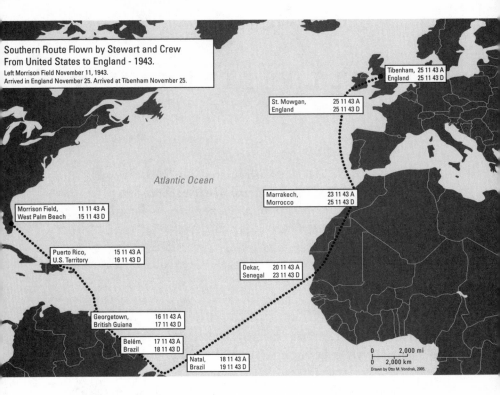

Southern Route Flown by Stewart and Crew
From United States to England - 1943.
Left Morrison Field November 11, 1943.
Arrived in England November 25. Arrived at Tibenham November 25.

Tibenham, 25 11 43 A
England   25 11 43 D

St. Mowgan,   25 11 43 A
England   25 11 43 D

Atlantic Ocean

Marrakech,   23 11 43 A
Morocco   25 11 43 D

Morrison Field,   11 11 43 A
West Palm Beach   15 11 43 D

Puerto Rico,   15 11 43 A
U.S. Territory 16 11 43 D

Dekar,   20 11 43 A
Senegal   23 11 43 D

Georgetown,   16 11 43 A
British Guiana   17 11 43 D

Belém,   17 11 43 A
Brazil   18 11 43 D

Natal,   18 11 43 A
Brazil   19 11 43 D

0   2,000 mi
0   2,000 km
Drawn by Otto M. Vondrak, 2005.

Squadron and had checked Stewart out on the Liberator when he first
arrived at Sioux City. Stewart wanted to fly overseas with a sure,
dependable flying officer who would share first pilot chores and still
allow him time for his duties as squadron commander.

Home base of the 445th Bomb Group was Tibenham, near the
village of Tivetshall in East Anglia, about 120 miles northeast of
London and 20 miles from the large city of Norwich. For the entire
flight, the Stewart-Sharrard Liberator was airborne for more than
fifty hours, flying mostly over water and jungle. Colonel Terrill also
flew the southern route to Tibenham. The ground echelon was
already there, getting the widely dispersed base ready for the incoming combat crews—that is to say, as much as the constant rain, cold,
fog, and mud allowed. The mud was slippery, deep, and everywhere.

This photo of vehicles struggling in the mud at Tibenham shows the conditions Stewart and his crew faced upon arrival.

The Wright crew, flying in the day after Captain Stewart's arrival—with eye-opening stories of stopovers at Belem, Natal, Dakar, and the harrowing approach to Marrakech, flying at 5,000 feet through a narrow pass of towering mountains above the plane. Like all other flight crews, they quickly moved into their Nissen-hut home, which can best be described as a big corrugated pipe cut lengthwise and turned upside down on a concrete slab. The latrine, strangely called the ablution room, was behind the hut. Two enlisted combat crews, six men each, were assigned to a hut. Nearby, in similar accommodations, the crew's officers were billeted, eight men to a hut. Captain Stewart, while at Tibenham, shared quarters with the commander of the 701st Squadron, Captain Howard Kreidler. Standard furnishings for the enlisted men in their Nissen huts were a small pot-bellied stove, cots, and a generous supply of blankets. The innovative and resourceful Wright crew quickly set about improving their home with a "requisitioned" larger stove, a radio for listening to the German propagandist "Lord Haw Haw," and the sexy voice and smooth music of "Axis Sally." They also built shelves for pictures, books, and personal items. The crew found a way to improve their meager supply of rationed coal for the pot-bellied stove, which was also used to heat water for shaving. But little could be done to relieve the bitter cold the American visitors encountered while on duty in the English countryside.

It has been wisely said that Americans, of all people, are quick to adjust to new and strange conditions and situations. To the bright, conditioned, and eager young combat crews of Colonel Terrill's bomber group, the traveling, briefings, training, and getting used to new situations in strange places and a different environment was old hat. After all, they had been going through this new way of life since they volunteered or were drafted into the Army Air Force. But, here in wartime England, with the blackouts and the German air raids at Tibenham, there was a new and strange element in their lives: Danger. Danger from an enemy. The clear possibility that another person in another plane, or sighting an antiaircraft gun from the ground, would seek to take their lives or cause them harm was fearsome. And there was the constant presence of the unknown.

To prepare these young Americans with the best training, the best equipment—and the psychological adjustment—to deal with this danger was the aim and purpose of Colonel Terrill, Captain Stewart, and other leaders of the group, as well as

The 445th Bomb Group's B-24 Assembly Plane "Lucky Gordon."

the Eighth Air Force itself. So, in the bitterly cold rain and fog of early morning darkness, the combat crews prepared for the enemy. The drill was on. The shakedown flights continued. Every day.

Sergeant Robinson of the Wright crew relates their situation:

> On the morning of December 5, a Jeep stopped by the hut, and a sergeant got out and came in. He told us we were scheduled to fly. We were to report to operations in the briefing room at 0900 hours, dressed out and ready to take off.
>
> We were ready to pull out of the hard stand, when a Jeep drove up, and Captain Jimmy Stewart got out.
>
> "Fellas, I'll be riding with you," he said.
>
> Stewart got into the aircraft and went to the flight deck. Wright taxied to the end of the runway. We went through the check list by the numbers. Everyone was on the ball. Down the runway we went and we had a good lift off.
>
> Jimmy Stewart walked all through the airplane, checking us all out, and returned to the flight deck. On the intercom he asked each crew position questions about our routine. He asked me, "What are you doing now, Sergeant Robinson? What do you see out the waist window? Can you see the supercharger gate position? Are the exhausts smoking? What color is the engine exhaust? How much fuel do we have on board? Are you checking it? Are the fuel gauges off and drained?"
>
> Stewart wanted to see each engineer on the flight deck. I went forward. Then more questions. "Robinson, can you fly as first engineer? Can you operate all turrets? Can you arm the bombs?" He had a question about everything. Stewart really knew this airplane. He wanted us to know it, too.

Stewart took Wright's position in the pilot's seat and put Buckey through the routine. We were to create a formation with other aircraft. We all would be forming on a lead or assmebly ship. The lead ship would be painted orange with black checks.

There was a thin cloud coverage and we flew up through it. We were all on oxygen. Buckey said the temperature was minus thirty degrees Fahrenheit. Stewart asked if all our heated suits were working properly. The flight test lasted four hours and fifteen minutes. We approached the airfield, touched down and made a perfect landing.

Stewart nodded in approval of Wright's smooth landing. "Good."

Wright taxied back to the hard stand, and we all got out of the airplane with a sigh of relief. Stewart got out and we were all sitting around under the wing, waiting for someone to come to take us to operations.

As we sat there, Stewart said, "Well—I suppose you fellas are going to make it okay together."

Of course, as important as training and shakedown flights were to the Wright crew, other things were on their minds in those early days at Tibenham. One was money. In one of the briefings, they had been told that the British pound was worth, in round numbers, four American dollars. There was no way to check this out because they had not been paid and had no money. Robbie said later:

Cross and I stopped by the finance building to see why we had not received our pay. The finance officer told us that he had not had the time to get to our pay records. He said, "You're not going anywhere. Come back next week."

We both walked out of the building, grumbling to ourselves about not getting paid. We walked on down the road, still grumbling. We ran into Jimmy Stewart. He must have noticed our expressions.

"How are you fellas doing?" Captain Stewart asked us.

Cross said, "Captain Stewart, we were just at finance to see why we had not been paid and the finance officer said to come back next week. He didn't have time to pay us." Stewart said, "You didn't get paid the first of December?" "No, sir," we chimed. "Well, now. Come on and we'll find out why he doesn't have time to pay you," Stewart said. We started walking briskly, side by side. Stewart had long legs and we had almost to run to keep up.

We all walked into the finance office together. With a clearing of his throat, Captain Stewart said to the lieutenant behind the desk, "Why hasn't Lieutenant Wright's crew been paid?" The lieutenant said, "They will be paid, sir, but it will take a few days to get to it." Captain Stewart put his hand to his chin and started rubbing it. Then he said, "Lieutenant, we just don't have a few days. I believe we ought to pay them right now. Not in a few days. I mean kinda like, now—in the next thirty minutes." Stewart looked at the lieutenant and then at us. He said to the lieutenant, I will be back in here in a little while, and, you know—if Lieutenant Wright's crew isn't paid by then, I believe that we will just have to find a new finance lieutenant for this one will be on his way out of here to the Infantry."

Stewart told us, "Stick around a few minutes. I think he is going to pay you now." Cross and I said quietly, "Thank you, sir." He halfway returned our sharp salute and said, "I'll see you around, fellas." Then he walked out of the finance office.

The finance lieutenant said for us to sign on a piece of paper. He gave us a month's pay. "Tell the other members of your crew to come by here as quickly as they can and get their pay," he said. We took the money, signed the paper and got ourselves out of there.

We rushed back to the hut and told everyone to get over to finance and pick up their money. We all were beginning to think this Jimmy Stewart was really an all right guy.

Things were gradually shaping up at Tibenham.

Slightly more than two weeks after arrival, on December 13, Jimmy Stewart flew with the 445th Bomb Group on its first bombing mission against Nazi Germany. The target was the naval docks at Kiel. Immediately upon arrival in the ETO, Colonel Bob Terrill laid on an extensive schedule of practice missions—formation flying, assembly procedure, and weather briefings—although nothing could be done about the horrendous English weather. New equipment was issued—oxygen masks, heated suits, throat mikes, and headsets. Classes and briefings were held in personal aggression, such as the use of a piece of wire, a shoestring, a rope, plus other methods for use in hand-to-hand combat.

A British flying officer from an RAF bomber squadron told the American crews what air warfare was like and how heavy the German antiaircraft fire could be. He called it flak. He said, "Yanks, the black bursts will be 88 mm shells. The 105 mm shells will make white bursts. When you get a burst near you, it will make a strange noise, and then you will hear small pieces of steel hitting your plane." The RAF officer went on to say, "There are 39,000 anti-aircraft guns on the Western front. There are more than a million men serving the guns and making up anti-aircraft gun crews, searchlight crews and barrage balloon crews. Ten percent of all the enemy population give all their time to the air raid services." He continued, "The bloody German fighter pilots are dangerous to all of us. There are enough of them for each of you to have several. So pick yours out while you can."

In spite of the freezing weather and frequent German air raids on the base, and, after the first mission on the thirteenth, the crews were settling into a steady routine. Then it was Christmas Eve.

Robinson reports:

Dawn briefing,
Eighth Air Force.
C.H. Freudenthal

Briefing started on a solemn note. Something was said about it being Christmas Eve, 1943.

Jimmy Stewart rose. "Fellas," he said, "this mission is uh—a very, very, important mission. We have to hit our target today. We have to plaster it. The Germans have some kind of—uh—it's a new rocket machine they've cooked up. They are going to use it to hit London and a lot of other cities over here in England. We have to stop it before they go that far."

He turned to the chart and picked up a long wooden pointer.

"We are going to fly in at 12,000 feet and hit these targets. Yeah. I said 12,000 feet. I—uh—know, fellas, that 12,000 is pretty low for us heavies. But—we just have to make sure we hit those targets today."

Stewart paused a minute and said, "Fellas, I'm going to make this voluntary. That means, anyone who doesn't want to go on a Christmas Eve mission does not have to go. You can just get up and walk out now. Nobody will hold it against you."

He looked around. "But—I'm going. Fellas, you can count on that. I intend to go along."

There was a long silence. No one left the room.

Stewart nodded. "Thanks, fellas."

Briefing officers said the weather would be good and we would have good fighter protection on this Christmas Eve. The target was Bonnieres, France. We would be hitting the Germans' secret rocket emplacements there. Thirty-five aircraft from the group would go. "Flak will be heavy," he said, "but you will see the English coast most of the flight."

We were dismissed. The walk to the truck didn't seem as bad as before. Maybe it was because we were not to be over enemy territory very long.

Flying over the target at only 12,000 feet was the big worry now. "That's not very high," somebody said.

The Christmas Eve mission was a success. Here is an account of it in the London newspapers:

CALAIS RAIDERS TOLD: SMASH SECRET TARGETS AT ANY COST

More than 2,000 Allied airplanes were used on Christmas Eve in a series of daylight operations against "special military installations" in the Calais coastal area of Northern France—believed to be the location of the German "secret weapon" concentration.

These attacks carried the non-stop air offensive from bases in Britain to a new high peak of intensity, and the fifth day of the monster blitz established two new records for the American Eighth Air Force.

It employed the largest force it had ever sent out, and the force of heavy bombers which attacked the chief target was the largest ever used on such an operation. In addition, the whole series of operations, which covered almost all the daylight hours, was carried through without an aircraft loss.

Brigadier General Ted Timberlake (middle), commander, Second Combat Wing.

*　　*　　*

The B-24 Liberators in the Eighth Air Force were assigned to the Second Bomb Division, commanded by Major General James Hodges. Under his control was the Second Combat Bomb Wing, commanded by Brigadier General Ted Timberlake. Comprising Timberlake's wing were three groups—the 445th, with Colonel Bob Terrill at the helm; the 453rd, commanded by Colonel Joe Miller; and the 389th, headed by Colonel Milton Arnold. All were relatively new to the ETO. Since its first mission against Nazi Germany, on August 17, 1942, the Eighth Air Force was in a constant growth pattern. From October, 1943, to January, 1944, the heavy bomber groups had increased from twenty-one to twenty-six, and more than 2,000 new Liberators and Flying Fortresses were in the pipeline and would soon be on their way to England.

On the 445th Bomb Group's first mission to Kiel, Captain Jimmy Stewart led the high squadron, going into the target at 27,000 feet, with good results and no losses. On Bremen a few days later and the mission to the Calais coast of France on Christmas Eve, Stewart turned in steady, capable, and conscientious performances that reflected a high degree of training and leadership ability.

Now, on January 7, 1944, it was Ludwigshafen, Germany.

Colonel Beirne Lay, in his *Saturday Evening Post* article of December 15, 1945, reported:

After leaving the target area in a two-group wing formation, Stewart, in command of the 445th Group, discovered with alarm that the group he was following was thirty degrees off course. He immediately called its leader on VHF and pointed out the error in navigation. The latter insisted that Stewart was mistaken.

At this point and in this situation, Stewart had few, if any, options. Colonel Lay continues:

He saw another formation leaving Ludwigshafen
on course, and knew that he could easily switch over

and tack on behind it, thus insuring the safety of his own group. But this would have meant abandoning to its lonely fate the group which was blundering away from the main procession—an easy prey for the fighters which were sure to single it out on the way home. And yet if he continued, for the sake of wing integrity, to follow a leader who was heading for disaster, he must accept the certainty of sharing concentrated fighter attacks and extensive flak damage. Wandering even a mile or two from the briefed course often meant that, instead of coming home without a flak hole, you arrived all shot up and minus six or seven good crews.

Colonel Lay, a veteran air force pilot who had flown on the first Eighth Air Force mission along with General Ira Eaker, and a number of combat missions since that time, drew on his own combat experience. He wrote:

It is easy to sit in comfortable chairs around a blackboard after a mission and say what a leader should or should not have done when faced with so awful a dilemma as confronted Stewart—a situation, incidentally, which illustrates perfectly the kind of decisions our air commanders had to face every day.

With a hollow feeling in his stomach and a heavy heart, Stewart called the other group. "Padlock Red leader to Padlock Green leader. We're sticking with you."

Fighter controllers of the Luftwaffe, eagerly plotting the track of the two groups that had become separated from the main force, vectored several fighter *Staffeln* toward the kill. Twenty-eight miles south of Paris, sixty Messerschmitts and Focke-Wulfs drove head-on attacks into the lead group. Jimmy Stewart grimly closed the 445th in for support.

Paying for a navigational error with his life, the leader of the other group was the first to go down under a fusillade of 20-mm cannon shells. Other B-24s of the lead group met the same fate. But the Focke-Wulfs which turned their attention to Stewart's compact formation didn't score any kills. Jimmy brought all his boys safely back to Tibenham.

At least one consideration which must have entered into Stewart's promotion to major later in January was the fact that he had already made a solid contribution on the Ludwigshafen mission to the sense of unity, hence combat efficiency, of the three groups in Timberlake's wing. By risking his neck to protect an erring teammate, he had probably saved the 389th from annihilation. More important was the factor of air discipline. He had served notice that he possessed a cardinal virtue of the soldier: Persuade your leader of his mistake, if you can, but follow him, right or wrong.

A few days after the January 7, Ludwigshafen mission, Colonel Terrill received the sort of letter a boss likes to get:

> *Headquarters, 389th Bomb Group (H)*
> 13 January, 1944.
> COL. ROBERT TERRILL,
> COMMANDING OFFICER,
> 445TH BOMB GROUP (H)
> *Dear Bob:* Please allow me to express the admiration of the personnel of the 389th as well as my

personal admiration for the splendid display of superb air discipline of the 445th on the mission of 7 January, 1944.

The good judgment of Captain Stewart, your Group leader, in maintaining an excellent group formation yet making every attempt to hold his position in the Combat Wing formation is to be commended.

Congratulations to you and the 445th,

Sincerely,

(Signed) MILTON W. ARNOLD,

Colonel, Air Corps, Commanding.

1st Indorsement

CAPT. JAMES M. STEWART,

C.O., 703D BOMBARDMENT SQUADRON (H)

1. It is extremely gratifying to me to receive letters of this nature. You are hereby commended for your good judgment and leadership ability as displayed on 7 January, 1944.

2. A copy of this letter will be filed in your 201 File and with your next regular efficiency report.

(Signed) ROBERT H. TERRILL,

Colonel, Air Corps, Commanding.

At the beginning of the new year of 1944, the Allied high level combat leadership was in place. This involved several major changes in the U.S. Air Force face cards, both in England and the Mediterranean. Every facet, every detail, every element in the changes of command and the ongoing buildup of American air power in the ETO was pointed to Allied air superiority over Germany at the time of the cross-channel invasion, which was sure to come, perhaps before the end of summer. Earlier, in December, 1943, President Roosevelt, Prime Minister Winston Churchill, and the Allied high military command had appointed General Dwight Eisenhower as the Supreme Commander of the Allied Expeditionary Force (SHAEF) with headquarters in London. For Eisenhower, this represented a far cry and a long way from the hot, wooded flatlands of the Louisiana maneuvers and a desk job in Washington.

Lieutenant General Carl "Tooey" Spaatz, America's top airman in the ETO, with battle experience in England and Africa, had been tapped to head the United States Strategic Air Forces in Europe (USSTAF). Out of West Point, class of 1914, Spaatz was a proven leader who brought to this new position vast experience from World War I onward and the respect and admiration of his Allied colleagues. With his longtime friend, General Ira Eaker, Spaatz had put the Eighth Air Force in action against Germany in 1942, and, Eaker went on to command the Eighth during the early and crucial days and the current buildup. Now he had been promoted to commander of the Mediterranean Allied Air Force in Africa and Italy, which included the Fifteenth Air Force. Both Spaatz and Eaker were graduates of Maxwell's Tac School and were strong advocates of daylight precision bombing, the raison d'etre of both the Eighth and Fifteenth Air Forces. General Jimmy Doolittle, after stellar work in Africa and Italy, had come up to England to take command of the Eighth Air Force, succeeding Eaker.

General Spaatz's operations officer at USSTAF headquarters at Bushy Park, code-named Widewings, just outside London, was Major General Fred Anderson. One of the most respected officers in the air force, Anderson was a West Pointer, class of 1928, and a graduate of the Tac School. He was forceful, bright, and tough; a true believer in precision bombardment in the daytime

General Carl "Tooey" Spaatz (right) and General Ira Eaker.

LEFT: Fred Anderson as a plebe at West Point.

ABOVE: General Fred Anderson as chief of operations for General "Tooey" Spaatz.

hours. If it can be said that only one man had the vision and carried the major responsibility for Allied air superiority at D-day, that man was Fred Anderson.

These were the senior air force officers who had the job of directing the American air offensive in Europe. But it had not been a piece of cake. Far from it. In the early stages of the war, the bombing doctrine of the United States, specifically the daytime precision tactic as taught in the Tac School—and in contrast to the Royal Air Force technique of saturation bombing at night—had come under heavy scrutiny and not-so-subtle criticism by British leaders, some in high places. And there was criticism in the British newspapers, importantly, from Peter Masefield, aviation editor of the *London Times*, who had severely lashed out at the use of the U.S. heavy bombers, the B-17 and B-24. Masefield wrote: "American heavy bombers are fine flying machines but not suitable for bombing Europe. Their bomb loads are too small, their armour and armament are not up to the standard now found necessary, and their speeds are too slow." Masefield was not alone. The *New York Times* had published a story about the differing attitudes on bombing strategy between the British and Americans, under a headline that read: "British Rift On Planes Holding Up Air Offensive."

This momentous difference in air strategic techniques between dedicated and common-purpose allies, as the *New York Times* headline stressed, was the cause of a major rift between friends. What was the solution? The British idea of a definitive role for the American Liberators and Forts in the war against Germany was anti-submarine patrol and RAF-type missions at night. This course of thinking was in total violation of the Army Air Force's long-range planning, aircraft design and construction, honest convictions, and deep-rooted air warfare philosophy. Historian Richard Davis wrote in his book *Carl A. Spaatz and the Air War In Europe*: "The abandonment of day bombing, the rock on which all AAF hopes stood, was unthinkable." The matter lay unresolved until mid-January, 1943, when President Roosevelt, Prime Minister Winston Churchill, and their combined

Roosevelt and Churchill at the Casablanca Conference, January 14, 1943.

chiefs of staff met in Casablanca in French Morocco. The key person in the dispute, or the settlement of it, was Churchill. As Davis reported:

> Churchill had not decided against daylight precision bombing, but the time was obviously fast approaching when daylight precision must begin to justify itself by deed rather than potential. Without results the Prime Minister could no longer accept the expenditure of resources devoted to the project. But the threat to halt the buildup of U.S. heavy-bomber groups could, in the end, jeopardize the whole experiment.

This was serious business. The whole concept of America's participation in the heavy bombardment of Germany was at stake. General Arnold knew it. General Spaatz knew it. The American delegation to the conference knew it. The astute Arnold, wise in the ways of political infighting, went to work. He had to convince Mr. Churchill of the ultimate value of American precision daylight bombing in concert with the RAF's nighttime raids. He knew that Churchill liked and respected General Ira Eaker, and he decided to make Eaker the spokesman for the American position.

Eaker was ordered down to Casablanca from his post as commander of the Eighth Air Force in England. General Arnold had requested an appointment for General Eaker to speak with Churchill, which was granted. Eaker planned to summarize his position paper, and he

Eighth Air Force commander Ira Eaker (shown here as lieutenant general). Eaker was later promoted to four-star general. Eaker convinced Churchill at Casablanca to support American daylight bombing of Germany.

also planned to leave a complete copy with the prime minister. General Eaker was a gifted, fluent speaker who had studied journalism in college. For two days, he put together the AAF position on behalf of daylight precision bombing with a strong emphasis on cooperation with the Royal Air Force in their nighttime bombing program. Churchill read Eaker's one-page briefing outline at the onset of the meeting. Eaker said later, "At one point, when he came to the line about the advantages of round-the-clock bombing, he rolled the words off his tongue as if they were tasty morsels."

The following is the concluding paragraph of Eaker's position paper:

> Day bombing is the bold, the aggressive, the offensive thing to do. It is the method and the practice which will put the greatest pressure on Germany, work the greatest havoc to his war-time industry and the greatest reduction to his air force. The operations of the next ninety days will demonstrate in convincing manner the truth of these conclusions. We have built up slowly and painfully and learned our job in a new theater against a tough enemy. Then we were torn down and shipped away to Africa. Now we have just built back up again and are ready for the job we all cherish—daylight bombing of Germany. Be patient, give us our chance and your reward will be ample—a successful day bombing offensive to combine and conspire with the admirable night bombing of the RAF to wreck Germany industry, transportation and morale—soften the Hun for land invasion and the kill.

Before the Casablanca conference was over, Churchill said, "Considering how much had been staked on this venture by the United States and all they felt about it, I decided to back Eaker and his theme and I turned around completely and withdrew all my opposition to the daylight bombing."

CHAPTER 9

A MISSION TO BREMEN

"Flak hit a B-24 behind us at 6 o'clock. It got a direct hit. A direct hit. My God. Look. it's going down. It's going down."

—Kenneth Dabbs, armorer-gunner, Wright crew

Never in the history of air warfare has there been a campaign like the heavy bombardment battles waged against Nazi Germany from 1940 through the spring of 1945. It had never happened before, and, as historian Cargill Hall has pointed out, would, perhaps, never happen again. The AAF doctrine for fighting a heavy bombardment war, that is, a formation of aircraft dropping bombs on a predetermined target, in daylight hours, with enemy forces defending that target with anti-aircraft guns shooting from the ground and defending fighter planes shooting in the sky. That doctrine was hammered out at the Tac School with little precedent from World War I.

The four-engine warplanes of Bomber Command headed by the redoubtable Arthur "Bomber" Harris of the Royal Air Force—the Lancasters and Halifaxes—had been bombing German targets at night for two years before the Eighth Air Force flew its first mission in the summer of 1942. Their experience was invaluable to the newcomers from America, such as the RAF Bomber Command veteran who had given the 445th group its orientation briefing. Yet, the American bomber crews had to learn for themselves. Moreover, their *modus operandi* was new even to the battle-hardened bomber command veterans—for the AAF doctrine called for precision bombing in the daytime. In short, the Americans had to learn by doing.

When Captain Jimmy Stewart led the 445th Bomb Group on its first mission to Kiel, Germany, on December 13, 1943, the Wright crew did not fly that day. Their first mission came three days later on December 16. To Bremen. Stewart led the mission with the Wright crew on his wing. Here is Robbie Robinson's account of the Wright crew's first combat briefing:

> Someone said, "Attention." We all stood up. Several officers walked to the front of the room.
>
> Jimmy Stewart was a head higher than all the others. He said, "Sit down, fellas, At ease. This will be the group's second mission. Maybe it will work out like our first one did. Without too, too much damage." He pulled the curtain off the big wall map. There was a red line all over the map. That red line would be our flight path over Europe. Stewart said, "The target today is Bremen."
>
> He pointed out the route and the known flak concentration areas along the route. He showed where we would enter the enemy coastline, how we would wiggle around between cities, then turn and go over the target and back out into the North Sea and back to base. We were to enter the coast through the Zuider Zee. After hitting Bremen, we would fly out into the North Sea near the Elbe River. All the twisting and turning in our flight route was to confuse the enemy defenses.

The briefings were held on the group level for the combat crews of all four squadrons. Colonel Terrill often led the briefings, and

Stewart, as a squadron commander, took turns with the other squadron leaders. On this Bremen mission, Stewart had the pointer, introducing the other briefers. Robbie:

> The gunnery officer pointed out all the places that we would receive flak. The intelligence officer was next. He pointed out all the escape routes, in case we went down. He pointed to a harbor city and said, "If you can make it to Kiel without getting caught, there will be an ocean vessel in the harbor with a pair of red long handle underwear hanging on its deck. Get on that ship and it will take you to Sweden. Do not let yourself be seen until the ship is away from port. Pick up your escape kits and passports when you leave the briefing room. They will help you to get through the country you go down in. There will not be an underground to help you in the area you are flying over today, which is Germany."
>
> The weather officer took over and reported the expected weather. He said, "The weather on takeoff will be poor: fog with less than a mile visibility. You will break through the clouds and fog at 3,000 feet. Waiting for you will be sunshine and clear skies. It will be clear where you cross the English Channel and enter the coast. There will be a weather front north of Bremen. The coverage will be under you as you leave Germany and go out over the North Sea. Your altitude will be 23,000 feet and the cloud coverage will top off at 15,000 feet. When you return to base, the weather here will be good. Do not delay your estimated time of arrival at Bremen. If you arrive as planned, the city will not be overcast. A cloud

coverage is expected to move in and cover the city shortly after you are scheduled to bomb it."

Jimmy Stewart got up next and said, "Well, fellas. This is it. I—uh—I want you all back here safe. That understood? Fine."

Someone said, "Dismissed." A sergeant standing by the medical officer was giving out the three morphine vials that went on the sleeve of our flight jacket. There were twenty-four aircraft sent out from our group. That was 240 men. Everyone was filing out of the briefing room in an orderly manner.

Robbie continues:

I walked outside into the cold. I was almost numb. Not from being cold. My feet moved forward but my mind and body urged me to stop.

I asked God, "Please, give me the strength to go and not to show everybody that I am afraid. Please, give me the ability to think and to return to my wife some day."

The ten of us on the crew got in the truck, still not saying anything. Everything just seemed automatic. The truck took us to the aircraft.

Wright started number three engine first because it provided all the auxiliary power.

He started the other three engines and pulled out to the taxi ramp. The ground crew was standing by the plane, waving goodbye. Wright came over the intercom, asking each position to report. Everyone confirmed that he was ready. Buckey came on the intercom with, "There goes the flare from the tower! The mission is on!"

*   *   *

The Liberators of the Eighth Air Force usually flew missions together in their own group formations. They would join other groups forming over the English countryside and would join wing, division, and, eventually, the entire Eighth Air Force in the bomber stream. A huge Circle F on the tail identified the Liberators of Colonel Terrill's 445th Bomb Group. They formed on the group's colorful orange-and-black formation aircraft, which, after completing the formation process, peeled off and returned to Tibenham. It was a tense, complicated, and dangerous undertaking that brought out the skill and poise of the pilots and the total cooperation of the crews.

Here are random comments from intelligence-interrogation reports and other sources by the Wright crew about the Bremen mission:

> We were beginning to climb to altitude. It looked like the 445th Group was going to be the lead group to Bremen. All of the B-24 groups were forming behind us.

> Wright said on the intercom, "Get on oxygen." I buckled up my mask. Each crew member confirmed that he was now on oxygen. I helped Dabbs and Cross to put on their flak gear and they helped me get into mine. Then we put on our steel helmets. I loaded a shell into the chamber of my gun so that I could fire it if the gun froze. The shell in the chamber would break the ice loose when the gun fired. If it froze without a shell in it, I wouldn't have a gun that would shoot on the whole trip.

> We were now at 15,000 feet and out over the English Channel. Wright said, "Check your guns and fire." We all fired several short bursts with our guns and then confirmed.

I was now beginning to feel the cold. I made sure that my heated suit was turned on. I turned the rheostat up for more heat. I was beginning to feel its warmth in spots. Everything was now working like it should.

We were now over the Zuider Zee. We were just entering land near a river when five black bursts, one after the other, exploded right in our formation, just left and in front of the lead ship and in front of our left wing. I could see our left wing passing through the black smoke. Then came sounds of steel fragments hitting the airplane, above the sound of the engines.

Buckey said, "Be on the lookout for enemy fighters. When our fighters leave, theirs will show up."

To the left and right in front of us there was a solid black cloud of flak bursts at about our elevation of 23,000 feet. Tyler called, "Flak at 2 o'clock." Lieutenant Wittman said, from the nose turret, "That's solid flak in front of us! We are going through it! Can't that guy in the lead ship see? Damn! What is wrong with him?" Before Lieutenant Wittman got the words out of his mouth, flak was everywhere. It was above us, below us and beside us. Steel was hitting the aircraft like it was raining.

The fighter escort planes were P-47 Thunderbolts, P-51 Mustangs, P-38 Lightnings and Spitfires. To the crews they were "Little Friends." American combat crews used the clock system for fast, concise directions. It worked like this: 12 o'clock was straight ahead, 6 o'clock was straight behind, 3 o'clock was dead to the right, 9 o'clock dead to the left. Example: 4 o'clock was lower right; 11 o'clock was high left, and so on. The IP is the Initial Point—a straight run into the target area.

Cook called out over the intercom, "Single line of fighters 11 o'clock high." At the same time, Tyler said, "P-47s approaching at 3 o'clock." The P-47s passed over us and headed straight for the line of fighters approaching from 11 o'clock. I could see dog fights taking place at 11 o'clock at a distance. The enemy fighters, which looked now like they were ME 109s, had dropped to a lower altitude with the P-47s after them. The P-47s were knocking the ME 109s out of the sky. They were going down everywhere.

We were now reaching our IP and from here on we would fly straight and level toward our target. Lieutenant Wittman looked out of the nose and said, "My God! There is nothing in front of us but flak. Miles of it at our altitude. It's black at our altitude and white above us. How can anybody drop bombs through this stuff?"

The bomb run had started. Wright opened the bomb bay doors and the wind was coming through the waist around us like a gale. The bulkhead door flew open between the waist and bomb bay. We would drop our bombs just as the bombardier in the lead ship dropped his. I could see the solid cloud front just north of the city of Bremen that the weather officer had warned us about. I thought, "That guy knew what he was talking about." The solid front had not covered the city yet. We were right on time. A few minutes later and the city would be totally covered by those clouds.

The black flak clouds were a real contrast with the distant white cloud front behind it. Wright told Wittman he could drop the bombs when he was ready. Lieutenant Wittman, in the nose, said, "I'll tell you when the lead ship drops his."

Flak was now bursting so close to us I could see the shells flashing between me and our left wing man's ship and bursting yards above us. The shells were making a trail through the smoke of the other anti-aircraft bursts around us. It was like a big fireworks show.

The cordite smell was so strong that I had to put my oxygen regulator on Full Oxygen position to keep from getting sick.

Dabbs called out, "Flak hit a B-24 behind us at 6 o'clock. It has a Circle "C" on its tail. It got a direct hit! A direct hit! My God. Look. It's going down. It's going down. It's going down." Dabbs kept saying that, over and over again.

I was trying to cover my private area by pulling the flak suit down as far as possible. I didn't think that I wanted to be hit there. I looked up at the front side of the waist window at the fuselage and—My God!—there were slashed holes in the aluminum skin. I could now see holes ripped in the horizontal stabilizer tail section.

I began to ask God, "Help get us out of here." I looked out the window and down at the city. I could see the parts of the city burning as we were crossing over the cloud front that was now under us. We had made it across the target. Several miles away, when I looked back, the black flak clouds could be seen above the fluffy white cloud cover. New black smoke from fires on the ground was now rising through the white cloud cover.

Seeing the black flak clouds in contrast to the white clouds recalled for the crew the apt description of the RAF bomber pilot at their orientation briefing:

I was beginning to feel that whenever I saw four fighters together in the distance, they were ours. As we flew along above the overcast, I could see nothing but clouds and our own P-47s.

The ice was getting thick on my flak suit and I kept trying to beat it off with my gloved hand.

The flak started again. This time, it was off to the side of us. We passed on by. Then Wittman yelled, "Here it comes again!" The next thing I knew, we were in the thick of flak bursting everywhere near us. It seemed that it took forever for us to get out of the flak area. It was not as thick as it was over Bremen but it was bursting too close to my airplane.

I asked the temperature and Wright said, "Thirty-seven below zero."

My gun was beginning to frost and turn white.

Ice was forming on my oxygen mask where my moist breath was coming out of it. I was breaking the ice away to keep it from closing up the discharge vent. I pulled my goggles over my eyes. Only a little skin on my face, between my oxygen mask and my goggles on each cheek, was now exposed to the frigid elements.

I punched Tyler behind me in the right waist position. He turned and looked at me. He had ice all under his mask, almost to his chest. I looked at Cross and he was the same way.

It is always demoralizing for a combat crew to see another plane go down, almost before their eyes. A combat crew's reaction to the falling B-24 on the way home was a natural and usual reaction.

In our formation over the target we had twenty-four ships with Circle "F" on their tails. Dabbs took a count and all twenty-four were with us, the best Dabbs could tell.

The formation soon crossed over the edge of the cloud front and there was the sparkling ocean, in the clear below us. We could see England coming up in the distance. We dropped to 8,000 feet in altitude and then down to 4,000 feet. I took my oxygen mask off and turned my heated suit off. I dropped my flak suit and took off my steel helmet. I felt like I had taken off a ton of equipment. I took my gloves off, down to my silk white gloves. I opened my heavy flight jacket. England was getting bigger in the distance and it was good to see it there.

Wright asked for a damage report. Everyone reported everything they could see. It looked like all the damage was on the left side of the aircraft. I could see several holes in the tails and in the waist walls in front of my window. It looked like a few tears near the left wing tip. We had come through pretty good.

We were soon near the field. The weather was clear, just like they had told us it would be. Wright peeled off and sat down on the runway. The ship taxied to our hard stand and parked. Wright cut the engines. I got out of the airplane and kissed the ground. The rest of the crew did the same thing, including Wright.

I walked alone to the mess hall and then to the hut. I had the feeling that I was all alone in this. It seemed that no one or nothing was ever going to make things go right again.

I told myself, "Get hold of yourself." I was actually shaking inside and out. I could still hear the flak bursting around me. I was talking to myself. Then I thought, "God, please help me."

I knew I must be losing my mind to be talking aloud to myself like this.

I realized I was at the front door of the hut and reaching for the door knob. "God, please help me," I said, over and over. I went into the hut and flopped on my bunk, totally exhausted.

I was scared as hell.

As the year 1944 unfolded, the mission field orders from wing and division headquarters came down nightly, with few standdowns, and Colonel Terrill had the group in the air almost every day—Ludwigshafen, Kiel, Brunswick, Frankfurt, Russelsheim—and the rocket launching pads on the French Coast. These launching sites were called "Noball" missions by the flight crews. A Noball target, although strongly built with reinforced concrete and heavily guarded, did not always count as a mission flown with credit awarded. Here is a typical flight crewman's reaction to a no-credit mission: "I thought, 'We get the devil shot out of us and the plane torn up and you are not going to count it as a mission?'"

In December, General Jimmy Doolittle, the new commander of the Eighth Air Force, had sent orders down from Pinetree, his headquarters near London: Starting immediately, all combat crews would fly thirty combat missions instead of twenty-five before being rotated to the zone of the interior—home. Heretofore, the popular Doolittle, with his flamboyant reputation as one of the world's greatest airmen, burnished by his heroic leadership of the B-25 mission to Tokyo, had widespread favor with combat crews throughout the Eighth. So it took a little time for the Doolittle missions to become just five more missions. Actually, Doolittle, like most commanders who have to send unpopular orders down the line, was only the messenger. The mission increase decision was made on the highest level in Washington. Ironically, some crews were lost between mission 25 and sweating out number 30.

The heat was on. The group had lost six crews since becoming operational in the middle of December. Sixty men missing in action in twenty-one days. One of the crewmen told an intelligence officer at interrogation after a mission: "the incendiaries were coming out of the airplanes . . . and blowing back through our own trailing forma-tions. I could see several of the incendiary bombs hitting B-24s behind us . . . one B-24 near us was going down . . . an incendiary bomb had hit its fuel tank and it was burning."

During these early days in the group's operational schedule, Jimmy Stewart flew often, most of the time as a flight leader. He told his squadron adjutant, Captain Bursic, "I just can't sit here and send these fellows to death without knowing myself what I am sending them into." It was in these early days of combat that Stewart's reputation as a "lucky" pilot who always seemed to bring his crew home safely began to circulate around Tibenham. In his book *Flight from Munich*, Donald C. Toye, a former 445th pilot, wrote: "The raids Major Stewart led were always successful. . . . We had faith in him. . . . That is to say, we found our targets, released our bombs with good effect and returned home safely."

But Stewart, acclimated to the balmy days and nights of Southern California, was not successful in dealing with the harsh English weather. His feet were always cold. Father Alex, back in Indiana, and always helpful and accommodating to his only son, began sending plastic pouches that Stewart filled with hot water, when he could get hot water. That helped. And he had friends. Last year, Robbie Robinson, writing from his Tennessee home, sent me this note:

> Jimmy Stewart came into our hut one night, walked to the end of my bunk by the potbelly stove, sat down and took his shoes off, and said, "Fellows, I just don't know how ya'll keep a red hot stove. It is always red hot when I come in here. I've just got to get my feet warm. I can never get them warm in my hut." Almost burning the bottom of his socks, he got them warm. Then said, "Ah! That feels so good." He put his shoes on, stood up looking at his feet and walked out, saying, "Goodnight fellows." We all wondered if he was trying to tell us not to steal so much coal from the Limeys' coal pile.

As the Stewart visit indicated, the Wright crew's Nissen hut was usually warm and cozy. They all worked at it, trying to make the hut as comfortable and home-like as possible. The steady supply of coal "requisitioned" from the communal coal pile guarded by the English caretakers kept the hut warmer than most of the others. The flight crews actually spent most of their time in combat airplanes or in the huts—writing and reading letters from home, listening to

Axis Sally's seductive music, and going to the nearby mess hall. The weather did not encourage outside activities. That was the situation when Captain Stewart paid another visit to the Wright crew's hut. Robbie Robinson said:

> After mess we were all lying around in the hut. I was writing a letter to Elizabeth and reading some from her that had come in today.
>
> In walked Jimmy Stewart.
>
> Dabbs called out, "Attention."
>
> "At ease, fellows," said Major Stewart before I could get up out of my bunk. He walked up to the pot bellied stove and started warming his hands and his back side. It was cold and raw outside. "Lieutenant Wright's crew has always got a good hot stove," Stewart said. "It's kind of bigger than some of the others."
>
> We waited.
>
> Stewart's eyes drifted around the hut. He strolled over to the pile of cots. He picked up the edge of one of the blankets. He carefully laid it back from the beer keg it had been covering. He turned and walked back across to my bunk. He took my canteen from the shelf above my bunk and carefully pulled the metal cup from the bottom of it. He put the rest of the canteen back on the shelf and walked back to the beer keg. He had not said a word since he uncovered the keg. He opened the spigot on the keg and filled my canteen cup with the beer that Dabbs had stolen from somewhere.

All military commanders have their own individual way of dealing with troops and handling disciplinary measures. Stewart was, by inclination, a non-confrontational man. Perhaps it was his personality and manner of living. Moreover, as a pilot, he was a flight crew member, flying missions and sharing the tense and dangerous life of his men. Thus, where discipline was concerned, Captain Stewart knew how to cut his men some slack. Robbie continues:

He stepped back over to the end of my bunk and sat down with a sigh. He drank the beer slowly, continuing to warm himself by the stove. Stewart just sat there, taking his time drinking the beer and wiping his mouth with the back of his hand.

He looked at me and said, "Well, this black English beer is pretty good—if you can't get anything else. Right?" I smiled. We all were silent. He got up and filled my canteen cup again and stepped back and sat down on my bunk.

He continued to slowly sip the beer and warm himself at the stove. He wasn't rushing. He was taking his time. He obviously was enjoying that second cup.

After a while, he said quietly, "Fellows, someone stole a keg of beer from the officers club a few days ago." He looked around. "Ah—you guys hear anything about that?" We shook our heads. We said we hadn't heard anything about it. Stewart shook the last drop of dark beer out of my empty cup that he had been drinking from. "I thought not," he said. He wiped the lip of it with his hand. Then he put the cup back on my canteen and carefully placed it where he got it, on the shelf over my bunk.

He walked over to the beer keg and pulled the blanket back over it. He tucked the blanket around the keg carefully. You couldn't see the keg in the pile of blankets anymore.

Stewart came back to the stove. He stood rubbing his hands together over the pot bellied stove. "Sure a nice sized stove."

Stewart cleared his throat and said, "I know that Lieutenant Wright's crew doesn't know anything about this. I'm certain they didn't have a thing to do with stealing a keg of beer."

He turned, wiping his mouth with the back of his hand. He zipped up his jacket and walked out of the front door without saying another word.

Stewart had been there for some time. We were all speechless, wondering what he was going to do when he finished his beer.

Dabbs said, "Whuuuu! I didn't know what was going to happen. Why didn't someone say something?" I sat there shaking my head. "What could we say?" We all thought it was funny but nobody was laughing. Stewart had made his point well. Dabbs sure wouldn't steal another keg of beer.

The beer keg incident was soon put on the back burner, and it never came up again. But there was something else to worry about. Everybody in the group knew that Major Stewart had been flying almost every mission, more than the other squadron commanders. Then the rumor started among the crews. All they really knew was that Stewart wanted to go on all the missions. Now they heard the high command was trying to put the reins on him, for his own protection. The higher-ups were doing this because the raids were going deeper and deeper into Germany all the time. But everybody kept saying it was just a rumor.

Meanwhile, the base was shaping up. Some roads were being paved. Retired Air Force Colonel William B. Robinson of Alexandria, Virginia, who had been a lieutenant at Tibenham in those days wrote to me recently and said, "Major Stewart was firm and friendly with all of us in the 703rd. He rode a bicycle around the base with the rest of us."

CHAPTER 10

BRUNSWICK AND BERLIN

"The courage, leadership and skillful airmanship by Major Stewart were in a large measure responsible for the success of this mission."
—Citation for Major Stewart's Distinguished Flying Cross for the Brunswick mission

As the deadly struggle raged day after day in the daytime skies between the American combat crews and the German Luftwaffe—General Spaatz and General Fred Anderson, at USSTAF headquarters, drew up a daring battle plan that laid the foundation for air superiority over the Normandy beaches on D-day. The code name was Argument. It soon became known as Big Week. Key to the operation was weather. Fortunately, the Allied meteorologists had predicted a rare spell of clear weather for most of the European continent, including Germany. That window of good weather embraced a few days in late February, 1944. Strategy of the Spaatz-Anderson-USSTAF-staff campaign had two main objectives: A concentrated precision heavy bomber assault on the German fighter plane factories, and bombing of German air fields to destroy fighter planes on the ground—and, to have American long-range escort fighters shoot down the Luftwaffe defensive fighters when they came up to challenge the B-24's and B-17's attack.

General Spaatz, at USSTAF, in addition to his control of the Eighth Air Force in England and the Fifteenth in Italy, also controlled the fighters of the tactical Ninth Air Force based in England. In the early stages of the war, the Eighth Air Force had encountered extremely heavy losses on DP (deep penetration) missions, mainly because of unopposed German air defense fighters. This changed drastically when American long-range escort fighters arrived in England in early 1944.

The arrival of the long-range escort fighters in the ETO made a major difference immediately. Shortly after these new fighters arrived, as a combat intelligence officer, I was interrogating a returning crew of my 453rd group, when one of the gunners exclaimed, "We sure like these little friends with the long legs." Dr. Wesley Newton, the air power historian, has stated that General Jimmy Doolittle made a vital decision that boosted the Big Week campaign. In a note to me, Dr. Newton said, "General Doolittle ordered that the escort fighters accompanying the bombers were to be 'freed'—which means—they were no longer just to protect the bombers but some were to seek out German air defense fighters as they formed up to attack the bomber stream, or attack German fighters before they could come within range of the bombers."

Big Week lasted a little less than one week—from February 20 through February 26, 1944. Dr. Newton pointed out, "In those six days the American bombers caused great damage to fighter aircraft production and assembly at places like Leipzig, Regensburg, Gotha, Brunswick, and the ball-bearing factory at Schweinfurt. The B-24s of the Second Bomb Division were especially effective on Brunswick. The damage inflicted by the bombers during Big Week was the most intense bombing thus far during the war, forcing the Germans to begin to disperse their aircraft production, making it less vulnerable but also less efficient."

During Big Week, Major Jimmy Stewart was in the thick of it. He was on the Gotha mission, was group leader on Nuremberg, and led the wing to Brunswick. For the Brunswick mission, Stewart was awarded his first Distinguished Flying Cross. Here is the citation from General Doolittle:

AWARD OF THE DISTINGUISHED FLYING CROSS

Major James Maitland Stewart, O-433210, Army Air Forces, United States Army. For extraordinary achievement, while serving as Deputy Leader of a Combat Wing formation on a bombing mission over Germany, 20 February, 1944. Having been briefed for instrument bombing with condition that should visual bombing be possible the deputy leader would assume command, the formation proceeded to the target, meeting heavy enemy fighter opposition. When the target was reached, it became apparent that visual bombing was possible and *Major Stewart* smoothly assumed the lead position.

In spite of aggressive fighter attacks and later heavy, accurate antiaircraft fire, he was able to hold the formation together and direct a bombing run over the target in such a manner that the planes following his were able to release their bombs with great accuracy. The courage, leadership and skillful airmanship displayed by *Major Stewart* were in a large measure responsible for the success of this mission. Entered military service from California.

By command of
Lieutenant General Doolittle.

While Big Week was successful and was certainly one of the pivotal air campaigns of the air war in Europe, the price was high. American bombers and crews were lost. American escort fighters and pilots were lost. But the German price was much higher. Dr. Newton: "Loss of German air defense fighters was extremely high from the bomber's gunners, and most importantly from the fire of the escort fighters. The Luftwaffe sent up its fighters in swarms to attack the bombers, and, to their peril, encountered the escort fighters."

The Germans were persistent in their efforts to get to the bombers and paid in their most precious asset: experienced, valuable pilots. Dr. Newton brings this loss into air battle focus: "They lost their aces, their formation and unit leaders. The Americans could now replace their bombers and long-range fighters. From a more effective training system, they could replace bomber crews lost and fighter pilots shot down. The Germans, in spite of the damage to their aircraft factories, could still replace their fighter aircraft. But they could not replace the experience of veteran pilots and leaders. Their training system had deteriorated. Loss of experienced pilots was their problem. Spaatz and Anderson realized that the Luftwaffe's continued loss of experienced flying personnel, and, hence, declining morale, was the key to winning the battle of attrition—and achieving air superiority."

Major Jimmy Stewart, there at Tibenham, and knowing the momentum was building, anticipated taking part in the next phase of the air superiority campaign—the missions against Berlin.

After Big Week, Spaatz and Anderson and their planning team at Widewings did not rest on their success for long. While pleased with the results of Big Week, the two generals were not convinced that the goal of air superiority over the Luftwaffe had been fully achieved. They both agreed that a knock-out blow, a tour de force—a combination of power and skill as well as strategy—was called for. Berlin was the answer—and the target. Intelligence reports and logic indicated that the Germans would fight to the end to defend their capital, sending up their fighters and best pilots to do so. The Spaatz-Anderson strategy was simple: With the momentum of Big Week, a series of maximum-effort bombing missions, with strong long-range fighter escort support, was laid on. The bombing raids would entice the German fighters to come up to defend Berlin. Once engaged, the Americans would have the planned opportunity to shoot them down, thereby adding to the casualty list of experienced German pilots. The assault on Berlin took place in March. As expected, the Luftwaffe came up in force to protect the city. Damage to both men and machines, on both sides, was extremely high, notably on the portentous mission of March 6, 1944.

In his description of the March bombing of Berlin by the Eighth Air Force, historian Newton has written: "This was the time that the air superiority in daylight passed from the Germans to the Americans. From then on, the enemy had to conserve men and planes and rise to the challenge only on certain occasions." Dr. Newton's views were also shared by General Doolittle in a letter of congratulations to General Bill Kepner, commander of the Eighth Fighter Command. Doolittle wrote: "It must be assumed that the German fighter units are broken but not utterly crushed and that the enemy has made a decision to conserve aircraft and pilots." In the aftermath of the March campaign, General Spaatz wrote to the air force chief General "Hap" Arnold in Washington: "We of course are all confident that the air battle is in our hands."

After the war, at the Nuremberg Trials, the commander-in-chief of the German air force, Marshal Hermann Goering, is reported to have said, "I knew we had lost the war when I saw the American fighter planes over Berlin." Captain Andy Low, who became Major Stewart's assistant when Stewart was transferred to the 453rd Bomb Group as operations officer in late March, 1944, told me: "I flew the D-day mission. We had the sky to ourselves at Normandy that day. We shot down the best German pilots during Big Week and the Berlin battles. They needed those pilots at D-day but they didn't show. We owned the air that day."

A personal note: Immediately after the end of the war, I was transferred from General Eisenhower's press staff at SHAEF in Paris to a special task force at AAF headquarters in Washington, headed by Assistant Secretary of War for Air Stuart Symington—working on behalf of a separate air force. General Fred Anderson was then the chief personnel officer for the AAF and a prime planner on the separate air force project. Thus, this remarkable officer was not only a major architect for air superiority in the war, but was one of the architects of the separate air force as well.

Major Jimmy Stewart was, as the British say, "mentioned in dispatches" back in the States for his leadership in the Berlin mission of March 22. After the mission, an ETO news release stated: "Major James Stewart, of Hollywood, California, flying as a wing commander, on his first trip to Berlin said: 'The flak was heavy and the fighter support was swell. I saw a few enemy fighters, but they kept their distance.' When asked if this trip was any more unusual than his others, Stewart exclaimed: 'Unusual? We hit Berlin, didn't we?'" Some of Stewart's colleagues on this Berlin mission were a little more specific: Staff Sergeant Alfonso Bruno of Brooklyn, New York, a tail gunner on Stewart's Liberator said: "Through breaks in the overcast I saw a helluva lot of smoke over the target. The Jerries stayed at least 1,000 yards away." Sergeant Thomas Fong of Oakland, California, a ball-turret gunner, said, "Flak, flak, flak, those Germans have a one-flak mind." First Lieutenant Albert Pearson, a pilot from North Providence, Rhode Island, who had seen Berlin action before said, "This was my third trip to Berlin. This was the heaviest flak I have ever seen." Captain T. H. Henley, a 445th navigator, reported: "Had flak for about 1-1/2 hours, could see our bombs hit the north central part of Berlin. Two planes went down over Berlin . . . fighter protection was very good . . . flew nine hours, half on oxygen."

As wing commander, Major Stewart filed a detailed mission report to the commander of the Second Bombardment Division. In this report, Stewart noted that flak was, "Moderate and accurate over target, and practically over entire course home." He described enemy fighters as weak.

Around the middle of March, the rumor about Major Stewart's departure as commander of the 703rd Squadron was in full circulation. Soon a name for his successor was mentioned—Major Maurice Casey. The rumor seemed to have a central theme—Stewart had been flying too many missions, the brass up the line didn't like it, and he was being transferred for his own protection. Soon the combat crews all over the group had heard the rumor. It was discouraging. Stewart was popular with the crews because of his skillful leadership of group missions. And from a personal standpoint, their own safety, they hated to lose him. As they discussed it, there seemed to be some credibility to the rumor. They all knew Major Stewart did not fly the first Eighth Air Force mission to Berlin on March 3. And he did not fly the Berlin missions of March 6, 8, and 9. These were important missions, which, they knew, he usually would have flown—that is, if he had not been ordered not to fly. Then the rumor got more specific: "that Stewart had been ordered to fly only one mission in every five, but he could pick the mission he wanted; he had been picking all the worst missions to fly. He skipped all the milk runs. High command did not like that."

Yet, on March 22, he had led the wing to Berlin. It was all confusing and discouraging. Not knowing made it worse. The crews did not want him to leave. As one of the squadron's flight crew members said: "Somehow he always made me feel that he was my friend. I knew when I had ten missions, Jimmy Stewart had flown five of them alongside or near me. He had a great feeling for all of us. You felt it when you were around him. Even when he was trying to give you hell for something you deserved, he got his point over without hurting you deep inside."

Then toward the end of March, the news came: Major Stewart had been promoted. After flying twelve missions with the 445th Group and commanding the 703rd Squadron, he was leaving to become the operations officer of the 453rd Group, at Attleborough (Attleboro), or Old Buc, only a few miles away from Tibenham. When the appointment was announced, nothing was said about "flying too many missions." The official word was that the 453rd needed an operations officer, and Major Stewart had been promoted to the job.

I was then a combat intelligence officer with the 453rd, and met Stewart for the first time upon his arrival at Old Buc. We immediately began working together in preparing details of the missions, operations, and intelligence, night after night, for the next morning's briefings of the combat crews before takeoff. Waiting for the field order to come down, we talked about a lot of things. Stewart never mentioned what

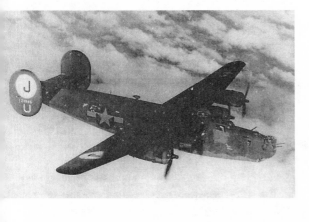

Stewart flew this 453rd Liberator (tail marking J) on bombing missions to Germany.

had led to his promotion. I never mentioned it. Since then, I have been asked many times about it. I must say that I think it highly unlikely that Stewart's mission schedule and high command's efforts to "protect" him had any bearing on his transfer and promotion. I do think the key player was Colonel Bob Terrill.

Stewart and Terrill had developed a close working and personal relationship from the beginning at Sioux City. I doubt that Stewart would have been appointed to the new job, leaving the 445th, without Colonel

Terrill's approval. Beyond that, I think the appointment was a routine air force change of assignment. Stewart was a mature, knowledgeable, and experienced air force officer with an operational and administrative background. And a stellar combat record. He knew the territory. In short, he was ready for promotion. And deserved it. Moreover, I had heard of a conversation that had taken place before Stewart's transfer between Wing Commander Ted Timberlake and Major General Hodges, the Second Division commander. Hodges had asked

Brigadier General Ted Timberlake, left, and Colonel Robert H. Terrill at Tibenham.

Timberlake who was leading the next day's mission. Timberlake had replied that it was Stewart. Whereupon Hodges said, "I always feel better when Stewart is leading. We always seem to have a good day." Thus, regardless of the rumors and their possible portent, and, with the confidence of his superiors, Jimmy Stewart was departing the 445th and leaving the staff. But he was not losing the guidance and friendship of Bob Terrill, the second officer after Colonel "Pop" Arnold who would shape and mold his air force career. Furthermore, in his new job at the 453rd he would still be under the high command of Timberlake and Hodges.

The Associated Press played the story straight, describing it as a routine promotion. Here is a copy of the AP story as it appeared in the *Washington Star* of April 1, 1944:

JIMMY STEWART RAISED TO OPERATIONS OFFICER

By the Associated Press.

A UNITED STATES BOMBER BASE IN ENGLAND, April 1, 1944—Maj. James M. Stewart—Jimmy Stewart of the movies—has been promoted from a squadron commander to operations officer of a Liberator bomber group, United States headquarters announced today.

In his new capacity, Maj. Stewart will direct the bombing operations of a group of at least 48 Liberators. He formerly led a squadron of 12 planes and participated in 11 missions over enemy territory including one trip to Berlin.

The promotion, effective March 30, still permits him to make occasional combat flights as a pilot.

So, after six months in the chain of command of Terrill's 445th, at Sioux City and Tibenham, Major Jimmy Stewart got in his Jeep and headed down the ten miles of narrow and twisting road to take up his new duties at Old Buc.

CHAPTER 11

NEW WAYS AT OLD BUC

It was Major Stewart's show . . . .
—Colonel Ramsay Pott's opinion regarding
his impressive new operations officer.

The Jeep ride from Tibenham was short. Major Jimmy Stewart arrived at Old Buc around the middle of the afternoon. A light rain was falling. There he met Captain Andy Low, the assistant operations officer at the 453rd, who was destined to be his confidant, lifelong friend, and one of the five air force officers who were instrumental figures in Stewart's military life. Low immediately took him in to see Colonel Ramsay Potts, the 453rd Group commander. The two airmen had met briefly before through General Timberlake, but it was only a passing handshake. Potts invited his new ops officer to share his quarters—a small, oblong block building next to the officers club with a bedroom at each end and a sitting room in the middle. Stewart accepted. The meeting was short, informal, with little protocol. Andy Low then took Stewart on a tour of the base, which was similar to Tibenham. After checking in at Colonel Potts' quarters, they visited the operations section, located in the headquarters building.

Early that night, Major Stewart returned to operations—lanky, slightly rumpled, wearing a leather A-2 jacket, a slightly askew overseas cap, and hightop shoes—ready to go to work. I introduced him to the operations and intelligence enlisted staff who would be working with us in planning the next day's mission. Major Stewart asked a lot of questions. About that time, the teletype bell sounded, and the field order began to come down. We worked all night putting together the details of the mission. With Andy Low at his side, Major Stewart took charge immediately. He was meticulous, precise, painstaking, exacting. It was obvious that he knew what he was doing. Colonel Potts came in and looked over the field order. But Potts believed that his operations officer was the play-maker, the fountainhead, the roller-bearing of the briefing team. It was Stewart's show.

At dawn, the combat crews of the 453rd discovered that their new operations officer was a good man with a pointer—a superb briefer. He knew the most intimate details of the mission, talked clearly, concisely, but in a low-key voice. He was easy to understand and to follow. Drawing on his skill as a performer, Stewart knew how to get and hold the attention of the crews. It was a well-planned and convincing presentation. No dramatics. Just to-the-point instructions dealing with an extremely important subject. One could almost feel the inspiration, the confidence, the galvanizing response in the air. It was not a pep rally but rather a provocative and reassuring kindling of spirit for young men who had recently suffered losses, and, who, again in mere hours, would be facing the deadly fury of a resourceful enemy in the air and flak from the ground.

The 453rd had been formed at Boise, Idaho, in the spring of 1943 under the command of Colonel Joe Miller, a West Point and Tac School graduate. After second- and third-phase training at Pocatello and March Field in California, the 453rd, flying the southern route, followed Stewart's 445th to England, arriving at Old Buckingham in constant rain and deep mud in early January, 1944. I was in the original cadre of the 453rd, joining the group in Boise, shortly after graduating from Combat Intelligence School at Harrisburg, Pennsylvania. Andy Low, a West Point–trained first lieutenant, joined the group at March Field at the beginning of third-phase training.

Just after the orientation flights at Old Buc, Colonel Miller had his planes in the combat zone, flying three missions in the first week of February. On his fourth mission, in mid-March, Colonel Miller went down on a raid to Friedrichshafen, Germany, which seemed to start a bad-luck cycle for the 453rd. In short order, Major Curtis Cofield, the group operations officer, went down in occupied France with his crew.

General Timberlake at wing headquarters moved with dispatch in appointing a replacement for Colonel Miller. He had experience in such matters. Few officers in the AAF had a more eclectic and distinguished background, even at this point, than West Pointer Ted Timberlake. He was the youngest general in the army since the Civil War; the original commander of the famed 93rd heavy bombardment group, renowned as "Ted's Traveling Circus"; the first commander to lead a formation of B-24 Liberators across the North Atlantic; and the leader of the first raid of the Liberators against Nazi Germany.

Timberlake was the chief planner of the seminal Liberator mission on the Ploesti oil fields in Romania. He was considered the leader of the Liberator cognoscenti, and for the commander's job at the 453rd he chose another top Liberator specialist who was rapidly gaining the reputation as a brilliant and promising young air force officer in the ETO—Colonel Ramsay Potts. Potts, out of the University of North Carolina at Chapel Hill, joined the Army Air Corps as a flying cadet before Pearl Harbor. With his wings and commission in hand, Potts fortunately soon came under the aegis and guidance of Colonel Ted Timberlake. He was in Timberlake's "Traveling Circus" in England and Africa, and on Timberlake's staff at Second Combat Bomb Wing Headquarters. Those of us at the 453rd knew of his reputation when Potts arrived at Old Buc. We thought he was a natural for the job as our leader. Bruised and battered as we

The 453rd's assembly ship, "Wham Bam."

were by recent unhappy events, we gave him a hearty welcome. Potts immediately took over with a sure, deft touch. He was confidence-inspiring, hands-on, and extremely hard-working. But one fact was clear: The group was not up to the task at hand, was not fully trained, had low morale, and was not fully prepared.

Potts grasped the situation straightaway.

He stood the group down. And immediately embarked on a sustained, around-the-clock schedule of reshaping, revamping, and leading a series of intense practice missions, starting with in-depth operational, intelligence, navigational, and weather briefings. The practice then included formation and assembly flying and reconditioning of combat crews, ground crews, backup personnel. Potts forged a team of fighting men by showing, by doing and setting an example. He seemed never to sleep, to be everywhere at once, leading, inspiring, working, working. The spirit spread from the flight line to the Nissen huts. It was inspiring to be a part of it.

Then the combat missions resumed. The operations officer went down. And Jimmy Stewart arrived at Old Buc.

Ramsay Potts has told me on more than one occasion that he didn't ask for Jimmy Stewart by name to fill the group operations vacancy at the 453rd. He has said, "I had been commanding the group long enough at the time to know the situation and what I needed in an operations officer. I made a list of the qualifications of the job as I saw it. I discussed this with General Timberlake, who was well acquainted with Stewart's background and qualifications through his work at the 445th, which was in his wing. So, General Timberlake sent Stewart to me. I have thanked him for it, time and again."

Here is an entry on Stewart's assignment from an official Eighth Air Force historical publication:

> The Commander, 2nd Combat Wing felt he needed to look across his Squadron Commanders to select a mature manager, a combat leader with substantial combat experience. On 30 March, Major

Stewart reported to the 453rd as the replacement Group Operations Officer. The recent loss of Commander, and then Operations Officer, was reflected in morale problems. Col. Potts and Maj. Stewart began immediately to turn the Group around. Major Stewart was thirty-five when assigned, brought the sophistication of his movie industry years to his military assignment, and most importantly, he brought his recent aircrew training and instructor flying experience in B-17 and B-24 units. He was an accomplished combat leader, on the ground and in the air.

Over the years since the war, I have talked with Potts frequently about Stewart. Potts offered his personal viewpoint: "Jimmy Stewart was a very good B-24 pilot; he had a steady hand and a natural feel for piloting the aircraft. His greatest strength, however, was in his ability as a combat leader. Stewart led many dangerous and difficult missions to such places as Berlin and, in the heat of air battle, he always maintained a calm demeanor. His pilots had absolute faith in him and were willing to follow him wherever he led."

Later, Potts added this postscript: "He had a tremendous rapport with crews, an easy, somewhat humorous way of putting them at ease in tight situations."

Potts and Stewart hit it off from the start. They were both highly motivated men, familiar with and accustomed to success, who had been moved, step-by-step, into the delicate art of leadership and the harsh ways of war, by master tutors—Timberlake and Terrill. It was now time to apply what they'd learned. The job called for experience, tact, understanding, force, and, as it turned out, the power of personality. Now, as a team, Potts and Stewart had a rare opportunity, in war or peace, to make a shining difference, to change a negative course and bring about a positive outcome. It was a rebuilding process. A process that would make the 453rd a winner. Colonel Potts found a ready and innovative ally in Major Stewart. They were on the job around the clock, constantly on the move, often in Stewart's Jeep, on the flight line, checking every detail, laying on practice missions—seldom leaving the base. Everybody worked. Everybody was overworked. Changes came. Morale was high. Spirits soared. Target proficiency improved. And, as Andy Low once said to me, "You were there, Starr. And as you know, the change at Old Buc after Ramsay and Jim came in was like daylight and dark."

Looking back now I can say, in recollection of those times, that Major Jimmy Stewart was a primal figure in the dramatic resurgence of the 453rd. And, as group operations officer, he was playing a cogent and pivotal role in the outcome of the war. Ramsay Potts was a highly experienced combat-tested officer—and a leader of the first rank. But he needed Stewart's help. Individually, they were natural-born leaders; together, they were a formidable team. Stewart was the point man, always on the firing line, working directly with the combat crews. He had a constant and steady hand in the preparation of the missions and briefed most of them. He was the man with the pointer, truly, in charge of operations. Stewart's confidence-inspiring presence and his reputation as a "lucky" pilot, with a skillful and sagacious sense of combat operations spread throughout the group.

The reason for being of a heavy bombardment group like the 453rd centered around the combat crews. It was the job of the group to support the work of these bold-spirited men who, at times, took off in the rain and fog and darkness to fly in dangerous skies to engage the enemy. Major Jimmy Stewart was their mentor, monitor, and leader. He knew the drill. He flew missions, although as ops officer that was not his main job; his primary concern was to teach and inspire the combat crews to successfully fly missions. In a manner of speaking, the combat crews were his "boys." Stewart was a winner. The crews knew it. And all of us at Old Buc knew it.

Working with the combat crews, moving around the sprawling base on my bicycle, I saw and felt the buoyant and bright mood, shared enthusiasm, and keen feeling of togetherness. I knew that this esprit de corps would be reflected in the mission reports; the battle is always the payoff. The interrogation sheets turned in by the intelligence officers after each mission indicated vastly improved assembly and formation discipline, more accurate gunnery, timely arrival over target, better bombing results, and, importantly, fewer losses.

Captain Bob Bieck was one of Stewart's combat crewmen and a lead pilot at Old Buc. He knew Stewart well, and even now his memory is vivid and clear. Colonel Bieck sent me this note from his retirement home in Lakeland, Florida:

> We soon found out that Major Stewart was no dumb figurehead. He was a gentleman and a very capable officer. Most important, he was a very good, well-informed pilot. He began giving the morning briefings immediately, and he spoke in that same low-key voice to which we had become accustomed in his movies. Interestingly, he flew his share of the missions irrespective of the target. It appeared to many of us the team of Potts and Stewart had brought an esprit de corps to the 453rd which heretofore had been absent. Major Stewart flew a great deal in the morning assemblies to insure that our formations were satisfactory. This was a difficult task due to the fact that we had a high turnover in combat crews. Even so, morale was unusually high and much of it was due to a very down-to-earth Jimmy Stewart.

My own personal relationship with Stewart was professional, not close, not casual. We were not buddy-buddy. I enjoyed working with him on mission preparations and especially briefing with him in the early mornings. I greatly admired his style and technique and skill with words. I liked the way he dealt with the crews. He was not condescending or imperious in an overly authoritative way. His manner was easy, a "Well, fellas" approach. Yet, he was not one of the boys. While it may have been that Stewart viewed the crews as "his boys"—it is quite another matter for Stewart, as ops officer and a man who was reserved by nature, to be viewed as "one of the boys."

I think the crews came to see him not as a famous figure, but rather as a leader who had made the combat scene, a man they admired, liked, and trusted. At briefings, he was businesslike, relaxed, genial. More than once, Stewart showed a ripping temper. He could handle the chewing-out process in a blistering top-sergeant-like tirade. There was the time a first pilot, who was constantly late for briefings, came slinking in and tried to slip into an empty seat. Stewart stopped the briefing and gave the pilot a tongue lashing, pulling no punches, in front of everybody. He was mad. The crews had never seen this side of Stewart. He laid it out to the pilot, sparing no words, telling him of the responsibilities of a pilot and officer—one of them being never to be late for the briefing of a mission. And, using the pointer, Major Stewart said, "You owe it to your crew, and you owe it to yourself."

At night, working with us preparing the details of the mission, Stewart was crisp and professional, never demanding, always cordial, always helpful. Stewart truly knew his job. Still, he asked a lot of questions and always rehearsed his remarks, standing in front of the big wall map in the operations building, before we went down to the briefing room on the flight line in the early mornings.

It was interesting to see him at the bar of the officers club after a tough mission and hear his discussions of the mission with the returning pilots, navigators, and bombardiers. Even then, he was reserved, never animated, but always quietly curious. This was in keeping with the Stewart persona. He went about his business with a cool, single-purpose approach, that did not call for close personal involvement. This, I think, was one of the reasons for his success in the war. He was determined to prove that he was more than an actor, more than a Hollywood star. He was determined to prove that now he could measure up as a man doing a really important job in the military crucible and not just a celluloid hero.

I had some good talks with Stewart, sitting in his little cubbyhole office waiting for the field order to come down. He was older by about twelve years. We had both passed through the intriguing city of Marrakech, French Morocco, on our way to England but at different times. With our crews, both of us had been weathered in there. It was hot in the daytime, but to escape the biting cold coming off of the Atlas mountains to our tents at night, we both found heat and comfort at the bar of the elegant and famous La Mamounia Hotel. Stewart liked to rehash that story, and he liked to talk about ways to keep feet warm. But never Hollywood.

While in Marrakech last year, I had lunch at the La Mamounia with the manager, Robert Berge. I told him the Stewart tent-and-bar story. He laughed and said, "My dear Starr, when Jimmy Stewart came to Marrakech on his way to England during the war, he may have stayed in a tent. But when he came back to Marrakech with Alfred Hitchcock to make a movie called *The Man Who Knew Too Much*, he had a suite here at La Mamounia, and I've been told he and his wife went to the bar every night for the La Mamounia's great dry martinis."

Although Stewart continued to fly missions, it was not like the times at Tibenham. The question of Stewart flying too many missions never came up at Old Buc, and he led the group and wing from time to time. His rhythm was different now, and his main interest was getting his crews in shape to fly deep penetration (DP) missions into Germany, bomb the target, and get home safely. In April and May, he led on Oberhofen and Siracourt and Troyes, France. In his *Saturday Evening Post* series, Colonel Beirne Lay wrote about the Troyes raid:

> But on the Troyes mission he finally messed one up. At least according to him. Between the initial point and the target, a railway marshaling yard, Stewart noticed that they were ten degrees off the briefed heading. He called his bombardier and navigator, but they were sure they were heading right for the target. While Stewart was busy talking to the

navigator on the interphone, his deputy leader tried to contact him on VHF and tell him he was going for the wrong target—a marshaling yard a few miles from the assigned target at Troyes, surrounded by misleadingly similar terrain features. But Jimmy, busy on the interphone, didn't switch back to his VHF channel in time to hear him. His bombs erased the wrong target that day.

At a subsequent wing critique, during which commanders were called upon to review the missions they had led, Stewart took all the blame for the turkey at Troyes. No mission that Stewart ever flew did more to win the respect of his colleagues than the one mission on which he missed the target and refused to alibi about it.

For Stewart's combat crews, flying bombing missions from Tibenham and Old Buc on the cold, dark days of those British winters of 1943–1945, the filtering sense and feeling of danger was never really out of mind. Neither was stark fear. Major Jimmy Stewart was no exception. Aristotle made the case that, "A courageous person is one who faces fearful things as he ought and as reason directs for the sake of what is noble." General Ira Eaker believed that there are two kinds of fear, physical and mental, and the physical can be more easily coped with than the mental. Eaker, who had flown thousands of hours as a pilot in more than fifty different aircraft, said, "the mental fear has to be handled very carefully. I always said to myself, if I worry too much about the past, it will decrease my ability to deal with the future. So when I would get morose over a past decision or a past engagement like one of the great raids, I would change my attitude by thinking about what I should do in the future. That's the way I cope with fear."

Robbie Robinson of the Wright crew at Tibenham finished his tour with thirty missions, many of which were the longest and most dangerous of all, including repeated raids on the "Three Bs"—Berlin,

Bremen and Brunswick. Robinson, in his book, never tried to conceal the fact that fear flew with him on every mission—regardless of the length or the danger of the target. It was my experience, working with the combat crews, that Robbie was not alone with his fear.

My longtime friend—the highly decorated Liberator warrior, Ploesti flight leader, retired Air Force Reserve major general, and Washington lawyer, Ramsay Potts—is given neither to emotionalism or hyperbole. On the matter of fear, he has said: "Flying combat missions in the ETO was dangerous business. The experience was so profound that even now one is reluctant to talk about it to people who did not go through it. They could think I'm overstating the case. But the fact remains that it was extremely hazardous duty and fear was always with you."

Edward R. Murrow, the renowned CBS reporter who had made live broadcasts describing German air raids from London rooftops in the Battle of Britain, was no stranger to fear. Or flying bomber missions with the Eighth Air Force and the Royal Air Force Bomber Command. On his famous "orchestrated hell" broadcast from an RAF Lancaster bomber, Murrow, while describing a German flak and fighter attack on a nighttime mission to Berlin, admitted, "I was very frightened."

In the May, 1993, edition of *AIR Classics* magazine, Jimmy Stewart was quoted: "Fear is an insidious and deadly thing. It can warp judgment, freeze reflexes, breed mistakes. Worse, it's contagious. I knew that my own fear, if not checked, could infect my crew members. And I could feel it growing within me."

Stewart has said the fear that haunted him the most was the fear of failure—of messing up a mission with a bad decision. In a talk with Richard Schneider for *Guideposts* magazine many years after the war, he remembered his feelings before a mission to Nuremberg, Germany. "Walking to the window, I pulled the blackout curtains and stared into the misty English night. My thoughts raced ahead to morning, all the things I had to do, all the plans I must remember for any emergency. How could I have a clear mind if it were saturated with fear?"

*   *   *

Where his combat crews were concerned, Major Stewart maintained the same high level of intensity at Old Buc that had been his hallmark as a squadron commander at Tibenham. The crews came first. Their deeds, their conduct in the air, and their well-being were his top priorities. When "his boys" were involved, Stewart's eye was always on the sparrow. Here's an excerpt from Andy Low's informal history of the 453rd, *The Liberator Men of Old Buc,* compiled after the war, that describes the return to Old Buc of a mission on May 30, 1944, to Oldenburg, Germany:

> The airfield at Oldenburg was the object of attention and received a grand total of over 95 tons of bombs. Bombing results were very good. The flak was intense and accurate, causing slight damage to six of the ships.
>
> Lt. Wilber Earl became caught in the slipstream of the preceding plane and lost control of his already battered ship and crashed on the main runway. The crew escaped injury, but the "Golden Gaboon" burned up.
>
> Lt. Lester Baer, forced to drop out of formation and reduce speed, flew the "Zeus" home at low altitude, leaving a trail of jettisoned equipment from the German border to the Channel. Upon arrival at the base he found the main runway blocked by the still burning "Golden Gaboon." Lt. Baer then prepared to land on the short, alternate runway, in a strong crosswind. Those on the ground, who were nervously, anxiously waiting, saw the plane touch lightly on one wheel, slowly roll along and reduce speed until the left wing tip dragged. Then suddenly they saw #1 prop dig into the ground off the runway and swing the ship around viciously. Amid a cloud of

dust and dirt, the plane laid still. With just his right landing wheel and receiving power from only two engines, Lt. Baer had made the most dramatic, skillful cross-wind landing that Old Buc has ever witnessed, thus saving himself and his crew from injury. All were able to walk away from the ship unaided, including Sgt. Smertelny and Lt. Bales, who had stuck to his navigation table throughout the mission.

Major Jimmy Stewart had watched Lieutenant Baer's bold and steadfast feat of airmanship from the control tower. He immediately made a recommendation to Colonel Potts that Lieutenant Baer be given special recognition for his undaunted deed. As a result of Stewart's recommendation, the event was recounted in *The Liberator Men of Old Buc*:

> Five hours and fifty-three minutes from the moment he returned from Oldenburg, Lt. Baer was awarded the Distinguished Flying Cross. In an informal ceremony without precedent, Brigadier General Timberlake, Wing Commander, accompanied by Col. Potts, Group Commander, and Major James Stewart, Group Operations Officer, made the presentation in the lounge of the Officer's Club.

Second only to enemy action is German fighter attack and flak, and the main fear of Eighth Air Force combat crews was having to ditch their bombers in the North Sea or English Channel. Major Stewart knew that the Liberator was not a dependable, seaworthy plane, and he always covered special ditching procedures at briefings. Roger Freeman, the British writer who, since the war's end, has become perhaps the leading historian on Eighth Air Force matters, wrote: "Ditching the B-24 was recommended only as a last resort. . . . From the very rare partially successful B-24 ditching in the North Sea only a few men had escaped."

In early spring, 1944, the Eighth Air Force laid a maximum-effort mission on the city of Berlin. As Dr. Wesley Newton has pointed out, the German High Command sent up the ME 109s and FW 190s in force at only certain times to protect the German capital. The raid turned out to be one of the most heavily defended missions ever mounted by the Eighth Air Force against Berlin. The 453rd history reported: "Major Stewart dispatched twelve planes for Berlin. The flak was terrific and returning crews reported savage encounters with the Luftwaffe, which was up in force in a vain attempt to protect the very heart of the Reich. Despite enemy action and undercast, results were thought to be good. . . . Lieutenant Davidson ditched his ship and he and his crew, with the exception of tail gunner Harold G. Oakes, were fished out of the water by the ever-alert Air Sea Rescue Squads." Lieutenant Davidson's Liberator was called the Ken O Kay. His radio operator was Sergeant Bob Krentler. In *The Liberator Men of Old Buc*, Krentler related his account of the ditching of the Ken O Kay and the rescue of the crew:

I can remember the sight of hundreds of heavy bombers flying in a formation that stretched as far as the eye could see. The tremendous skill our pilot Lt. Max Davidson had displayed on our previous eighteen missions was no cause to fear this mission.

As we approached Berlin we were attacked by the Luftwaffe in force. MEs and FWs were all around us. Our gunners reported two kills and one probable. As we began our bomb run, flak took over and it was savage.

Soon after dropping our bombs, but before we could leave the target area, we took a hit from flak, which caused us to feather two engines. With only two engines functioning, we began to lose air speed and altitude. Worse yet, we were required to operate the remaining engines at maximum RPM, thus using up our fuel supply at too fast a rate. As we battled loss of altitude, it became apparent that we wouldn't make it back to the base. At this point, I began to send out distress signals. What a surprise was in store for me: all the frequencies were jammed with S.O.S. signals. By this time we were over water but down to a couple thousand feet of altitude. Now I was really sweating. I kept turning my transmitter through the range of frequencies for air-sea rescue; still no reply. We were under 1500 feet when I finally got a response to my Mayday call. I locked down the transmission key and prepared to ditch. . . . Seconds later, the Ken O Kay hit the water.

Earlier in his narrative, Sergeant Krentler paid tribute to the "tremendous skill" of his pilot, Lieutenant Davidson. To ditch the Liberator, Davidson had to call upon all his considerable skills as a pilot. To keep the big bomber from breaking up at impact, he had to lose all air speed and virtually stall the aircraft into the water.

Krentler continues:

The next thing I knew, water was flowing in from the overhead hatch like a waterfall. I can remember fighting the force of the water with all my strength and finally getting my arms on the fuselage. Then the top turret began to sink and in the process caught the sleeve of my heated suit between the ring and the gears. Using what must have been super-human strength, I was able to rip the sleeve wires free from the turret and float away from the plane. I saw the crew in the water. Lake and Davidson couldn't swim. At this point, co-pilot Alan Kingston was a real hero— holding Lake above the water line and at the same time letting Max Davidson hold on to his Mae West straps in order to stay together.

I remember it was a bright, sunny day, the water seemed to have swells of about thirty feet. Friendly aircraft were circling overhead. I watched as the Ken O Kay slowly sank below the surface. All of this seemed like an eternity but probably took only five minutes at the most. The next thing I knew, an air sea rescue boat came roaring up to us. I thought it must be the one that answered my SOS call because his signal was very strong, indicating he was nearby.

The combat crews of the Eighth Air Force had a high regard, and almost a passion, for their "little friends." The fighter pilots who protected the bomber streams were first and foremost in their thoughts, thanks, and prayers. High on their list of friends as well were the British sailors who manned the Air Sea Rescue boats in the English Channel and North Sea. I remember one time at Intelligence interrogation after a mission, a young tail gunner, certainly no more than twenty years old, telling me: "Every time I cross the Channel and look down and see those little rescue boats I say a prayer."

Sergeant Krentler:

Just then a British sailor threw a cork ring into the sea and jumped overboard. He got into the ring and began to paddle toward us. At that time I still had some buoyancy left in my flying suit so I told him to pick up my buddies first. I could see Alan was having a rough time holding up Max and Lake. This was rather dumb on my part because the air quickly dissipated from my suit and my body became numb. I was struggling to stay afloat when he reached me and grabbed my hands, which were then secured to the inside of the life ring. This kept my head out of the water. Good thing, because I lost consciousness at this point and didn't wake up until we were almost to Portsmouth.

Sergeant Krentler's request that the British sailor rescue his buddies first because he felt they needed more immediate help is typical of the unity and spirit of cooperation and comradeship—and the overwhelming desire to take care of each other—that was characteristic of combat crews.

Shortly after Stewart came to Old Buc, Colonel Potts, perhaps because of my background as a journalist, asked me to be Stewart's unofficial press officer. This meant no publicity, no interviews, and no contact whatsoever with the hundreds of war correspondents eagerly seeking feature stories while awaiting D-day. About this time, I was in London on pass and went to the Churchill Club with my friend Charles Collingwood, the CBS war correspondent. The club was a VIP-type gathering place presided over by Pamela Churchill, the prime minister's then daughter-in-law. After the war, Pamela came to America and became well known, first, as the wife of Leland Hayward, Jimmy Stewart's best friend. She later married the famous diplomat and political figure, Averell Harriman, and, still later, she served as the American Ambassador to France.

On this night at the Churchill Club, Pamela introduced me to Lionel Shapiro, a Canadian war correspondent, and told him that I was a friend of Jimmy Stewart's. I hit it off well with Shapiro, had a drink or two with him at the bar, never mentioned Stewart, and that was that. Several days later, Shapiro turned up at Old Buc. Here is an account of Shapiro's visit to Old Buc from my book, *Only the Days Are Long—Reports of a Journalist and World Traveler*:

I told Shapiro that it was impossible to visit with Stewart. But since he had two hours before another train left for London, I took him to the flight line to watch the Liberators come in from the mission. Afterward, we went to the Officers Club. Stewart was there, standing at the bar surrounded by several pilots who had flown that day. It had been a deep penetration show and some of our planes were shot up but all returned safely. We stood at the edge of the group. Shapiro did not move closer. He never spoke, never took notes, never had any contact with Stewart—merely observed and listened to the animated conversation about the mission. Some time later, Stewart showed me a newspaper clipping and said some friends had sent it to him from the States. It was a well turned personality piece about Stewart with Shapiro's byline. Stewart kidded me about the story and wondered how Shapiro had gotten it.

As I recall it now, he was not displeased. After the war, Shapiro wrote *D-Day: The Sixth of June,* which was made into a movie starring Robert Taylor and Richard Todd.

CHAPTER 12

JIMMY AND ANDY— "THE BUZZIN' TWINS"

"As I look back on that training mission, I remember it as a really fun flight."
—General Jimmy Stewart

In the promising but unwavering days of late April and during the month of May—leading up to D-day in early June—the combat crews flew almost daily, the ground crews kept the Liberators ready for flight, and all Old Buc people felt the pressure and were proud of it. Happily, the weather turned and spring seemed only a heartbeat away. Living conditions were on the upswing and some at Old Buc were reminded of Robert Browning's gentle line, "Oh, to be in England now that April's there" and Kipling's "Give me back one day in England—for it's Spring in England now."

The Old Buc history tells of the times and the mood:

> Many changes have occurred but none have been greater than the physical change on the station itself. Overshoe Lane and Riverside Drive, once so deep in mud that even walking was difficult, have been paved with concrete. Three months ago where there was only mud, grass is now growing. Shrubs

and trees have been planted all around the living area. All together the Station now has that lived-in, well-kept look. The post theatre shows new movies, on the average of five times a week. The large, flat area directly in front of the Station Headquarters, has been converted to softball and football fields.

On April 14 the Aero Club opened with a grand celebration. General Timberlake and Major Mike Phipps represented the 2nd Combat Wing and Major Jimmy Stewart was master-of-ceremonies. The Aero Club, operated by the Red Cross, long awaited on this station, now operates at full blast. It fills the same niche in the lives of the enlisted men that the Officers Club fills in the lives of the officers.

The Officers Club has been greatly improved and several additions made. Here, too, dances are held for the young officers.

Promotions, always a great morale booster, have been coming in with regularity. The Combat officers, especially, are enjoying a great many promotions.

Food, long a point of argument here has improved at all messes. Fresh eggs and hot cakes, the supreme soldier breakfast, are found on the tables several times each week.

Many good men have been lost by the Group. Strange new feet are continually being placed on the bar rail at the Officers Club, the owners of which have joined the Group as replacements for the men who are gone.

The bomb record of this Group compares favorably with the efforts of much older and more experienced outfits in this theatre. Indeed, at one point during the last two-month period the 453rd led the entire Eighth Air Force in bomb hits on or near the target.

So . . . it might be recorded for history, that the 453rd Bombardment Group has suffered many losses, girded itself against the tragic repercussions caused therefrom, profited by its mistakes and even now is ready to carry out any mission to any point within its range.

At the officers club dances, I can recall many times when spirits were high and glasses were raised. Major Jimmy Stewart would play the piano and the entire company would gather around him and sing the great old American and English show tunes, including his own favorite, "Ragtime Cowboy Joe." I seem to remember that the most vivacious people in the room were the piano player and the English lady guests. This was about the time of the infamous "Buzzin' Twins" incident.

Looking back, nobody seems to know why Major Jimmy Stewart, the solid and non-flamboyant pilot's pilot decided to take a four-engine Liberator bomber up for a joy ride. He could have been seeking a tension release from the long, grinding night-and-day work schedule of the past weeks. Or, the trip could have been a celebration of the excellent bombing results in recent reports. Or perhaps Stewart, who loved to fly the big bomber, wanted only to make a non-business flight on a spring day, taking along his assistant and cohort, Captain Andy Low as copilot. In any event, news of the Stewart-Low flying escapade soon spread to the Eighth Air Force bases and stations. It immediately became known as the mission of the "Buzzin' Twins." While the flight was widely known and discussed by the combat crews around the pot-bellied stoves of the Nissen huts, it was not written about or committed to paper until forty years later.

This is how the "Buzzin' Twins" incident became a part of the informal history of the Eighth Air Force in England in World War II: In the summer of 1983, Jimmy Stewart, now a retired brigadier general of the Air Force Reserve and his wife, Gloria, attended the reunion/convention of the Second Air Division Association at Norwich, East Anglia. Andy Low, who had retired earlier as an air

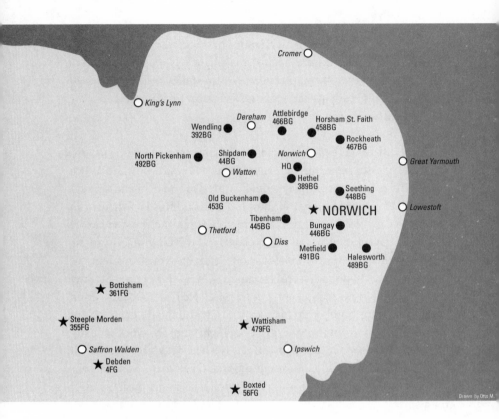

Liberator territory in East Anglia.

force major general and his wife, Helen, also attended the convention, along with over 500 Liberator veterans of the Second Air Division and their families. General Low, a career air force officer, had maintained his close Old Buc friendship with Stewart throughout the years since the war. He was president of the association that year and was especially happy to have Jimmy and Gloria at the Norwich meeting.

Norwich was considered the "Mother City" of the fourteen Liberator groups stationed near that North Sea city in the war years. It was to Norwich that the Liberator men made their Liberty Runs by trucks from Tibenham, Old Buc, and the other B-24 bases with names like Bungay, Rackheath, Seething, Shipdham, Horsham St. Faith, Wendling, Hethel, Metfield, Hardwick, Attlebridge, North Pickenham, and Halesworth. The American airmen came to Norwich on off nights for dancing at the Sampson, Lido, and Hercules ballrooms; movies; and an occasional traveling stage show. Drop-off and pick-up point for the Liberty Run trucks was the Bell Hotel, and many of the ladies who attended the Liberator base dances came from Norwich.

The Liberty Run always went in to Norwich for Sunday church services. Thus, the strong and loving bond, forged in wartime, between the people of Norwich and the Liberator men and women of the Second Air Division has been closely and meticulously maintained, with mutually precise attention and devotion, on both sides, throughout the years. The Second Air Division Memorial Library with its Roll of Honor has been established in Norwich. Every few years, to re-live the wartime memories and re-seal the deep bonds of friendship, the Liberator veterans, fewer each visit, make their pilgrimage to the Mother City by the North Sea.

So it was that Stewart, Low, and their Liberator compatriots found themselves, once again, in Norwich in the summer of 1983. Jordan Uttal of Dallas, Texas, who, during the war, served on the headquarters staff of the Second Air Division and as a former president of the association, was general chairman of the Norwich convention. He had planned well. The week-long reunion was mostly social in nature and featured receptions, formal dinners, informal lunches, dances, high teas, extensive library-museum visits and tours of the area—all carried out by Norwich hosts and American visitors in a warm and gracious atmosphere of heartfelt camaraderie. Perhaps for Jimmy, Andy, Gloria, Helen, and other 453rd veterans and their families, the highlight of the reunion was a visit to Old Buc. The Norwich newspaper took note of their return:

> The Yanks went back to Old Buckenham yester-
> day . . . and were given a heroes' welcome by scores
> of villagers.
> A red carpet greeting awaited the visitors as they
> turned back the clock for an emotional trip to their

second world war flying base.

There were reunions, memories, even a few tears—and for the ex-airmen and their families it was a day to cherish forever.

The Americans, in Norfolk for the 36th annual convention of the 2nd Air Division Association, had a chance to view their wartime airfield from above and saw a lasting memorial to lost comrades officially opened.

One of fifteen coach trips to Norfolk and North Suffolk, air bases of the last war, the Old Buckenham visit more than lived up to its promise of being one of the convention's stand-out events.

From the moment when the coach from Norwich arrived in the village, residents pulled out all the stops to salute the men whose daring exploits played a large part in the USAF's campaign in the skies between 1942 and 1945.

And there was an interview with Stewart:

Jimmy Stewart, from Indiana, Pennsylvania, could to an outsider have easily been just another of the former airmen making a nostalgic return to Old Buckenham.

And that's just the way James Stewart, Hollywood legend and Academy Award–winner, would have wanted it.

In his hometown last week he was honoured with colourful public celebrations to mark his 75th birthday.

In Norfolk yesterday he was a distinguished ex-airman paying tribute to lost colleagues.

He spoke to the people of Old Buckenham, thanking them for their welcome, and helped to plant

LEFT: Captain Jimmy Stewart at Tibenham, shortly after his arrival in England, 1943.

RIGHT: Forty years later, Jimmy Stewart takes an early morning stroll in Norwich, England, during a Second Air Division reunion in 1983.

Jimmy Stewart's family (circa 1916), clockwise from top left, Elizabeth (mother), Virginia, Alexander (father), Jimmy, and Mary.

Jimmy, as a young boy.

Jimmy Stewart grew up in this house in Indiana, Pennsylvania. *Starr Smith*

Three generations of dapper Stewart men stand in front of the family hardware store in Indiana, Pennsylvania: Alexander and Jimmy "bookend" James Maitland Stewart, after whom Jimmy was named.

Allied leaders Roosevelt and Churchill and the Combined Chiefs of Staff discuss Allied strategy in Morocco at the Casablanca Conference, January 14, 1943. Chief of the Army Air Force, General "Hap" Arnold, is at the extreme left, and General George Marshal, U.S. Army Chief of Staff, stands directly behind Roosevelt.

Stewart's boss and friend in Sioux City and Tibenham, Colonel Robert H. Terrill, commander, 445th Bomb Group.

Jimmy swears loyalty to God and Country along with several other army draftees at Fort MacArthur, California, March 22, 1941.

Private James Maitland Stewart, March 1941.

Party time at Tibenham and Old Buc, with Jimmy Stewart leading the singing surrounded by combat colleagues and English guests from the Norwich area. One song that Stewart especially liked to play was "Ragtime Cowboy Joe."

703rd Squadron, staff officers including (center back row) Captain Jimmy Stewart, commanding officer.

Jimmy Stewart was the quintessential airman. He loved airplanes and he liked the people who flew and worked with airplanes. At both Tibenham and Old Buc he seldom left the base, and spent a lot of his time on the flight line. He flew as command pilot frequently, and was just leaving on a mission with this crew when the picture was taken.

Lieutenant Stewart makes a point with wisecracking rookie Charlie McCarthy (along with Edgar Bergen) during a camp show, 1942. Unlike some Hollywood celebrities during the war, Stewart was not content with entertaining. He was determined to see real combat.

Major Jimmy Stewart serving the troops at Old Buc, Thanksgiving 1944, with General Ted Timberlake, left, and Colonel Ramsay Potts, center.
Francis Thomas

The novelty of having a movie star in their midst soon wore off among
Stewart's men. He was popular and comfortable with crews, despite being
10 to 12 years older than most of the men.

Sharrard Crew officers who flew to England with Captain Jimmy Stewart in late 1943: (front row, left to right) Stewart and pilot, First Lieutenant Lloyd Sharrard; (back row, left to right) Lieutenant Jim Kidder, Lieutenant Charles Wolfe, Lieutenant Rowland Swearnain, and Lieutenant Donald Daniel. The photo was taken in Marrakech, French Morocco, enroute to the 445th base at Tibenham.

Stewart on active duty in the ETO.

Stewart (front row, second from left) with fellow officers of the Second Air Division, England, 1944.

Major Jimmy Stewart: mentor, monitor, leader of men. He had a special feeling and rapport, a true bond, with both the combat crews that flew the daily missions and the ground crews that kept the Liberators in top flying condition.

Major Jimmy Stewart interrogates returning combat crewmen about their mission, May 1944.

Jimmy Stewart receives his first Distinguished Flying Cross (order of General Jimmy Doolittle, commander of Eighth Air Force, for Brunswick mission).

Colonel James Stewart travels home from England, along with 16,000 other American soldiers and airmen on board the *Queen Elizabeth*.

Stewart the officer: fervent but calm, passionate but controlled. He spent a lot of time on the flight line and was always at the control tower sweating out the return of his combat crews—and the mission's result.

Jimmy Stewart with his parents during his homecoming from the war in 1945.

Featured in *LIFE* magazine, this photograph captures Jimmy Stewart after the war in the family hardware store in Indiana, Pennsylvania. The original photograph hangs in the Stewart Museum. *Peter Stackpole*

Jimmy Stewart is reunited with his mother and father at the St. Regis Hotel in New York after returning from ETO in 1945.

LIFE

WELCOME JIM

OLONEL JIMMY STEWART

SEPTEMBER 24, 1945 **10** CENTS
BY SUBSCRIPTION: TWO YEARS $8.50

LIFE magazine cover featuring Colonel Jimmy Stewart in his hometown,
Indiana, Pennsylvania, September 24, 1945. *Peter Stackpole*

Jimmy and Gloria were married in Hollywood in August 1949. After meeting at Gary Cooper's house, they courted for little more than a year before marrying. Gloria had two young sons from a previous marriage, while it was Jimmy's first (and only) marriage.

Left to right, movie director John Ford, Colonel John F. Harvey, and Stewart, November 1960. Ford and Stewart had just finished filming *Two Rode Together* in Brackettville, Texas, and were at Laughlin Air Force Base awaiting a flight back to Hollywood.

Stewart receives a briefing on the partial pressure suit while visiting Laughlin Air Force Base while filming the western *Two Rode Together* on location, November 1960.

Colonel Stewart stands tall while on duty with the Air Force Reserve.

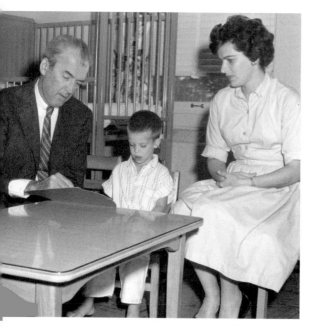

During a visit to Laughlin Air Force Base in Texas, Stewart takes time out to chat with a youngster in the base hospital, November 1960.

Jimmy Stewart, with pilot Major John Irving, after his Hustler flight at Carswell Air Force Base in Fort Worth, Texas. The flight earned General Stewart his Mach 2 pin.

General Stewart at a briefing for a Vietnam mission.

General Stewart returning to base after a Vietnam mission.

Andy Low and Stewart, both retired air force generals, during a personal reunion in Pennsylvania.

Stewart and Andy Low plant a tree in memory of their fallen comrades at Old Buc during a 1983 visit to Norwich.

The Jimmy Stewart statue in downtown Indiana, Pennsylvania. *Starr Smith*

Ramsay Potts at the Eighth Air Force Museum, March 2001.

Jimmy leads the bands at the 1983 Norwich reunion, while Gloria applauds.
Under Stewart's direction, the band played mostly Glenn Miller music.

Jimmy Stewart and Gloria at the Norwich dance reunion.

Jimmy Stewart walks on the crumbling runway at Old
Buc for the last time in 1983.

A pilot's farewell.

This Jimmy Stewart bust is on display at the Eighth Air Force Museum in Savannah, Georgia. *Starr Smith*

an American tulip tree in the village hall grounds.

Mr. Stewart, who flew from Old Buckenham during the war and was a commanding officer of the 703rd Bombardment Squadron at Tibenham, told a reporter, "Coming back reminded me of being here during the war.

"We got a wonderful reception, which represented a great deal of hard work on the part of the people here. It was a great tribute."

Chairman Uttal had planned a formal banquet as a grand finale of the convention with an orchestra playing World War II music. He told me later that he planned to ask Jimmy Stewart to lead the band in a medley of Glenn Miller songs. It was to be a surprising feature of the closing dinner. Here is a newspaper account of the event:

IMAGE OF THE PAST

"Moonlight Serenade" had never been so potent with nostalgia as it was last night at the Norwood Rooms.

It was the final banquet of the 36th annual convention of the Second Air Division of the Eighth Air Force and the talk was rife with times remembered.

Even so, "Moonlight Serenade" provided a unique moment. The leader of the Ray Shields Orchestra, who dress like the Glenn Miller Band and play like the Glenn Miller Band, invited James Stewart, the Hollywood veteran, who once came to Norfolk to help fight a war, to step up and conduct.

And there was this beloved, legendary actor doing what we had all seen him do in the 1953 film "The Glenn Miller Story," in which he had played the title role.

It was his 75th birthday, too, and the company of 560 sang their best wishes.

What with all of this, what with the Lord Mayor, Mr. Len Stevenson, remembering those "beautiful, virile and brave" young men who came from the U.S. more than forty years ago, and what with Mr. Stewart, by his very presence, reminding us of some of the best films we ever saw—remember "The Philadelphia Story," "Mr. Smith Goes to Washington," and "Rear Window" in a long list—it was a heart stirring occasion.

Earlier in the week of the convention, a Norwich couple—June and Edward Trafford—true-blue aficionados of the Liberator tradition in East Anglia, gave a dinner party. They invited the Lows; the Stewarts; Jordan and Joyce Uttal; Evelyn Cohen, a vice-president and longtime helmslady of the association; and a few other American and English friends. As Andy Low told me years later, it was a lovely and bountiful time. Late in the evening, over convivial brandy, Jimmy and Andy took turns telling the buzz story. June Trafford, ever the thoughtful and congenial hostess, announced that the story was so good and well told, it should be written down for everybody to enjoy. She suggested that Jimmy and Andy, in turn, should each tell his own version of the story. Indeed, as June Trafford suggested, the long-ago episode was written down and first published by editor Ray Pytel in the Second Air Division Association *Journal*. Here it is as it appeared in print:

STEWART & LOW—THE BUZZIN' TWINS!
Part 1—By Andy Low

Somewhere on a bomber base in England, late in the afternoon of an April day in 1944, the Operations Control Room of the 453rd Bombardment Group (H) under the direction of the Group Operations Officer, the Major, and his assistant, the Captain (that was me) was slowing its activity. The Major was winding up last-minute operations reports to higher headquarters on the results of the morning mission to Hitler's Fortress. The Captain was anticipating the next day's mission. The call would come for a maximum effort—every available aircrew and every available aircraft. There would be a short interlude in group activity as the staff awaited target intelligence and arming instructions.

With hardly a break in shuffling the mound of paperwork, the Major, in his low key manner, simply said, "Andy, find us a minimum crew and an airplane and we'll go shoot some landings." With a quick "Yes, Sir," I headed for Base Operations. For staff pilots, who generally flew in the co-pilot's position of the lead aircraft during combat missions, getting to "shoot some landings" was a welcome break.

At Base Operations I filed an aircraft clearance form and questioned the regulation which specified a minimum crew for any training operator. It was a poor time of day to locate crewmembers. Both the Major and I were "green card" and instructor pilots on the B-24 Liberator aircraft. Both of us had many flying hours as instructors in both B-17 and B-24 aircraft in the U.S., thus my rationalization on finding additional crew members for a local area training mission was simple—make up some names. I listed the Major as pilot and myself as co-pilot. Using combinations of our names, I filled out the remainder of the crew positions. I signed the authorization. We were cleared! No questions!

I phoned the Major to indicate the parking hard-stand where the aircraft was located. The aircraft was coming out of major maintenance and the crew chief had systems that he wanted us to operate and check during our flight. I gave the aircraft a quick inspection, kicked the tires, signed the paperwork, and confirmed the aircraft was ready for flight.

Soon the Major pulled up in his jeep. He first asked about the minimum aircrew requirements. I ran over my rationalization on this subject. The old barracks proverb, "the exigencies of the situation being such as to preclude compliance with appropriate regulations," etc., could apply. The Major was a very silent guy. Without comment we mounted up with him in the pilot's position and myself as co-pilot. We cranked the engines, received our clearance by radio from the control tower, taxied out and were on our way. Exhilarating! Off we went into the "wild blue yonder!!" The B-24 Liberator responded like a homesick angel.

We could not have been up to 1,000 feet on the climb when the Major pulled back on the power. He looked over at me with a wry smile and above the noise of the aircraft engines he shouted, "My former group commander always has his nap about now. Let's go wake him up!"

The Major had just come to our group from a base less than ten miles away. Before I could comprehend his intentions, we were in a gentle dive toward his former base. We swooped below the surrounding treetops, below the ridgelines of the barracks. The Major then deftly pulled up in a beautiful "Chandelle" maneuver to his left.

"Well that will wake him up. Now let's GET him up!" said the Major as he rolled expertly into another dive. Again we dipped below the treetops, the barracks ridgelines, and then up again into another "Chandelle" maneuver, this time to the right. As a normal thing the Major had a very subtle smile, but by this time he was smiling broadly, with a steely glint in his eye. "He's up now and will want our aircraft tail number, so let's go up one more time!"

The control tower operator at the base continually called to inquire why we were flying in his control area without a clearance. And below specified altitude minimums. Handling the radio, I looked to the Major for guidance. "Ignore them, don't answer," the Major instructed.

At each dive, the control tower operator became more adamant. He wanted the name, rank and serial number of the pilot. We were reminded that they had our aircraft serial markings. The bureaucracy would soon know who we were.

After the third swoop, the Major looked over to me with almost a mad twinkle in his eye and with his taciturn drawl calmly said, "I could make those operators get out of that tower!" We rolled into another dive. The control tower was mounted on an elevated platform above the maintenance hangar. Access was by an external ladder for the last twenty feet. Down to the tower level we dove and around the tower we zoomed. Transmissions from the tower became more rapid, almost frenzied and staccato. Would the pilot of the B-24 kindly report his name, rank and serial number! We remained silent. The second diving pass was from the opposite direction, but just as close to the tower. On the third pass, the transmission from the tower ceased. The three occupants could be seen scrambling down the ladder. The Major broke into a broad grin.

We returned to our home base. The Major practiced some takeoffs and landings. We ran through the system checks requested by the crew chief. We changed seats and I then had an opportunity to check my proficiency. Our mission was over. We came to a stop on landing, taxied in, and parked the aircraft. We made the necessary entries in the flight logs, reported to the crew chief, and returned to our office. It had been a most satisfying and relaxing training mission.

An hour later, we went to the officer's mess for our evening meal. Suddenly the group commander strode into the room and came directly to where we were seated. We jumped smartly to our feet and the commander began to regale the two of us; pity the poor example set by his operations officers, those charged with developing and enforcing safe air operations.

Here in the story I have difficulty recalling the exact details of what happened next. So, I defer to the Major—Major James M. Stewart, Group Operations Officer. Major Stewart was known to us principally as a talented pilot and inspirational combat leader. To the rest of the world he was Jimmy Stewart, already an acknowledged movie star.

Part 2—By Jimmy Stewart

Well, it's been forty years.

I recall the incident. In fact, I recall when I wished I could have forgotten it. It happened much as Andy has written. In his telling, perhaps the airspeed seems a little faster, the altitude a little lower and the Chandelles more perfect, given the passage of so much time. So, there may be some embellishment.

It fairly relates what happened on a late afternoon in April 1944. He's right, Colonel strode into the mess. Normally he was a most mild-mannered man. Highly decorated, he had already been through much of the air war. Though much younger than I, his combat experiences had induced a maturity far beyond his years. Obviously he had recently been severely chastised and I guessed immediately that he had been called by the Brig. General commanding our combat wing. The word of our training mission—escapade—had been reported to higher headquarters. Well, I tried the explanation that we were highly qualified instructor pilots who had been cooped up too long in a stuffy headquarters. Suddenly we had a chance to fly, and were momentarily carried away with the exhilaration of being free. We did nothing dangerous, only getting a feel of the airplane. So we tried to explain. The more I struggled for words (the Colonel did not give me much opportunity to speak), the more I realized that what we had thought was a grand idea some three hours earlier now seemed pretty dumb. So we switched rationale. I say "we." Andy just stood there. He did try to remind the Colonel that we were very experienced pilots and did nothing dangerous.

Then I remembered the old barracks proverb, "when you are at the bottom of a hole, don't dig." I assured the colonel that there had been only a momentary lapse in good judgement. This we regretted and such a lapse would not happen again.

Flushed and upset, the Colonel strode out of the mess without stopping for his evening meal. After that, our evening meal didn't taste very good either. We returned to the office. Shortly after arriving, a telephone call came from Wing Headquarters for me. It was the Commanding General. As a Major I was pleased to be called by the General, but it soon turned out to be a continuation of our encounter with the Colonel. How could we do such a dumb thing? Weren't we supposed to be setting a proper example for the younger crews? Suppose they were tempted to repeat our mission and kill themselves in a high-speed stall.

I had learned from our session with the Colonel to limit explanations. Now they did not make too much sense. I assured the General that a lapse of good discipline and training would not occur again. At least, not with us. Finally he hung up.

It wasn't over yet. The phone rang again. It was my former Colonel, and he was most upset, particularly about his control tower operators. I was most humble and contrite of heart. I assured him we regretted the stir we had caused. We were convinced it was unprofessional. Reluctantly we listened and hung up.

I was glad the operations instructions for the mission the following day began to come in. At least it changed the subject.

As I now recall the incident, and the furor we provoked, I recall I was fortunate to have had so much theatrical training behind me. I was called on to play many different roles in a very short time. But the air war went on.

A month later, in May 1944, I was promoted to Lt. Colonel and Andy was promoted to Major. Obviously, the bureaucracy had not taken a vengeful stance. I was moved up to Combat Wing Headquarters and assigned as Executive Officer to the Commanding General. Andy moved up in the bomb group to replace me as Operations Officer.

Somehow, I guess the bureaucracy has forgiven our iniquity.

As a postscript to our war story, I can report that one of my early tasks was to publish, in the General's name, a memorandum calling attention to the regulations requiring a minimum aircrew, which forbids flying without proper clearance in a control zone and descending below safe operating altitudes for any reason.

In reflection, over the past forty years I have done a lot of flying in many kinds of aircraft, and for many diverse reasons. As I look back on that training mission, I remember it as a really fun flight.

The Players:

Brig. General Ted Timberlake,
   Wing Commander
Colonel Ramsay Potts
Colonel Bob Terrill, Stewart's
   commanding officer at Tibenham
Major Jimmy Stewart
Captain Andy Low

CHAPTER 13

D-DAY—THE SIXTH OF JUNE

*"There will be four missions, first briefing at 23:00.
Take off at 03:27."*

—D-day briefing instructions for
Old Buc combat crews

Sergeant Major Eugene Lipp was the ranking 453rd non-commissioned officer at Old Buc. He operated out of base Headquarters. Here is his recollection of D-day as recounted in Andy Low's *Liberator Men of Old Buc*:

> It was two o'clock in the afternoon in northern England on a mid-week day, June 5, 1944. I was at my desk doing my duties and meeting my responsibilities as the 453rd Bomb Group and Air Base Sergeant Major when my phone rang. I was quickly informed, "Sergeant, this is General Griswold, 2nd Air Division." "Yes, General—Yes, sir," I replied. The General was the Deputy Commanding General, 2nd Air Division.
>
> General Griswold asked for Colonel Ramsey Potts, base commanding officer, and . . . I replied that he was not anywhere in headquarters. He said, "Very

well, Sergeant, you will have to act in his absence. I will hold you fully responsible, do you understand?"

"Yes sir, yes General," I said in response. "Sergeant," he said, "I am ordering you to close the base as soon as I finish here. I want the base closed in the next ten minutes, and nobody, absolutely nobody, may leave the base. You may allow officers and enlisted men to come back on the base where they belong, that only. Do you understand Sergeant?" "Yes, General, I do indeed sir, and I am ready now to implement your orders, sir," I replied. "Very well, Sergeant. I am holding you fully responsible." "Yes sir, I understand General. Goodbye, sir." With that I immediately called our base Provost Marshall, a Captain, and the equivalent to a chief of police in civilian life. The Captain quickly understood the orders from General Griswold. Within ten minutes the base was closed. I made the announcement on the P.A. system that operated from my office in the headquarters compound. In England the P.A. system was known as the Tannoy.

Unlike the navy, we did not address our base personnel with "Now hear this." My announcement always began with "Your attention please," a slight pause and again, "Your attention please," and then the announcement. This day the announcement centered upon the instructions from General Griswold, and I made it very clear that the base was closed upon the orders of the deputy commanding general, 2nd Air Division. It was the first official action, the prelude to the commencement of D-day the next morning, June 6th.

The base closure announcement did indeed cause a really gripping tenseness that dominated,

yes, permeated the minds and hearts of the entire
base population because "invasionitis" and D-day
talk had been prominently in the forefront of general
daily conversation for many weeks. Our base personnel sensed we were very, very close to D-day, and
the announcement fully convinced them. "This is it
guys, at any moment."

At 06:28 the next morning, the combined air,
water and land strike commenced. The code name
for this huge venture was "Operation Overlord."
True, the base was closed, but it was anything but
down. Come dusk, then darkness, the base was
certainly alive, really humming, just plain peaking
with activity. Mission briefings began well before
midnight for all four bomb squadrons comprising
our 453rd Bomb Group. Takeoff of the B-24
bombers, and then the rendezvous of the four
squadrons, as the Group began about 03:30 a.m.,
June 6th.

Sergeant Major Lipp pointed out in his narrative that the 453rd flew
four missions on D-day, dispatching its planes time and again to the
skies over Normandy. Each plane carried fifty-two one-hundred-pound
anti-personnel bombs. All four missions were under the direction of
group operations officer Lieutenant Colonel James M. Stewart. Stewart
had been promoted to lieutenant colonel only hours before D-day.
The new colonel briefed all four missions and flew on one of them. The
453rd bombed St. Laurent, St. Lo, Caen, and Coutances.

After the base was closed on the eve of D-day, Sergeant Major Lipp
went back on the Tannoy and announced a meeting of all Old Buc
personnel on the flight line. This is how I remember that long-ago
meeting: Colonel Potts was in charge. He began by emphasizing how
the ground attack depended on the attacking aircraft disrupting the
defense on the beaches to achieve a successful landing. He read a

Colonel Ramsay Potts and General James H. "Jimmy" Doolittle.

message from General Doolittle that asked for an extraordinary performance of duty by all personnel. A communications from General Eisenhower called for a noble effort as the "Crusade in Europe" began. Colonel Potts said that the first air attacks were to be completed by 06:28 because time for the landings was 06:30.

Throughout the hectic hours of preparation and leading up to the series of D-day briefings, the man in charge was the omnipresent and charismatic Potts. Younger than Stewart and only a few years older than the combat crews, the youthful colonel, with tremendous presence, radiated confidence, experience, and quiet enthusiasm. He was present at all briefings but left actual instructional details to Jimmy Stewart. The chief briefing officer for all four missions was Stewart. I must say it was a bravura performance—as if he had been rehearsing all of his life, and, now, finally, the big moment was at hand. I worked with Stewart on two of the missions, and it was a memorable experience.

A young navigator officer, Lieutenant Leon Helfand, was at Stewart's side all night long, the detail man in preparing the missions. Last year, at a 453rd reunion, I asked him to tell me about that night. He wrote to me several months ago from his home in Woodbridge, Connecticut. Here is his letter:

> My crew was shot down on the night of April 22. Our pilot was Jim Munsey, and only five of us survived with me the most badly injured. I

still had bandages on my hand and [was] unable to fly, and so was readily available for briefing the navigators (and other assignments). I knew that Major Stewart would be doing the briefing.

At about 7:00 p.m. on June 5th I heard the teletype clicking away nearby, and went into the teletype room. Looking over the shoulder of the operator the first thing I saw was coordinates for OMAHA BEACH, UTAH BEACH, and some others. I knew instantly that this was what we were waiting for, and went to call Major Stewart.

We went over it together. The 453 was assigned to a section of Omaha Beach. H-hour was 6:30 a.m. No bombs were to be dropped after 6:28. The bomb load was to be anti-personnel type. The secondary target was St. Lo, or Caen. (I don't recall.) None of the invading forces were to shoot at any aircraft in the area as they would be 100% ours.

Major Stewart and I went to work starting with approximately 6:25 a.m. and working back from there by calculating time from base to target, time from take off to altitude, breakfast, briefing, to wake up of the crews which I vaguely recall was 1:30 a.m. We knew that it would be very dark at time of take-off until approximately crossing the south coast of England. We also knew that it could be dangerous to form up by circling the base in darkness, so we devised a plan using "G" navigation for position, rate of climb, and time for the flight.

The planning was complex, but the flying was easy, and it worked. All aircraft arrived at the designated point on the South Coast at the same time even though they had taken off one minute apart.

The second mission followed the first. I believe the target was Caen.

(Note: On the first mission, the target had been described by Intelligence as a defending position 300 yards offshore, about ten miles northwest of Bayeux and one mile north of St. Laurent. Its complement was probably forty men with machine guns, two-inch or three-inch mortars, and anti-tank guns. Knocking out this locality in support of the landing forces was of the utmost importance.)

I handled the interrogations for several returning combat crews. To a man, they were excited, exuberant, and anxious to talk. It was as if they felt their dark and dangerous work was beginning to show results. However, flying above an almost solid overcast, they were disappointed that only in an occasional break in the clouds were they able to see the invasion going on beneath their wings.

Here is the intelligence report that was filed:

At the interrogation, the crews plainly showed their disappointment. They were told that they would see the Allied Navy standing offshore lobbing their shells onto their targets. They were told that they would see the invasion barges just waiting their turn to slither onto the beaches. The water would be filled with big ships, little boats, vessels of all varieties, leaving hardly any space for water. The undercast was solid with breaks almost completely absent, hiding all from their view. However, they could sense the magnificence and magnitude of the spectacle below them. As a consolation perhaps, they did see the air filled with fighters, medium and heavy bombers, and an endless chain of troop transports and gliders, all heading for the invasion coast. Everything that could fly or float was in the air or water.

CHAPTER 14

ED MURROW AND
JIMMY STEWART IN LONDON

*"Colonel Stewart, all of us in England are aware of
your fine work with your bomber groups."*
—Ed Murrow's remark to Jimmy Stewart
when they first met in London

A fter D-day the bad weather continued. But despite the undercast, Lieutenant Colonel Stewart kept his Old Buc Liberators in the skies over the Normandy beaches day after day, attacking railroad bridges and airfields in the beachhead area. For nine days following the successful landings, Allied bombs dropped continuously in an effort to disrupt the German communications system. Stewart kept the 453rd in the thick of this ongoing campaign in support of the Normandy advance. The group history noted that Argentan, an important communications center forty miles south of LeHavre, was hit on June 7 by twenty-three Old Buc Liberators carrying sixty-nine tons of high explosives. On June 8, Avranches and Redon were attacked. The group flew two missions on June 10, Evreux and Dreux. The airfields at these two locations were targets for the thirty-four Liberators that Stewart dispatched that day. Weather still dogged the group's efforts on June 11. The railroad bridge at Le Port Boulet across the Loire River about fifty miles southwest of Tours was the first target for the day. But the twenty-four ships dispatched were turned back because of weather. That afternoon, twelve ships bombed the airfield at Cormeilles En Vexin. On D-day plus six, with clearing weather, two missions were dispatched—a railroad bridge at Montfort and the airfield at Conches.

June was a record-setting month for the 453rd. Thirty-three missions were flown. Four aircraft were lost to enemy action.

On June 29, 1944, the 453rd observed a signal anniversary. On that date, one year earlier, the group had been formed in Boise, Idaho. One year later, on June 29, 1944, the 453rd flew its ninety-eighth mission, dispatching a record number of forty-eight aircraft, marking a full year of combat operations against Nazi Germany. Shortly after D-day, I had been transferred from Old Buc to my new post as a press officer at General Eisenhower's Supreme Headquarters (SHAEF) in London. I went back to Old Buc for the anniversary celebration, which was presided over by Colonel Potts and (newly promoted) Lieutenant Colonel Jimmy Stewart. Cries of "Hear, Hear," rang from the rafters when Major Andy Low raised his glass and proposed a toast to "the gallant airmen of the Eighth Air Force and the RAF who, during Big Week and the Battles of Berlin, denied the vaunted Luftwaffe from keeping its rendezvous over Normandy Beach skies on D-day." The celebration turned out to be Jimmy Stewart's last official function at Old Buc. Three days later, on July 2, he was transferred to Second Combat Wing Headquarters at Hethel as General Timberlake's executive officer. The staff work at Hethel, directly under General Timberlake, was quite a contrast to combat duty at Tibenham and Old Buc. The stakes were high but different and on another military plateau. Timberlake became the fifth air force officer—after "Pop" Arnold, Bob Terrill, Andy Low, and Ramsay Potts—to enhance Stewart's career and become his friend.

Stewart's transfer to wing headquarters prompted two rumors— that the promotion was in recognition of his salient work, under Potts, in the resurgence of the 453rd, and the resultant superior bombing reports. The second rumor was more intriguing: that Stewart was being groomed for a group commander's job and

General Timberlake wanted him by his side at wing headquarters, for the time being.

I had heard the group commander rumor in air force circles in London. It all seemed to make good sense and I must say it was thrilling news, deserving and in keeping with the usual logical progressive order of military procedure.

But it never happened.

The timing, as fast-moving events developed in Normandy, was not propitious. After D-day, and the success of Overlord, the role and the rhythm of the heavy bombers was changing to more tactical options and missions. Yet there can be no doubt that the Jimmy Stewart–group commander promotion had attention in high places. After the war when I was working with General Jimmy Doolittle on the separate air force project in Washington, and Stewart was back in Hollywood, the general spoke highly of him and once said to me, "We were getting ready to give Jimmy a group when the war ended." In his post-war book, Doolittle wrote: "If the war had gone on another month, Jimmy would have become a group commander, which was the most important job in the Air Force. . . ."

Stewart stayed with the Second Combat Wing Headquarters for his remaining months in the ETO. He served as executive officer, operations officer, chief of staff, and, finally, wing commander. He put on the eagles of a full colonel on March 29, 1945, slightly less than a year from his promotion to lieutenant colonel. At Hethel, Stewart was General Timberlake's right-hand man. The work was different now, and his duties, while still operational, did not call for flying routine combat missions. However, he would often slip over to the 389th, the Pathfinder (radar) group also based at Hethel, or Jeep down to Tibenham or Old Buc to fly occasional missions. At Old Buc, he sometimes flew on the wing of Major Andy Low who had succeeded him as the 453rd operations officer. That is, before Andy was shot down.

One of Stewart's friends at Hethel was the Nebraska journalist Captain Carroll "Cal" Stewart (no relation), Timberlake's aide and author of *Ted's Traveling Circus*—the story of Timberlake's 93rd

Bomb Group, which had performed so notably on the Ploesti mission of 1943. Cal Stewart was also a coauthor of *Ploesti*, the definitive book on that historic mission. Another of Jimmy Stewart's Hethel friends was Mike Phipps, the twenty-goal polo player who was the wing intelligence officer and had already flown eleven combat missions and was one of the planners of the Ploesti raid. Now retired in Lincoln, Nebraska, Cal Stewart told me: "Jimmy was a superb pilot, never overlooking a detail, never shirked, a tireless operations officer who got along with the young flyers. He was proud of his military service but did not want to parade it around."

During his time at Tibenham and Old Buc, Stewart was committed to a seven-days-a-week working and flying schedule. Now at the wing, his job was less hands-on, and he could get away for an occasional trip down to London.

I was based in London for a few weeks after D-day before moving on with the Eisenhower press staff to Paris, after the Liberation. One night I was having dinner at the Savoy Grill with Ed Murrow, the CBS correspondent, and his colleague, Charles Collingwood. Colonel Jimmy Stewart and several American and British friends came into the restaurant and took a nearby table.

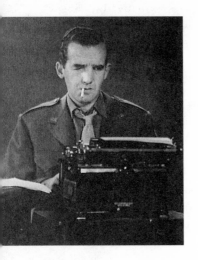

I knew that both Jimmy and Ed had a professional admiration and respect for each other although they had never met. As a friend, it seemed a good time to bring them together. I had heard Ed comment on Stewart leaving Hollywood behind and turning to the difficult and dangerous life of a bomber pilot in a combat situation on a Liberator base in the English countryside. He once said, "It seems to me that Stewart

Edward R. Murrow at the BBC Studios in London working on his "This is London" broadcast. *CBS Photo* came over here to fight." On his side, Jimmy admired Ed's work and courage and had learned a great deal about the war in Europe from his broadcasts and seldom missed his "This . . . Is London" reports while in Boise and even more so after arriving in Sioux City when it looked like he was headed to the ETO. I knew that both men had a lot in common, notably a small-town background—Jimmy in Pennsylvania, and Ed in North Carolina and later in the Washington state. Both had grown up with a strong and strict family influence, Ed under his mother, Ethel, and Jimmy under his father, Alex. They had a mutual interest in airplanes. Ed, of course, had flown bombing missions with the Eighth and the RAF, and his brother, Lacey, was an air force general. Jimmy was aware of this and Ed knew about Jimmy's civilian flying days in California before the war and the little Stinson two-seater. While Jimmy and Ed had made great reputations as public performers, both were essentially private, reserved, and taciturn men who were not given to casual camaraderie and badinage.

After checking with Ed, I went over to Stewart and told him I'd like to bring Murrow over to his table for an introduction. He stood up and said, "Yes. Yes, Starr, of course. I would like to meet Mr. Murrow but I want to go over to *his* table." Which we did. The introduction and following conversation was probably the shortest on record, even for two private and reserved men. It went like this—Murrow: "All of us in England, Colonel, know about your work and your missions with the bomber groups. Congratulations." Stewart: "Mr. Murrow, your reports meant a lot to all of us in the States. I listened to your broadcasts all the time before I came over here. Thank you." After I had introduced Stewart and Murrow, I could not help thinking that, other than General Eisenhower, they were perhaps the most famous Americans in England.

Later, after the war, I was to recall this Stewart-Murrow encounter when I heard of the first meeting of two other private and non-talkative people—my fellow Mississippians, William Faulkner and Eudora Welty.

*　　*　　·　*

It has often been said and written, mostly by those who were there, that London during World War II was the most exciting, exhilarating, and glamorous city in the world. The constant unfolding drama and ultimate climax—interposed by the mortal danger of the earlier German air raids, and, later, Hitler's V-1 buzz bombs and V-2 rockets— marked every thought, every word, and every movement in a great and overflowing city at a time that would be forever talked about and remembered. Eric Sevareid, who was there, has observed, "In the war, London was a truly singular and memorable experience."

There was a never-ending stream of uniforms, many carrying the distinctive Eighth Air Force shoulder patch. The American airmen would come down to London from their bomber and fighter bases with their crisp uniforms, crushed hats, silver wings, and, some might say, a confident, even cocky, attitude. The Liberator men would come in on three-day passes, arriving at Liverpool Street Station or King's Cross Station, and many of them would immediately take a taxi to Piccadilly Circus, then fan out to the Red Cross clubs, hotels, restaurants, bars, and theaters of the West End. They could be seen at Albert Hall, St. Paul's Cathedral, and the great London museums. The lively music halls were popular and crowded. The men strolled London's streets and viewed the historic sights—Buckingham Palace, Big Ben, Parliament, Marble Arch, Hyde Park Corner, Trafalgar Square, The Mall, The Tower, and the Thames. And, of course, the Americans were not the only men and women in uniform—the RAF and British army and navy, Free French, Czechs, Poles, Canadians, and Australians. New Zealand, South Africa, India, and other faraway nations of the British Commonwealth were represented in uniform on the streets of London in those times, a colorful parade of Allied unity.

Leading up to the invasion, the influx of men in uniform swelled daily. One British woman was heard to say, "Piccadilly is a thrilling place these days. All the uniforms of all the nations seem to be there." While Piccadilly Circus was usually the starting point for the American airmen, the entertainment avenues of those London times led in many directions. At the Ambassador Theatre, throughout the war, was a music revue that was perhaps the favorite of the Americans. It was called, at various times, "Sweet and Low," "Sweeter and Lower," and "Sweetest and Lowest," and featured music, comedy, and dancers. Perpetual star of the productions was Hermione Gingold, who was such a favorite that she came to America after the war and had a great success on Broadway and television.

Jimmy Stewart had few opportunities to savor the theater during his combat duty at Tibenham and Old Buc. As an actor, he liked the London theater and greatly admired the stage productions in the West End. After transfer to wing headquarters, his London days and nights were more frequent and, for the most part, centered around theater visits. As it turned out, London theater life was gaining momentum after a lull brought on by the grim days of the Blitz and the Battle of Britain. The years of 1943–1944 found the production of almost half of Shakespeare's canon on the boards in the West End, including the major pieces—*Hamlet, Macbeth, King Lear,* and *Midsummer Night's Dream.* George Bernard Shaw's *Arms and the Man, Androcles and the Lion, Pygmalion,* and *Candida* were also in production, along with Henrik Ibsen's *A Doll's House* and *Hedda Gabler.* The American playwrights were much in evidence in those years—Robert Sherwood, John Steinbeck, Thornton Wilder, Eugene O'Neill, Cole Porter, Maxwell Anderson, and, in late November of 1943, Irving Berlin brought his all-soldier revue to London.

The perennial London attraction of those times, Noel Coward, continued to beguile his audiences with *The Happy Breed, Private Lives, Present Laughter,* and, later, *Blithe Spirit.* The American servicemen, not always accustomed to live theater, came in large numbers to the West End where they especially liked the shows of Ivor Novello—*Perchance to Dream, The Dancing Years,* and *Arc de Triomphe.* The theaters were sold out many times and always crowded with the military uniforms of Allied nations and London civilians. London's eclectic theater life in those war years of 1943–1944 also included productions of *The Vagabond King,* the *International Ballet, The Merry Widow,* and Sigmund Romberg's *The Desert Song.*

General Jimmy Doolittle entertains the King, Queen, and Princess Elizabeth at an Eighth Air Force base in 1943.

The war documentaries, Noel Coward's *In Which We Serve,* and *London Can Take It,* with a commentary by the American journalist Quentin Reynolds, played to large audiences in the movie houses. In the early stages of the war, older Hollywood movies like *Destry Rides Again,* with Jimmy Stewart and Marlene Dietrich, were shown. Later, newer movies like *Goodbye Mr. Chips, Mrs. Miniver,* and *The Wizard of Oz* began to appear on the London screens. I shall never forget one London night seeing the movie based on the Ernest Hemingway novel, *For Whom the Bell Tolls*—and the next night having a drink at the Dorchester bar with Mary Welsh, the *Time* war correspondent who introduced me to the famous author. Hemingway was in the ETO as a correspondent for *Collier's* magazine. Mary later became Hemingway's fourth wife and widow.

London dining places favored by the American airmen included Simpson's in the Strand, Mulatta's in Half Moon Street, The Savoy Grill, Prunier's, and Cafe Royal, just off Piccadilly Circus. The favorite was Rainbow Corner. Colonel Clyde Bradley, of North Carolina, now retired from the air force, vividly remembers his London three-day passes with his crew. He told me: "After the first two or three visits, sightseeing and strolling around, we would take several rooms at the Strand Palace on Piccadilly Circus, and just hole up for three days—drinking, playing poker, taking baths, sleeping, and getting room service."

Major Glenn Miller brought his air force orchestra to London just after D-day in 1944. Following his first concert in a London theater,

Major Glenn Miller, with trombone, leads his famous orchestra at Eighth Air Force bomber base, in the fall of 1944. *C.H. Freudenthal*

which was broadcast over the BBC, the Miller band was a triumphant success and seemed to be a mutual bonding channel between the English and their American visitors. General Jimmy Doolittle, always a favorite with the Royal Family, invited King George, Queen Elizabeth, and their daughters, Princess Elizabeth and Princess Margaret, to an Eighth Air Force base for a Glenn Miller concert.

As the war was winding down, Colonel Jimmy Stewart came more often down to London from Hethel, putting up at the Savoy, going to the theatre, and entertaining friends at the hotel. It was at the Savoy, after the war was over, that Stewart had a poignant and joyful reunion with Colonel "Pop" Arnold—his friend from their Boise days.

CHAPTER 15

THE BOMBING OF SWITZERLAND

"Yeah, yeah. That's all right, dear. Just take your time."
—Colonel Stewart consoles a frustrated
young court reporter

O n June 1, 1945, just days after World War II ended in Europe, Colonel Jimmy Stewart, chief of staff of the Second Combat Wing of the Second Air Division, presided over the court-martial of two combat flyers of the Second Division who were accused of bombing neutral Switzerland. This was by far Stewart's most important assignment at wing headquarters, and, because of the grave charges against the officers, perhaps the most significant of his wartime career.

This is the story:

On March 4, 1945, only a short time before the war ended in Europe, an American B-24 Liberator on a bombing mission to Nazi Germany inadvertently bombed a large city in neutral Switzerland. This tragic and untoward event caused an international episode that resulted in this headline in a Swiss newspaper, "American Flyers Hunt Nazis in Switzerland," and a general court-martial for two American flying officers. Before the spiraling developments of the unfortunate event reached their ultimate closure months later, the circumstantial network had embraced President Roosevelt; General George

Marshall; General Eisenhower; General Carl Spaatz; Congressional Medal of Honor recipients General Jimmy Doolittle, Eighth Air Force commander, and General Leon Johnson, commander of the Fourteenth Combat Wing; and Colonel Jimmy Stewart.

The two defendants in the historic court-martial were First Lieutenant William Sincock and First Lieutenant Theodore Balides. They were assigned to the 392nd Group of the Fourteenth Combat Wing, Second Air Division of the Eighth Air Force. Home station for the 392nd was Wendling in East Anglia, some seventy miles from London, near the city of Norwich and the North Sea. On that fateful day in March, 1945, the 392nd dispatched twenty B-24 Liberators on the primary target of a tank factory in Aschaffenburg, Germany. Before reaching the target, a squadron of seven bombers of the group, led by Pilot Sincock with Balides as navigator, were lost due to extremely bad weather and faulty navigational equipment. Knowing they could not bomb the primary target, and far off course, Sincock and Balides, in the lead plane of the lost squadron, now sought a "target of opportunity." That target, so they thought, was Freiburg, Germany, near the Swiss border. The informal mantra for Eighth Air Force crews at the time was, "Any bomb on Germany is a good bomb." So, for Sincock and Balides, the decision seemed clear. But the forty-eight 1,000-pound bombs of the lost squadron did not fall on Freiburg, Germany. The bombs fell on Zurich, Switzerland.

The war was almost over. The Eighth Air Force dropped its last bombs on Germany on April 25, 1945. Even so, Lieutenants Sincock and Balides were charged with violation of the 96th Article of War. Specific charges against Sincock read in part, "while in command of and piloting a B-24 aircraft . . . in the position of squadron leader . . . did . . . at or near Zurich, Switzerland . . . wrongfully, negligently . . . cause the plane he was then leading to drop bombs upon and near the city of Zurich, Switzerland . . . a nation friendly to the United States." The charges against Balides, while dealing mostly with his duties as navigator, were essentially the same as those against Sincock, "wrongfully, negligently." These charges were serious enough to call for a general court-martial. Punishment, if convicted, included dismissal from the U.S. Military Service, forfeiture of all pay due, and confinement at hard labor for life.

All units and personnel involved with the incident belonged to the Second Air Division. Therefore, the court-martial was convened at Ketteringham Hall, the division headquarters, with Colonel Jimmy Stewart as president of the court. Captain Jackson Granholm,* group navigator of the 458th Group of the Fourteenth Combat Wing, was appointed defense counsel, assisted by First Lieutenant Max Sokart, an intelligence officer with the 458th, and a lawyer in civilian life from New London, Connecticut.

The international incident claimed the official attention of Washington all the way to the White House. Richard G. Davis, in his book *Carl A. Spaatz and the Air War in Europe,* reported the reaction of Chief of Staff George C. Marshall:

> The March bombing . . . elicited a strong response from Marshall, who cabled Spaatz direct-ly: "The . . . bombing of Swiss territory . . . demands more than expressions of regret." He ordered Spaatz to leave immediately for Geneva and to present to the appropriate Swiss officials information as to the cause of the incidents, Spaatz's plans for corrective action, and "a formal apology." Marshall further requested that Spaatz undertake the mission in "maximum secrecy" with "no publicity."
>
> This message reached Spaatz on March 6. By March 8, in Bern and in the company of U.S. Minister to Switzerland Leland Harrison, Spaatz extended official and personal regrets to the Swiss Foreign Minister, the Minister of War, the Commander in Chief of the Swiss army, and the Chief of the Swiss Air Corps. He briefly explained the difficulties of winter bomber operations,

---

*Captain Granholm is the author of the book *The Day We Bombed Switzerland,* published in 2002.

emphasizing the prohibition, previously agreed to by the Allies, against bombing within 50 miles of the Swiss border.

He promised to set up two zones: one from 150 to 50 miles outside Switzerland within which he would forbid attacks without positive identification, and the other within 50 miles of the Swiss border, where no attacks could be made without his express permission. All this appeased the Swiss. In keeping with their neutrality, they agreed to keep the forbidden zones strictly confidential in order to keep the Germans from moving additional tempting targets close to the Swiss borders. The Swiss, for the purposes of domestic public opinion, issued a communiqué after Spaatz's departure describing the visit in general terms. To Marshall, Spaatz reported, "It seems evident to me that with the present restrictions which have been established, plus the fact that the importance of these incidents has been most forcibly impressed on our Air Forces, there should be little danger of any recurrence of any such violations of Swiss sovereignty."

Stewart had spent most of his time in the ETO in personal involvement with combat crews. As presiding officer of the court-martial, he had a highly responsible role in a vital military procedure concerning two combat crewmen. He did not know Sincock or Balides, and had no personal knowledge of the matter at hand. The testimony of the court-martial centered around the laborious details of wintertime weather and the precise technical techniques of wartime navigation. From all accounts, Colonel Stewart handled his razor-edged and well-defined duties with professional balance and even-handed understanding and compassion.

At one point in the court-martial proceedings, Colonel Stewart did provide a brief glimpse of his familiar movie style. Corporal

Dolly Palmer, a young WAC secretary, was drafted as a court reporter. As the testimony became more and more rapid, complicated, and technical, she became frustrated and began to cry. Colonel Stewart interrupted the proceedings. "Well, just a doggone minute here! Let's just hold it up here a bit. This poor lady is snowed with all this big technical talk. Yeah, Yeah, that's all right dear, Just take your time."

The court-martial ended with a not-guilty verdict on all counts. Lieutenants Sincock and Balides went free.

CHAPTER 16

A FAREWELL TO THE ETO

*"Sound judgement ... outstanding performance ... patri-
otism ... loyalty ... initiative ... as evidenced by participation on bombing missions ... and ... staff work."*
—Excerpts from Commendation for
Colonel James Maitland Stewart prior to
his departure from ETO in fall of 1945

The Eighth Air Force dropped its last bombs on Germany in the second week of April, 1945. On April 16, General Carl Spaatz informed General Jimmy Doolittle that the "strategic war was over ... the Eighth Air Force (and Fifteenth in Italy) would henceforth operate with the tactical air force in close cooperation with the ground forces."* Less than a month later, President Harry Truman in Washington and Prime Minister Winston Churchill in London proclaimed May 8, 1945, V-E Day. The war in Europe was over.

A few days later, Colonel Jimmy Stewart went down to London from his 2nd Combat Wing headquarters. The visit was in the nature of a celebration, and he checked in at the Savoy Hotel. As it turned out, the visit developed into a momentous occasion in Stewart's life. It involved an old friend, Colonel Walter "Pop" Arnold, his commanding officer at Boise, who had made the pivotal Sioux City call to Colonel Terrill, setting the wheels in motion that eventually brought him to England—and combat with the Eighth Air Force. Colonel

*from *I Could Never Be So Lucky Again*—General Jimmy Doolittle's autobiography.

Arnold later was given command of his own Liberator group in Italy. His daughter Kathleen tells the London story:

> Dad was coming home after being released from the German POW camp at Moosburg. Pop's best friend, Irwin "Bull" Rendle, flew to Paris to pick Pop up and then flew him back to London. Pop was still physically sick and weak from being seriously wounded when his B-24 was shot down and eight months internment in German POW camps. Coincidentally, Jimmy Stewart was staying at the same London hotel as Pop and Bull. When Jimmy found out that Pop was at the hotel he immediately came to his room. Jimmy rushed in and greeted Pop with a great big bear hug, which lifted Pop right up off the ground. Jimmy was having a party in his room with a mixture of both military and famous people and he insisted Pop and Bull join him. Pop felt embarrassed because he looked so bad and begged off but Jimmy wouldn't take no for an answer and he physically, pulled Pop to the party. Jimmy kept his arm around Pop the whole time, supporting him, never leaving his side. Jimmy introduced Pop as the best pilot in the air corps and told everyone how he had taught him to fly. He told everybody that Pop saved his life several times in near crashes. He told everyone what a great Commander Pop was, and about their times together in Boise, and how Pop had helped him advance in his career. Jimmy made a real big deal, turning all the attention on Pop and making him sound like some sort of hero. Pop said he was a bit embarrassed by all the attention and he didn't feel very heroic at all. Jimmy made a toast to him and he was totally

overwhelmed by the atmosphere of celebrities and
by the genuine display of friendship from Jimmy.

Stewart said later that the totally unexpected and joyous reunion
with Pop Arnold on such a positive and propitious occasion there in
jubilant London, coupled with the mountainside incident in Boise,
was one of his most emotional memories of the war.

Upon his return to Hethel after the V-E celebration in London,
Stewart learned that General Timberlake was leaving for a new
assignment. He was being replaced by the former commander of the
389th group at Hethel, Colonel Milton Arnold.

The wartime shadows were getting shorter now in East Anglia, but
things were still busy and upbeat. General Doolittle authorized
30,000 Eighth Air Force ground personnel to make aerial tours of
Germany "to see with their own eyes what they had helped to bring
about."* Stewart had always looked with great favor and deep respect
on the ground crews that kept the big bombers flying mission after
mission, many times repairing flak holes and other damage throughout the night in order to have the Liberators ready for the next day's
mission. He took personal charge of many Liberator fly-overs to
Germany for his wing ground crews, arranging background briefings
before the tour and follow-up sessions after the return.

About this time Stewart received two career-enhancing developments. One was a commendation. The other was a promotion as
commander of the Second Combat Wing.

THE COMMENDATION:
HEADQUARTERS, 2ND COMBAT BOMB WING (H)
SUBJECT: Commendation.
TO: Colonel James M. Stewart.
1. From July, 1944, to December, 1944, and from
February, 1945, to May, 1945, you were assigned to the
2d Combat Bomb Wing of the Eighth Air Force as
Chief of Staff. In that capacity, as in the other

*Ibid

positions in this Command which you held, including squadron commander of the 703d Bombardment Squadron from August, 1943, to March, 1944, Group Operations Officer of the 453d Bomb Group (H) from March, 1944, to July, 1944, and Operations Officer of this Wing from December, 1944, to February, 1945, your performance of duty was outstanding.

You were responsible for the administrative organization and the efficiency of the many component parts of this Command and their co-ordination into one of the greatest striking forces of the entire Air Force. Throughout the period of your incumbency as Chief of Staff of this Command the bombing efficiency of this Wing, according to figures published and released by ORS, Eighth Air Force, and the figures prepared separately and released by 2nd Air Division, improved until for the period from August, 1944, to May, 1945, the 2d Combat Bomb Wing was first of all Wings in the 2nd Air Division in the 1,000 and 2,000 foot circles. This in itself is a direct reflection on your work and efforts as Chief of Staff.

Throughout the time you have been associated with this Command you have displayed the most intense loyalty and patriotism as evidenced by your own participation on nineteen important combat missions and encounters with the enemy in addition to your staff work. Your initiative, sound judgment, personality and sincere devotion to duty has contributed immeasurably to the smooth operation of this Headquarters and the morale and efficiency of the men of this entire Command. Your keen interest and unselfish devotion to duty has been exceptional, and I desire to take this opportunity to commend you for an outstanding performance of duty. It has been a sincere pleasure to serve with you and to be associated with you.

(Signed)   MILTON W. ARNOLD,
         Colonel, Air Corps,
         Commanding.

As summer came, Stewart was promoted to the last and biggest job he held during the war, commander of the Second Combat Wing, a position formerly held by his friend and mentor Ted Timberlake. The cycle was now complete. All of his service in the ETO had been in the Liberator Wing—squadron commander, group operations officer, wing executive officer, wing chief of staff, and, now, wing commander. His primary job was supervising the myriad arrangements for taking the wing back to the United States. In short, Stewart was given the job and responsibility of getting the boys home. A wing commander's job called for the rank of brigadier general.

Meanwhile, back in the States, the welcome mat was out in Indiana, Pennsylvania. In late August, the *Post-Gazette* of Pittsburgh reported: "Every time the phone rings at the A. M. Stewart home in Indiana, Pa., Mrs. Stewart hopes it's Jimmy. 'It's been a long wait for me—two years,' Mrs. Stewart said. But she disclosed that the reel hero who became a real hero and full colonel via the Eighth Air Force expects to be home soon. 'I don't know whether he's going to fly or come by ship,' his mother said. 'I think maybe he's coming by water with his outfit, the Second Bomb Wing.' But she thinks she'll be seeing her famous son soon because she had been notified not to send any more mail to England."

In September, 1945, under the headline, "Jimmy Stewart Back from the Wars, Real Reel Hero On Home Soil Again," the *Post-Gazette* announced: "It might be today and it might be tomorrow, but anyway it won't be long until Colonel Jimmy Stewart is back home in

Indiana. After talking long distance to the war and movie hero in New York City, his sister Virginia, concluded Jimmy would arrive with his parents. The important thing for his sisters (Mary's the other one) is 'Jimmy said they're coming home.' His leave began . . . after docking with his Second Bomb Wing. Mr. and Mrs. Alex M. Stewart wanted to greet their son in New York . . . so that they wouldn't have to wait any longer than necessary to see him. 'It's been two years now,' Mrs. Stewart said. In those two years, Jimmy, who had entered the army as a buck private, rose to the rank of full colonel."

The Pittsburgh newspaper had it right. Colonel Jimmy Stewart and his Second Combat Wing airmen arrived in New York on a fall weekend after a five-day voyage from England on the Queen Elizabeth. Bessie and Alex were waiting for their son at the St. Regis Hotel, just as they were at the terminal to say goodbye in Sioux City at Stewart's departure for the ETO—twenty-two months earlier.

Before leaving New York City by car with Bessie and Alex for his Indiana homecoming, Stewart held a press conference in the office of the commander of the New York Port of Embarkation. Here is the *New York Times* report of September 2, 1945:

STEWART FROWNS ON ANY WAR FILMS
Former Star Now Army Officer Says He'd Like to Make Comedy When He's Civilian

Problems of readjustment to civilian life are not troubling Col. James Stewart of the Army Air Forces, who arrived from Europe on Friday on the Queen Elizabeth.

"I haven't lost any sleep worrying," the former film star explained here yesterday. "On the contrary, I'm sort of looking forward to civilian life."

The 37-year-old officer, whose hair has become tinged with gray since he went overseas, said that he hoped to return to motion pictures as soon as possible. Before he goes back to Hollywood to face the cameras, he will spend a week with his parents, Mr. and Mrs. Alexander Stewart, at Indiana, Pa., leaving with them today by automobile.

Explaining that he was anxious to go back to his old work before the cameras, he said that he might need a little time to get over camera shyness.

"There's a lot of technique you forget—like any other skill—which I'll have to learn again. I would like to make anything except a war picture. Everybody's had enough of that stuff for a while. A good comedy would be better."

Asked whether he preferred American or British girls, Colonel Stewart replied, "I don't consider myself qualified to say." He is not married or engaged or planning to be either, he added hurriedly. As to the slight graying of his hair, he explained, "I don't care what color it gets as long as it stays in."

The former film star was overseas twenty-three months and flew twenty missions. He wears the Distinguished Flying Cross with cluster, the Air Medal with three clusters, six battle stars and a French medal.

Jimmy made it clear that he did not want any special attention at his homecoming. Alex passed along his request to a disappointed chamber of commerce. There was no parade. Yet, the town was glad to have him home if only for a few days. Jimmy was not only a popular son of the city but a movie star as well. Now he was a decorated war hero, and his presence in the town was not ignored. The center of attention and activity was the hardware store with a beaming Alex, who had decorated the store's window with some of his son's wartime memorabilia, over Jimmy's objections. Stewart spent most of his terminal leave in Indiana, just taking it easy, unwinding, enjoying his family, and trying to make a graceful transition to civilian life.

A crew from *LIFE* magazine came to town, headed by the renowned photographer Peter Stackpole. They planned a cover story with many pictures. The story ran in *LIFE* on September 24, 1945.

Toward the end of September, Colonel Jimmy Stewart went to Andrews Field in Washington. He was relieved from active duty and returned to civilian life. At that time, he accepted a commission as a full colonel in the Air Force Reserve.

In the first week of October, Stewart returned to Hollywood and began to make the professional moves toward resuming his movie career.

He had been gone—in uniform—for almost five years.

His first movie after returning was *It's A Wonderful Life*.

$$\varsigma V \varsigma$$

POSTSCRIPT A

GLORIA

*"Life means more than just a book of phone numbers.
. . . I need a family to come home to at night."*
—Jimmy Stewart

After a lifetime of bachelorhood and a not-so-subtle reputation as a womanizer and Hollywood man-about-town, Jimmy Stewart, at 41, was married on August 9, 1949, at the Brentwood Presbyterian Church. While he was working with Stewart at Old Buc during the war, Andy Low said that they often talked about marriage. Low, who was married and a recent father, has said that Stewart was more than mildly interested, and asked many questions about marriage and family life. Yet in spite of this wartime talk about love and marriage, back in Hollywood after the war, Colonel Jimmy Stewart, more glamorous and appealing to women than ever before, was extremely active on the social scene and in gossip columns.

Still, in those immediate post-war days and living "in a place that swarmed with beautiful girls," many of Stewart's friends had the impression that after courting the film capital's most glamorous and charming ladies, he was ready to retire his prodigious and well-used black book. Stewart himself was widely quoted on the subject of love and marriage, saying, "Life means more than just a book of phone

Jimmy Stewart and his wife Gloria.

numbers. I need to put down roots and have a permanent relationship and secure marriage with the woman I love. I need a family to come home to at night."

Many of the ladies in Stewart's black book bore names that dazzled on movie marquees at theaters all over the world and were no strangers to newspaper headlines—Ginger Rogers, Norma Shearer, Olivia de Havilland, Dinah Shore, Anita Colby, Eleanor Powell, Loretta Young, Shirley Ross, Marlene Dietrich, Virginia Bruce, Wendy Barrie, Rita Hayworth, and even more. Stewart's friend and former roommate Burgess Meredith has described these friendships as "light love affairs."

However, when Stewart decided to make the marriage move, he chose a tall, willowy 31-year-old divorcée and sometime model from the East Coast with two small sons. Gloria Hatrick McLean was a dark-haired, vivacious, witty, beautiful, and gracious woman who did not have to lower her green eyes in the presence of Hollywood's brightest and most compelling stars.

Stewart and Gloria met for the first time in the summer of 1948, shortly after her divorce from Ned McLean and her arrival in California with three-year-old Ronald and two-year-old Michael.

Gloria Hatrick was born in 1919 in Larchmont, an upscale community just outside New York City. Her father was Edgar Hatrick, a ranking executive in the William Randolph Hearst empire. Gloria attended Finch College for Women in New York City and, after part-time modeling and a career in fashion design, met socialite Ned McLean, the son of wealthy Evelyn Walsh McLean of Hope diamond fame. They were married in 1941. Gloria was somewhat to the manner born in show-business circles and, consequently, was neither awed, intimidated, or overly impressed with the Hollywood crowd. Moreover, she was extremely beautiful, elegant, friendly, appealing, and was seen at the right places on the arm of Hollywood's most popular and eligible bachelor, Jimmy Stewart.

Before that fateful 1948 summer night when he met Gloria for the first time, Stewart was hearing not-so-subtle views about finding the "right woman" from buddies Henry Fonda; Leland Hayward, then married to the dramatic actress Margaret Sullavan; and Burgess Meredith, who was later to marry Paulette Goddard, the glamorous actress and international star. Stewart was now frequently flying back to Indiana in his Piper Super Cub, where his father, in typical Alex style, had no shyness or hesitation about discussing with his only son a per-manent romantic life and, as time was slipping rapidly by, the lack of it. And there was another factor. Many of Stewart's friends were already married—Gary Cooper, Dinah Shore, Josh Logan, Fonda, Hayward, Dorothy McGuire, as well as his own two sisters, Mary and Virginia. To offset these suggestions and reminders from Indiana and Hollywood, which, fortunately, never reached the full-court-press stage, was the simple fact that Jimmy Stewart was a loner and, as Meredith once put it, "Jimmy is a self-contained man. He can live totally within himself." Obviously, he was not going to rush into anything.

Still, clearly, when the dinner invitation arrived from Gary and Rocky Cooper, he accepted forthwith. The dinner apparently was not planned as a matchmaking conspiracy but other than Stewart, Gloria McLean was the only single at the party, which included the Ronald Reagans and the Leland Haywards. Afterward, some of the guests went to Ciro's nightclub for dancing. The Nat King Cole Trio was playing. This was long before Cole became a world-famous romantic balladeer; that night he was leading his trio at the piano. The Coopers had put Gloria next to

Jimmy at dinner, and she noticed that he seemed quiet and reserved at the table. On the dance floor, there was a different Stewart. Ginger Rogers, when she was dating Jimmy, said he danced as well as Fred Astaire, and Gloria had been a dancing instructor. All went well, and Stewart had his own version of the events of that first night: "Gary and Rocky Cooper gave the dinner party where I met my wife, Gloria, and we have all remained very good friends, even after Gary's death. I was seated next to Gloria at that dinner, and then I asked him if I could take her home afterward, which I did. This started us off."

Their courting was marked by long days on the golf course, dinners at Chasen's, and Stewart's gradual departure from his routine life as a single loner. Almost immediately, since that night at the Coopers, there was a glowing and embracing *simpático* between them. Now Stewart was faced with another unknown factor—establishing a relationship with Gloria's sons, Ronald and Michael, which, as it turned out, never became a problem in all the years of their lives together. Gloria and Jimmy became engaged in May of 1949, Stewart's forty-first birthday, after little less than a year of courtship. The wedding three months later, was, by Hollywood standards, small and exclusive. The fifty guests included both sets of parents, David Niven, the Coopers, Spencer Tracy, George Murphy (later to become a U.S. senator), and a few other close friends.

Hawaii was to be the ultimate honeymoon destination. But there was a detour to the Bendix Air Races at Columbus, Ohio. Always the airplane-lover and airman, Stewart had acquired a surplus-property World War II fighter plane—a P-51 Mustang. He knew the Mustang well. On his deep-penetration bombing missions to Germany and especially to Berlin, the P-51s had provided escort cover and vital protection from oncoming German fighters, the blazing M-109s and FW-190s. Stewart's Mustang was entered in the Bendix Air Races. The race began in California's Mojave Desert and ended in Columbus. His Mustang won the race, setting a new record of four hours, sixteen minutes. The pilot, Joe DeBona, presented the Bendix trophy to the cheering Gloria and Jimmy as a wedding gift.

At first, the newlyweds, with Ronald and Michael, lived in Gloria's house in Coldwater Canyon. Now, in a manner of speaking, Stewart had to master three missions, or, to put it another way, he had to keep three balls in the air—first and foremost, his new role as husband and father. Then there was his day job making movies.

Also, Stewart still had his Air Force Reserve assignment as a colonel, which meant training sessions several times a year and two weeks of active duty. This was serious business with Stewart, who, for the most part, did not discuss military matters and especially his wartime service with reporters, but he did tell an interviewer: "I want to get as much training as I can. If I'm called to active duty, I want to be ready." He kept his hand in as a pilot and was flying regularly. After the Bendix victory, he sold the Mustang and bought a Beechcraft Bonanza and flew occasionally to Indiana. And the happy pilot lost little time in flying his beautiful new wife to visit his family and friends at home. Gloria made the first of many visits to Indiana in September after the August 9, 1949, wedding.

Jimmy was so respected and loved by his hometown that, upon arrival, Gloria had an instant reception of approval. Linda Moore Mack, Jimmy's longtime friend who later became a founding member of the Stewart Museum in Indiana and a member of the 1983 seventy-fifth birthday celebration said, "Gloria is a gracious, down-to-earth, and charming lady with a wonderful sense of humor. Her love and support of Jimmy is very evident." Elinor Blair, wife of Jimmy's great boyhood friend, Hall Blair, described Gloria as being, "absolutely perfect for Jim. He always said how gorgeous she looked. She was very elegant, had a wonderful sense of humor, a very fancy girl. She never pushed herself forward to be with Jim unless she was invited. She had a good sense of that."

Back in Hollywood, in due course, the little Stewart family moved from Coldwater Canyon to a Beverly Hills house where the famous director King Vidor had once lived. It was a Tudor-style house with five bedrooms and an impressive address at 918 North Roxbury Drive. They all set about making their new home livable, likable,

homelike—a grand piano, a modest art grouping, a large book collection, a backyard garden, and, later, a sensitive and convincing portrait
of Gloria painted by family friend Claudette Colbert. Importantly,
there was a wing for the boys. As the years passed, the house on
Roxbury became, like many longtime family homes, a sheltering and
secure sanctuary. It was to be Gloria and Jimmy's home for the rest of
their lives, in gladness and grief. Perhaps it was in this house that
Gloria and Jimmy came to the full realization of the wisdom of
Thomas Wolfe's words, "the countless measure of . . . loss—the
countless measure of . . . gain."

The twins Kelly and Judy were born on May 7, 1951. The girls had
a French governess, attended Westlake Academy, and later went to
school in Switzerland. Summers were spent *en famille* on family
ranches in Nevada and California.

Even with Jimmy's increasingly successful movie career and growing
bank account, the Stewarts did not live lavishly. Their lifestyle could
perhaps be best described as American upper-class, quietly affluent.
There were no Mercedeses, Cadillacs, or Jaguars at 918 North Roxbury.
Jimmy drove a Volvo for years, which allowed enough head room for
his lanky frame. In the early 1950s, the Stewarts bought the house next
door, tore it down, and put in a garden that remained Gloria's delight,
a meditative retreat for the rest of her life.

As the kids grew older, went off to college, and began to form lives
of their own in several different locations, Gloria and Jimmy began
their never-ending worldwide travel. About this time, they made the
fortunate friendship of Kirk and Bess Johnson of Fort Worth, Texas.
Kirk and Jimmy were business partners, and the two couples soon
became lifelong traveling companions. The Johnsons were veteran
travelers, knew the ropes, and introduced Gloria and Jimmy to exotic
Africa, which became their favorite and most enticing destination.

In the late 1950s, Andy Low was commander of the Fortieth Bomb
Wing at Schilling Air Force Base in Kansas, a B-47 outfit. He had orders
to fly some of his planes to England for temporary deployment and
knew that Stewart was about ready for his active-duty reserve tour that

year. Andy told me he called Jimmy in Hollywood and proposed that he do the active duty stint in England with the Fortieth Wing. He said that Jimmy was all excited and promised to work out the details. Andy said he called back a few days later and said, "Sorry, Andy. Got to pass. I promised Gloria I'd take her to India. And I've got to do it."

With her winsome wit and engaging personality, daughter Kelly went on to a remarkable career. After Stanford and a PhD from Cambridge University in England, she became associated with gorilla expert Dian Fossey in Africa. In 1977, Kelly was married to a Cambridge professor, Alexander "Sandy" Harcourt, in London, with the reception at the Savoy, one of her father's favorite hotels. Both Kelly and her husband now teach at the University of California, Davis.

After college, Judy also spent time in Africa, where the twins had gone for the first time when they were fourteen. She graduated from Lewis and Clark, a small liberal-arts college in Portland, Oregon. In 1979, Judy married a San Francisco banker, Steven Merritt. They are now divorced. Their sons, John and David, are college students.

Both Ron and Michael attended Black Fox Military Academy in Los Angeles in their early years. For prep school, Michael went to Mercersburg, Jimmy's old school back in Pennsylvania. Michael then went on to Claremont in California, where he studied political science, and later enrolled at Oxford University in England.

Ron indicated no interest in either Mercersburg or Princeton, and for prep school went to Orme in Arizona. He later majored in business at Colorado State.

It is perhaps noteworthy that Jimmy was a Princeton trustee from 1958 to 1962 and spoke out against admitting women. In 1969, Princeton changed the rules, and women were accepted as students. It has been said that by that time Jimmy had changed his views. In any case, neither Kelly nor Judy went to Princeton.

After Colorado State, Ron went into the marines, received a commission, and within months was fighting in Vietnam, where he was killed in action while leading a patrol. The date was June 11, 1969. Ron was 24.

THE GENERAL

"I personally like Jimmy Stewart . . . but popularity should not be the yardstick by which we promote officers."
—Senator Margaret Chase Smith in her objections to Stewart's promotion to general

Charlton Heston, the Hollywood actor best known for his roles in *Ben Hur* and *The Ten Commandments*, was a longtime friend of Jimmy Stewart. In his book *In the Arena—An Autobiography*, Heston wrote:

> The Ritz is one of the great hotels in the world. . . . One of several where actors, if identified, were denied lodging. . . . Jimmy Stewart, who'd remained in the Air Force Reserve after his sterling service in World War II, came to Madrid to do his annual month of active duty at Torrejon Air Base. He'd reserved a suite at the Ritz, where they had no idea this J. Stewart was *the* J. Stewart. As he signed the register, the manager sidled over, discombobulated. "Ahh, Señor Stewart . . . I am honored to meet you, but . . . ah, you are an actor, of course. We, ah, do not, ah, cater to actors, you see."

> Jimmy looked at him coolly. "'Zat so? Waal,
> lemme tell ya. For the next four weeks, I'm Brigadier
> General James Stewart, United States Air Force." He
> picked up the keys and turned to the elevator.

The Madrid incident passed with no press attention. Stewart was completely correct in dealing with the hotel manager but somewhat out of character. In his slightly less than ten years as an Air Force Reserve general officer, doing his active duty stints, Stewart was never one to throw his weight around or pull rank. As a celebrated Hollywood star who, over the years, had carefully nurtured and astutely developed his career, Stewart knew well the responsibility he had to his fans and the publicity value that drove his career. While he was always cooperative with his studio's public relations people, granting interviews to movie reporters and making promotional tours, he was always essentially a private man, never flaunting his celebrity, saying little. In Madrid, the hotel manager touched a nerve. Stewart was in Spain, not as an actor, but as a ranking American military officer in the service of his country. He expected to be treated with respect and dignity, and he quietly demanded it.

On active duty in the air force, wearing his general's uniform, Stewart mostly remained in the background. But, he wasn't exactly a face in the crowd. After all, he was over six-feet tall, slim, and wore his general's uniform, not with a flair, but with well-dressed distinction. Then there was the face, perhaps one of the most recognizable in the world, made famous by dozens of movie roles, some of them memorable. Retired Colonel Capers Holmes, an Eighth Air Force and B-24 veteran of World War II, knew Stewart from the Pentagon days when the general did his active duty. Holmes told me, "You couldn't help but notice him. The secretaries were thrilled to see him and the men would glance his way. He was very businesslike but friendly. In uniform or out, people recognized him."

Colonel Ned Sparks, a retired fighter pilot, knew General Stewart on his active-duty tours at the Pentagon. He remembers: "A gentleman.

Soft spoken. At meetings he was well briefed, always prepared. Very courteous. I did see him raise his voice once or twice. He was a pleasure to work with. I liked him."

In truth, Stewart loved being an air force general. He liked to be called General Stewart. He liked the trappings of flag rank, but did not revel in it. Stewart was a man of immense pride who asked no favors. Remember that at a crucial time in his military life, early in the war, after intense training and grinding work as an instructor pilot, and fearful that he would not see overseas duty, Stewart pleaded with his commanding officer for help in getting a combat assignment. He wasn't requesting a favor, but, based on training and experience, he was asking for a chance to fight.

In forging a notable career as an actor, Stewart learned his craft by hard work, paid his dues, and won an Academy Award, the highest honor in his field. After wartime duty, Stewart entered the Air Force Reserve as a full colonel in 1945, doing his reserve duty in various capacities for more than a decade. In 1957, he was nominated for the rank of brigadier general in the Air Force Reserve by President Eisenhower. Colonel Stewart saw this nomination to flag rank as a great honor, and it was especially poignant when viewed against the background of his early military days as a private soldier on KP duty, his promotion to corporal, the war years in England, and his twenty combat missions against Nazi Germany. Truly, it would crown his military career. Only a few months earlier, President Eisenhower had invited Stewart to deliver the Veteran's Day speech at Arlington National Cemetery. But soon the celebrated Hollywood movie star, combat bomber pilot, war hero, and dedicated American patriot would be introduced to the political ways of Washington.

Stewart's nomination to the rank of general touched off a media-driven controversy in Washington that soon made headlines throughout the country, and gave him unwanted, awkward, embarrassing, and, worst of all, unfavorable publicity. And most of it was unwarranted.

Question: Was Air Force Reserve Colonel James Maitland Stewart qualified for promotion to brigadier general in the Air Force Reserve?

One member of the Senate Armed Services Committee did not think so. This was Senator Margaret Chase Smith, a highly respected Republican from the state of Maine, and herself an Air Force Reserve officer. Senator Smith objected strongly to the Stewart nomination. In simple terms, her objection seemed to center around a shortage of participation in active-duty training, which a reserve officer is obligated to undertake. In short, Stewart had not pulled enough fifteen-day active-duty tours and lacked proper training for his reserve assignment. Moreover, a few months earlier, Stewart had a starring role in the popular movie *Strategic Air Command*.

To further complicate the somewhat complex issue, Stewart's reserve, or M-Day, assignment was deputy director of operations for Strategic Air Command, a vital defense position. While this important post gave knowledge, authenticity, and creditability to Stewart's role in the movie, it did not, in the senator's view, add a solid foundation to his one-star nomination. She said, "I personally like Jimmy Stewart, the actor, as do thousands of his loyal admirers. . . . but popularity should not be the yardstick by which we promote officers."

The battle raged on, much of it in the press. It was a Washington and Hollywood firestorm that created coast-to-coast media coverage, from the *New York Times* to gossip and political columns. For his part, Stewart refused to engage the senator, staying above the fray. At one point, he did say, "I was honored to receive the nomination from President Eisenhower and the air force. Whatever the outcome, I intend to do my best and fulfill my duty." The air force stood solidly behind Stewart and the nomination. It seemed to be a losing battle. Under the headline "No Star for Jimmy," *Newsweek* magazine reported on September 2, 1957:

> Lt. Gen. Emmett "Rosy" O'Donnell Jr. is a rough and ruddy fighting man who led the first Superfortress raid on Tokyo during the war. But this hard-bitten soldier is also the devoted fan of a movie actor—James Stewart. For lanky Stewart is a

flier of note, too, and has long been a reserve colonel in the Strategic Air Command. (He starred in the 1955 film of that name.) O'Donnell was determined that this year Colonel Stewart should get the star of a brigadier general. The actor's name was on the list of eleven scheduled promotions that has been hanging fire for weeks in the Senate Armed Services Committee, which must approve them.

Last week, before the committee, Rosy O'Donnell went to bat for Stewart. But he ran up against a tough adversary in the person of the Senate's only woman, Republican Margaret Chase Smith of Maine. She likes and admires Stewart personally, she said, but he just hadn't put in enough training time—nine days in the past eleven years—to justify this promotion. O'Donnell's spirited defense of Stewart was in vain. By a vote of 11 to 2, the committee rejected Stewart's promotion.

There were those who suggested that Mrs. Smith's bitter-end opposition stemmed from the fact that her administrative assistant, William C. Lewis Jr., who is also a colonel in the Air Force reserve, had been omitted from the list of promotions. Nonsense, said Mrs. Smith. Her only interest, she insisted, was in the morale of the Air Force.

In any case, the matter moved along, unresolved, for almost two years. Finally, perhaps in a compromise with Senator Smith, the air force reassigned Stewart from his SAC post. In his new assignment, he became deputy director of the Secretary of the Air Force Office of Information. In July of 1959, Stewart's promotion to brigadier general was confirmed by the entire United States Senate, with Senator Smith's support.

Throughout the whole affair, Stewart had maintained his usual composure, saying little, but watching the events unfold in

Washington with more than casual interest while making movies in Hollywood. In a 1961 interview, he said:

> The promotion was approved, leaving me to wonder whether Senator Smith was mad at me personally. I didn't think she was. She was protesting against giving a movie actor an important rank because she didn't think I had done enough recent flying to qualify for a star. I'm not sure that the senator fully understood that nobody was expecting me to climb into a modern jet bomber and fly it. Anyone who knows that my next birthday will be my 53rd will agree that jets have made the pace too hot for my slowing reflexes. . . . Even before Senator Smith squared the jaw at me, I was in line for a more suitable assignment—deputy director of the Office of Information.

An amusing footnote in the promotion story came from Ramsay Potts, Stewart's wartime commander and personal friend. The Washington lawyer, already a brigadier general in the Air Force Reserve, was up for promotion to major general on the same nomination list as Stewart. He told me, "After it was all over and we were both promoted, I kidded Jimmy about holding up my promotion."

After Stewart's promotion was confirmed by the entire Senate, he served for almost ten years, from 1959 to 1968, as a reserve brigadier general. As deputy director, holding an M-Day assignment, in the Office of Information (now Public Affairs), Stewart worked to foster better understanding between the military and civilian communities. He was, in many ways, an ambassador-at-large, articulating the military position in speeches and interviews.

He was an extremely popular speaker for civilian audiences and air force dining-in celebrations and attended a number of reunions in this country of his old wartime outfit, the 453rd Bomb Group. In 1983,

Stewart and Gloria traveled to Norwich, England, for a Second Bomb Division reunion, and went with Helen and Andy Low down to Old Buc where they planted a tree in memory of their fallen 453rd comrades.

Stewart served in Vietnam during active-duty tour as a general. He flew a bombing mission and said later, "I piloted the aircraft but didn't take part in the actual bombing."

In the spring of 1960, only a few months after his promotion, General Stewart put on his uniform for two weeks of active duty. He spent a few days of the tour at Thule Air Force Base in Greenland, which had only recently been taken over by the Air Defense Command. While at Thule, General Stewart went out for the day to the 931st Aircraft Control and Warning Squadron, located on Panlarsut Mountain about twenty miles from Thule. After being driven by truck out to the squadron atop the mountain, General Stewart spent the day with Technical Sergeant Glenn Hood. Sergeant Hood, who retired from the air force as a master sergeant and now lives in Chipley, Florida, told me about General Stewart's visit to the mountain:

"After a short briefing by our C.O., Captain Hilderbrandt, General Stewart told the captain that he wanted to see the nuts and bolts of the operation. Because I was in charge of supply and support of ground-to-air missiles, the captain turned the general over to me. At the site, we had a little chit-chat, then General Stewart had a lot of questions—stocking the spare parts for the radar systems, the microwave tower, special-purpose vehicles and the pipeline time to get critical parts. He wanted to know about the generators and if they generated enough power to run the site, and what about emergency plans? Things like that."

Hood said the general had asked earlier about how well the troops were fed. Then at lunchtime, he said, "There is one way to find out, let's go to lunch. So, with my assistant, Sergeant Brown, we went over to the mess hall and had lunch with the men."

Over lunch, Sergeant Hood said that General Stewart wanted to know about recreation facilities, church services, how often the men could go into Thule, and if they had access to radio and movies.

Sergeant Hood told me he had the feeling that General Stewart was as concerned about the treatment of the enlisted people as he was about the operation of the site, and said, "He left me with the sense that his view was that if the troops were maintained, that the mission would be met with full force and be accomplished." This is Sergeant Hood's summary of the day on the mountain with General Stewart: "Sharp, sharp. Really down to earth. General Stewart presented himself as well dressed as a recruiting poster and as relaxed as could be. He sat down, propped his feet up, and engaged myself and Sergeant Brown in a relaxed and informal discussion. A right guy."

Neither Hood nor Baker had served in World War II. They had no way of knowing that they were seeing, at close range, the Stewart manner with both officers and other ranks that had become almost legendary during the war years. I remember when the word was out that he was coming to Old Buc as the new ops officer, we had already heard from Tibenham about his easy style and popular reputation with combat crews and coworkers. I noticed it firsthand and early on. At group headquarters were a number of corporals and sergeants. They liked to work with Stewart, handling the details of the mission briefing preparation, and, later, at the briefing room on the flight line as we briefed the combat crews at dawn.

One element of Stewart's manner was his almost imperceptible, muted, sense of command—his assiduous preparation, knowledge of the subject, and the feeling that he was able to impart the importance of the task to others. This was especially true in his attitude, relationship, and rapport with the combat crews. It was as if he had adopted as his own credo, the modus operandi of the Roman general Marius, as described by the historian Plutarch: "What they admire in a leader is the willingness to share their danger and hardship, rather than the ability to win them honor and wealth, and they are more fond of officers who are prepared to make efforts alongside them than they are of those who let them take things easy."

Stewart pulled his two weeks of active duty time at various air force bases around the country and overseas. Perhaps his most memorable reserve tour, other than the Vietnam mission, took place at Carswell Air Force Base, at Fort Worth, Texas. At Carswell, he had a flight in the supersonic B-58 Hustler with instructor pilot Major John Irving. The flight caused quite a stir in aviation circles around the country. Major Irving had given a first-person account to *Flight Journal* magazine. Andy Low had called and told me about the flight, and Sam Schloss, a veteran Southern civilian pilot, had sent a copy of the magazine. Here is Major Irving's story:

> One of the highlights of my career was meeting and flying with Jimmy Stewart. He came down to Carswell for his two weeks of active duty [Stewart, a former B-24 pilot during WW II, stayed in the Air Force Reserve into the 1970s, eventually rising to the rank of Brigadier General]. He was making a movie in Dallas on the record-setting flights of the B-58 called "Champion of Champions." Brick Holstrum, my wing commander, said, "John, you're going to be his aide for two weeks." I said, "Great! I'd love to!" It was my job to familiarize him with the aircraft and take him over to Dallas every morning.
>
> At the end of his two weeks, I was to give him a ride in a Hustler. We had a procedure in the manuals that I don't think anyone up to that point had ever executed. It was a maximum-performance takeoff. The standard takeoff was attention-getting all by itself. Normally, you'd take off with all four burners lit, and when you reached 425 knots indicated, you'd pull back to military power and climb at 425 until you got to cruise altitude, when you'd transition to .91 Mach. The max-performance takeoff called for you to leave the engines in burner till you got to the top of the hill [35,000 feet]. I said to Brick, "Boss, do you mind if I show him a max-performance takeoff?"

He said, "I don't give a damn what you do with him." I said, "OK!"

That was the wildest ride I ever took! Jimmy and I strapped on a TB-58 [the training version of the Hustler] and taxied out to the runway. "Ready?" I asked. He said, "Yup." I lit those burners, and before you know it, we lifted off. Just like that! Up came 425 knots, our normal climb rate. Well, I kept pulling the nose up to stay at 425 or below. I had the stick pretty far back and I just kept pulling and pulling and pulling, and pretty soon, we were going straight up! The gyro spilled, and the whole panel was going nuts. It took just three minutes from the time I released the brakes to the time I pushed the nose over at 35,000! Right then, I heard this sigh of relief from the front seat. Stewart said, "This ain't no airplane, it's a goddamned missile!"

One of the requirements of the flight was that I get Jimmy his Mach 2 pin. But when I got up there and pushed the throttles into burner again to go supersonic, one of the damn engines wouldn't light. I thought, "Oh, hell! He's gonna get to Mach 2 one way or another!" So, I pushed the nose over with the three burners lit and went almost straight down. We zoomed through Mach 2 and I pulled everything back and leveled out and said, "OK, you've been there!"

John Irving is now retired from the air force and lives in the Washington area, where he's a travel guide and popular storyteller. I had dinner with him last year at the National Press Club, where I insisted that he retell the Stewart flight story. At the end, he said, "We had a big party that night at the Carswell Officers Club, and everybody was toasting Jimmy and admiring his Mach 2 pin. After a while, his wife, Gloria, called me over to one side and said, 'John, I want you to know you made Jimmy really happy today.' Then she said, 'I thank you'" Later that night at the Press Club Bar, John told me, "You know, I'll never forget that meeting with Jimmy, and I like to tell this story. I'll tell you, that guy's not even acting when he's in a movie. That's just the way he is all the time. He's a great fellow, the nicest, slowest talking guy I've ever met. I just ate that assignment up, enjoyed the hell out of it."

Brigadier General James Maitland Stewart's military career ended at his retirement in 1968, after 27 years of active and reserve service, in war and peace. He was 60. At retirement, General Stewart was decorated with the Distinguished Service Medal—only the second time in American military history that the award had been presented to an air force reserve officer. The citation states:

> The singularly distinctive accomplishments of General Stewart culminate a long and distinguished career in the service of his country and reflect the highest credit upon himself and the U.S. Air Force.

THE JIMMY STEWART
MUSEUM IN INDIANA

"I'm grateful I had the chance to honor the man who has brought me a lot of joy and provided me an example of a true hero."

—Entry in visitor's book at the
Jimmy Stewart Museum

W hen the Jimmy Stewart Museum opened on May 20, 1995, in Indiana, Pennsylvania, the program stated: "This is the loving result of the inspiration and vision of many individuals who saw in James Maitland Stewart, a man among men, whose character, values, and achievement deserved preservation and study, so that future generations may embrace the very best that America, and, indeed, the world has to offer."

It is highly doubtful that the city of Indiana will ever see another weekend like the one that marked the opening of the Jimmy Stewart Museum. Due to failing health, Stewart was not there, but he was represented by his twin daughters, Kelly Stewart Harcourt and Judy Stewart, who had come from California for the event. Stewart's natural modesty and aversion to self-acclaim did nothing to encourage the establishment of a hometown museum to bear his name. On the contrary, he was dead-set against the idea. But his reluctance waned, and an agreement was reached when Stewart was convinced that the museum would draw tourists who, in turn, would financially benefit

A plaque in his hometown of Indiana, Pennsylvania, outside the Jimmy Stewart Museum.

the community and surrounding area. He asked for only two stipulations—that the museum be modest in approach and presentation, and that it be located in downtown Indiana. In the matter of tourist attraction and financial gain, Stewart was acting in the civic spirit of George Bailey of *It's a Wonderful Life* by helping to boost the economic life of his hometown.

The museum is on the third floor of the Free Library Building in downtown Indiana, just as Stewart wished. Within walking distance are the Stewart historic landmarks, tactile footnotes of his early life—his birthplace at 965 Philadelphia Street, with its marker; the site of the Stewart family hardware store, now a bank; and up Vinegar Hill, at 104 North Seventh Street, Stewart's boyhood home. On the lawn of the new courthouse, only a block from the museum, is the remarkable larger-than-life statue of Stewart, dedicated on his seventy-fifth birthday. A short distance away, at the old courthouse, is the clock that served as the backdrop for Stewart's famous *LIFE* magazine cover picture by Peter Stackpole.

A glowing proclamation on Stewart and the museum had earlier been issued by then-Governor Tom Ridge of Pennsylvania. With the Stewart children as honored guests and the focal point, the weekend, built around Stewart's May 20th birthday, moved along in glamorous fashion—a parade with bands along Philadelphia Street, a gala dinner, a ribbon-cutting and champagne brunch at the museum, and a ceremony on the steps of the new courthouse near Jimmy Stewart's statue.

Heading into its tenth year in 2005, the museum, even with the sadness of Stewart's death in 1997, has moved forward with vision to enhance the community. The compact, well-organized, colorful, and varied collection includes movie props; posters; many pictures; a statue of Stewart; awards, including his Academy Award nominations; mementos of Hollywood times and friends; air force uniforms and flying suits; wartime medals; General Stewart's one-star flag; his personal American flag; framed photographs; and a retrospective of Stewart's World War II combat bomber pilot service. The collection is truly a visible, distinct memoir of a life well lived. I must say that on my visit to the museum in the fall of 1998, I was most impressed. Fortunately, as Stewart envisioned, and with George Bailey's paradigm, the economic impact to the Indiana area has been substantial and is consistently increasing.

American icons Charles Lindbergh and Glenn Miller, portrayed on the screen by Stewart, perhaps because he was both a flyer and a musician, and their momentous lives and times, have an honored place in the museum. Starkly visible from Stewart's action movies are the rifle from *Winchester '73* and a propeller from the cast and crew of *The Flight of the Phoenix*. It has been reported that Gloria came up with the idea of Jimmy doing the film, a strange story of a small transport plane crash in the desert. The adventurous, eclectic crew and passengers decided to piece together and rebuild the crashed plane into flying condition and fly it back to civilization. Stewart played the pilot and was later cited in the press for his stellar work. This was yet another role with Stewart as an airplane pilot, along with *Strategic Air Command* and *The Spirit of St. Louis*.

Last year, the museum received a glamorous addition direct from Hollywood, which was a clear-cut memento of Jimmy's times in California. For years, with Gloria, he was a frequent guest at Chasen's—the illustrious Beverly Hills restaurant owned by his close friend Dave Chasen. When he saw Clark Gable early in the war while both were home on leave, they had lunch at Chasen's. And, Jimmy and Gloria frequently had Thursday night dinner at the restaurant. After Chasen's closed, the directors of the museum procured the personal Gloria-and-Jimmy leather booth and installed it in a place of honor.

After Stewart finally agreed to the museum, he took a personal interest in the items to be displayed. Jay Rubin, the Indiana lawyer who headed the museum foundation's board of directors, said, "Talking with Mr. Stewart about plans for the museum, and viewing many of the items that he wished the museum to have, was probably the greatest highlight of this endeavor."

In 1998, director-curator Elizabeth Salome asked me to do a retrospective of Stewart's military career for the museum. In the fall of that year, when the task was finished, she arranged a weekend in Indiana for the presentation. Ramsay Potts and Andy Low, Stewart's best friends from the war years, came to Indiana for the occasion—Potts from Washington and Andy from his home in Rhode Island. It was a time of stirring memories and sensitive nostalgia for three of Stewart's wartime comrades— coming to his town, seeing his sights, meeting his friends, walking his streets, and visiting his museum.

Ramsay Potts, left, and Andy Low in front of the Jimmy Stewart statue at the Stewart Museum in Indiana, Pennsylvania after his death.

In addition, as a journalist, I was interested in the comments in the visitors' book:

> —"Such a thrill to see Jimmy Stewart's life unfold before our eyes. We'll never forget this great man."
>
> —"Jimmy, keep wing tips up and nose pointed to the sky."
>
> —"Jimmy, your goodness will never be forgotten. Thanks for the memory."
>
> —"Jimmy Stewart brought much happiness into this world. God bless him."
>
> —"I'm grateful I had the chance to honor the man who has brought me a lot of joy and has provided me an example of a true hero."
>
> —"This is a great tribute to Jimmy Stewart, a great human being."
>
> —"I was always impressed at what a great American and genuine person he was."

It is provocative that in a setting filled with colorful reminders of Hollywood glamour, including the booth from Chasen's, that the centerpiece and signature attraction at the museum is a large photograph of Colonel Jimmy Stewart in his Eighth Air Force uniform. It is an informal picture of Colonel Stewart made in his father's hardware store immediately after returning to Indiana from combat duty in Europe at the end of World War II. The picture was made by Peter Stackpole. It is perhaps the best-known of all photographs ever made of Jimmy Stewart in air force uniform.

In the museum is a picture of Stewart's twin daughters, Judy and Kelly, probably made when they were in Indiana for the museum's opening. While there, they told a charming story of their father calling them into his study for a "talk" before they left for college. Not knowing what to expect and hoping it would not be a birds-and-bees talk, they apprehensively sat across from their father waiting for him to begin to speak. When he did, it was typical Jimmy Stewart, short and to the point. He merely said, "Be nice to people and they will be nice to you."

THE MIGHTY EIGHTH AIR FORCE HERITAGE MUSEUM

If it can be said that Jimmy Stewart had a spiritual home, other than his beloved Indiana, it was, perhaps, the Eighth Air Force.

In south Georgia, about twelve miles west of Savannah, just north of the intersection of interstate highways 95 and 16 and near the little town of Pooler, is the Mighty Eighth Air Force Heritage Museum, which opened in 1996. Although the handsome white building, with a lake, reflecting pool, and flying flags in the foreground, blends gracefully with the low, rolling countryside of Chatham County, the museum's presence at this place was not mere happenstance. In uncertain times—slightly more than one month after Pearl Harbor, on January 28, 1942, in an armory on Bull Street in Savannah—the Eighth Air Force was born. Soon afterward, in those dark days of a new year and a new war, the fledgling organization, flying on the wings of destiny, arrived in beleaguered England. Using airplanes borrowed from the RAF, the Eighth was soon airborne and flying missions against Nazi Germany. It was in this early commitment to combat that the new organization began its seminal role in World War II. When victory came three years later, the Eighth had become

LEFT: The Mighty Eighth Air Force Heritage Museum, Savannah, Georgia

RIGHT: Eighth Air Force birthplace plaque in Savannah, Georgia.

the largest and most formidable air armada in the annals of warfare, and in the course of those momentous events, its combat bomber crews and fighter pilots were engaged in the most deadly air battles in aviation history.

The Eighth Air Force did not fold its wings after the great victory over Germany in the spring of 1945. In 1946, the Eighth joined the Strategic Air Command (SAC), and its magnificent record continued to be enhanced through the Korean Conflict, the Cold War, Vietnam, and Desert Storm. But its memories and the deeds of Eighth Air Force warriors in World War II are forever enshrined in the museum that bears its name—only a few miles from downtown Savannah, where it all started.

If it can be said that if Jimmy Stewart had a spiritual home, other than his beloved Indiana, it was perhaps the Eighth Air Force. He often said that the war was the most portentous and meaningful time of his life, even more than his Hollywood days. And he spent the most essential part of his war years in England flying combat missions in B-24 Liberators of the Eighth Air Force. To mark these times and to commemorate his deeds, a bronze bust of Stewart was unveiled in the rotunda of the museum on October 1, 1999, alongside those of the great wartime generals of the Eighth Air Force—Spaatz, Eaker, and Doolittle. Ramsay Potts, Andy Low, and Lloyd Prang, 453rd veteran and custodian, came up with the idea for the bronze bust and ramrodded the deal, which was underwritten by Stewart's 453rd compatriots and other admirers. A tribute at the base of the bust states:

> JAMES MAITLAND STEWART
> Brigadier General, Air Force Reserve—Retired
> 1908–1997
>
> The Comrades-in-Arms of General Stewart of the 445th, 453rd, and 389th Bombardment Groups (Heavy), and the Second Combat Wing, are proud to recognize his outstanding record of exemplary achievement while serving with these combat units during World War II.
>
> PRESENTED TO THE
> EIGHTH AIR FORCE HERITAGE MUSEUM
> AS A LABOR OF LOVE
>
> BY THE MEMBERSHIP OF THE
> 453RD BOMB GROUP MEMORIAL PROJECT

Stewart was never actually assigned to the 389th Group at Hethel. As Andy Low wrote in a note: "I included the 389th, as both Jim and I flew many combat leads in the PFF squadron of that Group." The 389th was assigned the responsibility of providing radar bombing "pathfinder" crews and aircraft for the Second Air Division. These crews and airplanes led all Second Division radar bombing operations, utilizing special equipment, beginning in early 1944. Hence, the PFF (pathfinder) designation. As Low mentioned, Stewart flew a number of missions

Lieutenant General E. G. "Buck" Shuler and Colonel Starr Smith at the dedication of the Jimmy Stewart bust at the Eighth Air Force Museum in Savannah, Georgia, October 1, 1999.

with pathfinder crews, and when Low was shot down, he was flying with the pathfinders of the 389th. After Ramsay Potts left the 453rd, he commanded the 389th for several months, before moving on to Eighth Air Force headquarters.

The unveiling of Stewart's bust in the rotunda of the museum in the fall of 1999 was not the first time he had been honored by his Eighth Air Force comrades and colleagues. In 1997, the Brigadier General James M. Stewart Award was established. The award is given for outstanding airmanship. Criteria for the award state:

> The Eighth Air Force Heritage B/G James M. Stewart Award is given on an annual basis in honor of General Stewart and to an individual or group of individuals in recognition of distinguished contributions to United States civilian or military aviation for exceptional airmanship and leadership involving aerial flight. This award recognizes uncommon aviation skills, dedicated leadership and high competence of aviation minded men and women whose actions are distinctively noteworthy. The recipients of this distinguished award represent the finest aviators in the world. Selections for this prestigious

award are made by the Board of Trustees of The Eighth Air Force Heritage Museum.

The award includes a trophy, life membership in the Eighth Air Force Heritage Museum, and placement of the recipient's name on the Wall of Honor in the museum. The first three Stewart Awards were presented to: a veteran present-day Eighth Air Force pilot, the Chief of Staff of the U.S. Air Force, and an air force colonel who was the first woman to pilot a space shuttle on a mission.

The first B/G James M. Stewart Award was made to Colonel John H. Beard, USAF, at the Eighth Air Force Heritage Museum on September 12, 1997, for leading the longest combat mission in history. As mission commander, Colonel Beard led a flight of seven B-52Gs that flew from Barksdale Air Force Base, Louisiana, to the Persian Gulf on January 16–17, 1991 to launch conventional cruise missiles against command control and air defense targets in Baghdad, Iraq. With five air refuelings, the flight of B-52s was able to return to Barksdale AFB on the non-stop mission of 35 hours duration.

Colonel Beard is a native of Kansas City, Missouri, and a 1973 graduate of the Air Force Academy, the Air War College, and the Naval War College. At the time of his historic flight, Colonel Beard, a command pilot, had logged more than 4,600 hours. He is now retired.

General Michael Ryan, chief of staff of the air force, was the honoree of the second Stewart Award. He is the second member of his family to serve as chief of staff. His father, General John D. Ryan, a legendary World War II veteran, bomber pilot,

Colonel John H. Beard, awarded the first Jimmy Stewart Award in 1997.

LEFT: The second Jimmy Stewart Award is presented to General Michael Ryan, chief of staff, United States Air Force in 1999, by Lieutenant General E. L. "Buck" Shuler, chairman of the Eighth Air Force Museum, and former commander of the Eighth Air Force, Barksdale Air Force Base, Louisiana.

RIGHT: Colonel Eileen Collins, awarded the Jimmy Stewart Award in 2000.

and commander of the Strategic Air Command, was chief of the air force in the mid-1970s. General Ryan's distinguished military career of almost forty years was cited by the museum's board of trustees as the reason for honoring him with the Stewart Award.

General Ryan entered the air force after graduating from the U.S. Air Force Academy in 1965. He has commanded at the squadron, wing, numbered air force, and major command levels. He flew combat in Southeast Asia, including 100 missions over North Vietnam. He also served in staff assignments at the major command level, Headquarters U.S. Air Force and the Joint Staff. As Commander,

Sixteenth Air Force and Allied Air Forces Southern Europe in Italy, he directed the NATO air combat operations in Bosnia Herzegovina, which directly contributed to the Dayton Peace accords. Before assuming his current position, the general was Commander of U.S. Air Forces in Europe and Commander, Allied Air Forces Central Europe, with headquarters at Ramstein Air Base, Germany.

The third recipient of the Jimmy Stewart Award for outstanding airmanship was astronaut and shuttle commander Colonel Eileen Collins, of the United States Air Force. Colonel Collins became the first female space shuttle pilot in 1995. In 1999, she became the first female shuttle commander on mission STS-93.

The official Brigadier General James M. Stewart Award citation for Colonel Collins stated: "This award recognizes uncommon aviation skills, dedicated leadership and high competence of aviation minded men and women whose actions are distinctively noteworthy."

Houston Chronicle reporter Bob Tutt, in his story on the presentation to Colonel Collins of the Stewart Award, wrote:

> Two problems could have prematurely ended the 1999 mission led by Collins: loss of electrical power to the shuttle's center engine and a small hydrogen leak not detectable by the flight crew but spotted by the monitoring ground crew.
>
> "Fortunately, the engines are very robust," and continued functioning, Collins said. "That caused an orbit seven miles lower than expected," but the aircraft was able "to climb to the proper altitude to carry out the mission.
>
> "I did have some concern, but more than my concern was my confidence level. We knew that whatever happened, we had a plan to complete the mission and get back home safely."
>
> Serving as shuttle commander "was a tremendous challenge because I knew I'm setting an example for

other women," Collins said. "It was important for me to set a precedent because more women want to be shuttle pilots and commanders."

It is my impression that placing the Jimmy Stewart bust in the museum's rotunda and establishing an award for aviation distinction bearing the name of Jimmy Stewart are significant and glorious celebrations of years gone by and times yet to come.

Just as the articulate and visionary Texan General Ira Eaker is considered the father of the Eighth Air Force, another adroit and far-sighted Southerner is the motivating force behind the Eighth Air Force Museum. He is retired Lieutenant General E. G. "Buck" Shuler Jr., who commanded the Eighth Air Force at Barksdale Air Force Base in Louisiana before his retirement in 1991. Lanky, silver-haired, and innovative, Shuler is a Citadel and National War College graduate who, for over 32 years, flew jet bombers, fighters, tankers, and support aircraft. Shuler flew more than 7,600 hours in twenty-six different

types of airplane. Shuler's combat record includes Vietnam, the Pueblo crisis in Korea, the Just Cause action in Panama, and Desert Shield and Desert Storm in the Persian Gulf. Few air force commanders have had Shuler's wide-ranging and diverse experience. While on active duty, his command experience embraced two squadrons, two B-52 bombardment wings, two SAC air divisions, and a numbered air force, as well as director of operations for the Strategic Air Command. And now, after heading

Lieutenant General E. G. "Buck" Shuler, former commander of the modern-day Eighth Air Force, chairman, and guiding light of the Mighty Eighth Air Force Heritage Museum in Savannah, Georgia.

the modern Eighth Air Force on active duty, Shuler, as chairman of the board of trustees, is leading the Eighth Air Force Museum in retirement.

Under Shuler's leadership—and with the help of a resourceful and prestigious board, an experienced staff, a dedicated corps of World War II buffs and air force/aviation aficionados who form a dependable force of volunteers—the museum, in just over eight years, has become a national historic treasure house and a timeless shrine of emotions and memories of the "good" war. It is truly a compassionate and poignant rendezvous point for the more than one million American men and women who have served in the Eighth Air Force since 1942, in war and in peace. Opened in May of 1996, the museum has become one of America's leading reunion destinations for World War II veterans and their families.

Shortly after it opened, I went to Savannah and toured the museum. Later, I wrote a column about it for my newspaper, *The Montgomery Advertiser*. Here are excerpts from that column:

> I had the high honor and extremely good fortune to fly with the Eighth Air Force in those momentous war years in England as a combat intelligence officer, posted with the 453rd Bomb Group, a B-24 outfit stationed near Cambridge in East Anglia. Some weeks ago, on a gray Saturday, I spent a few hours of muted excitement and somber reflection at the museum. Time remembered.
>
> The huge Eighth Air Force insignia had been inlaid into the floor of the rotunda; the banners flying overhead represented every bomber, fighter group and wing of the Eighth, and plaques detailed every unit. Some of the treasures included a World War II jeep and an English bicycle, like the one I used to ride around my bomber base. The Schweinfurt-Regensburg exhibit showcased flight

artifacts. There were also the detailed diorama of an American bomber base in England, the Nissen hut so like the one I entered on cold English mornings for a few hours sleep after briefing the flight crews on that day's mission. . . .

Perhaps the museum's major attraction is a large exhibit area linked with a story line that takes visitors from the pre–World War II days right up to the present-day Eighth Air Force and its current assignments. Three main theaters tell the story: Freedom, Mission Experience, and the Battle of Britain. Since intelligence was my primary interest in the Eighth Air Force days, I was deeply moved by the prisoner of war, escape and evasion exhibits. Equally dramatic and moving was the Memorial Gardens with its Wall of Valor, which already has more than 400 plaques honoring Eighth Air Force veterans and crews. . . .

Suspended from the ceiling of the museum's largest exhibition hall is a P-51 Mustang fighter aircraft, which the bomber crews called their "little friend" on fighter escorted bombing missions deep into Germany. Placed beneath the Mustang is a German jet fighter plane, which came into action late in the war. . . ."

The museum is designed like a huge wagon wheel for the most part. At the center is the combat gallery, with a grouping of warplanes—set off by contrast—with a P-17 Stearman training plane. Like the spokes of a wheel, more than a dozen static and interactive galleries surround the combat gallery. These galleries include dioramas, replicas, scaled exhibits, models, a British telephone booth, and countless articles and objects, both symbolic and sentimental, that tell the gallant story of the valor, deeds, exploits, and memories of the men and women of the Eighth Air Force.

Andy Low is honored with a memorial window. The uniforms of Major General Fred Anderson, Eighth Air Force operations chief, are on display. The brilliant strategic airpower skills of General Anderson have been chronicled, not only by this writer, but also in what is perhaps the definitive book on the air war in Europe, Wesley Newton and Steve McFarland's *To Command the Sky*. There is a wall display honoring African-Americans in aviation, centered around the World War II exploits of the famed Tuskegee Airmen. A special gallery honors the airmen of the Eighth Air Force who were awarded the Congressional Medal of Honor—America's supreme recognition for valor.

General Shuler says, "The museum is a living history lesson for people of all ages, particularly the young. This lesson of history, especially the unique role of airpower in wartime, is not presented anywhere else to the degree the Eighth Air Force Heritage Museum presents it."

The 90,000 square feet of the museum are well planned and laid out. The spacious, two-story rotunda sets the tone for visitors, with its bronze sculptured images of Spaatz, Eaker, Doolittle and Stewart, and on the wall is a plaque with these words, written by General H. H. "Hap" Arnold, wartime commander of the Army Air Forces:

> He lived to bear his country's arms. He died to save its honor. He was a soldier . . . and he knew a soldier's duty. His sacrifices will help to keep aglow the flaming torch that lights our lives . . . that millions yet unborn may know the priceless joy of liberty. And we who pay him homage and revere his memory in solemn pride rededicate ourselves to a complete fulfillment of the task for which he so gallantly has placed his life upon the altar of man's freedom.

FOLDED WINGS: WITHDRAWAL IN BEVERLY HILLS, A FUNERAL WITH FULL MILITARY HONORS

And, at the end, the clear bell-like tones of "Taps."
—Kelly Stewart Harcourt's vivid memory
from her father's funeral

In the fall of 1993, Jimmy Stewart learned that his wife, Gloria, had lung cancer. She decided to forego extended chemotherapy and died on February 14, 1994. She was 75. Stewart was devastated. A strong, astute, and noble woman, Gloria had been the love of his life and his constant and enduring companion for 45 years. It was as if her departure from Stewart's life set off a haunting signal to withdraw into the seclusion of his home on North Roxbury Drive in Beverly Hills and admit nobody into his sad, grieving, and private world—except his daughters, Kelly and Judy; his stepson, Michael; and their families. He received few visitors, accepted few phone calls, and encouraged none. Household retainers of long service took care of his primary needs, and Stewart seldom left his room. His close friends made overtures at first—and then understood.

One Stewart friend was reminded of Thomas Wolfe's words:

> Something has spoken to me in the night,
> burning the tapers of the waning year;

something has spoken in the night, and
told me I shall die, I know not where.
Saying: To lose the earth you know, for
greater knowing; to lose the life you have,
for greater life; to leave the friends you
loved, for greater loving; to find a land
more kind than home, more large than earth—
whereon the pillars of this earth are founded,
toward which the conscience of the world is
tending . . . a wind is rising and the rivers flow.

Stewart's health had faltered badly in recent years, and his hearing was almost totally gone. Gone, too, were his early family and many friends—his mother and father, Bessie and Alex; his sisters, Mary and Virginia; his stepson, Ron, lost in the Vietnam war; his boyhood Indiana friend, Hall Blair; his longtime Hollywood friends, Henry Fonda, Gary Cooper, John Ford, Leland Hayward, Margaret Sullavan, Jack Benny, Rosalind Russell, Dave Chasen; and his Texas business associate and traveling companion Kirk Johnson. Many more were gone. And now the most vivacious and life-giving of all the people in Jimmy's life, his beloved Gloria, was gone.

After the war and upon his return to Hollywood, Stewart had bought a twin-engine plane and flew it at every opportunity, especially on his visits back to Indiana before Gloria died. Because of his declining health and hearing loss, Stewart had grounded himself and closed out his pilot's logbook. His commanding officer at Tibenham, Bob Terrill, had retired from the air force in 1964 as a lieutenant general and lived in the March Field–Riverside area of Southern California. Stewart was very fond of the man who had given him a combat job, and they stayed in touch, visiting back and forth as the years went by. Terrill died in 1992.

Brigadier General Jimmy Stewart died at his home in Beverly Hills on July 2, 1997. He was 89.

The funeral was held on a Monday. On a cool, sunny Southern California morning at Forest Lawn. Kelly Stewart Harcourt told me about that day: "It was a private graveside funeral. Only our immediate family and Dad's personal friends from home who had taken care of us all for a long time—Ann Coyle, Cecelia Drapper, and Connie Cerrito—were there."

Over the years since 1997, the memories of that day at Forest Lawn have remained near and vivid for Kelly. She remembers the quiet dignity and muted seclusion as her dad was laid to rest with full military honors; the uniforms, white gloves, and shining belt buckles of the Presidential Air Force Honor Guard from Washington; the American flag draped on the casket; the twenty-one-gun salute; and how the flag was meticulously folded into a triangle and presented to the family. She remembers President Clinton's note, "with Deep Appreciation from a Grateful Nation." And, at the end, the clear, bell-like tones of "Taps."

Later that day, there was a memorial service for the general at the Beverly Hills Presbyterian Church. Here is the Associated Press account of that service:

STEWART'S FRIENDS, FAMILY SAY GOODBYES

(AP) Co-stars, family and friends turned out Monday to pay respects to Jimmy Stewart, with the Oscar-winning actor's daughter quoting from "It's a Wonderful Life."

Speaking at the memorial service for her father, Kelly Harcourt told the 350 friends and relatives: "Like him, we might take a cue from his favorite film—'No man is poor who has friends.'"

The line is from "It's a Wonderful Life," the most popular of Stewart's approximately 80 movies.

The half-hour service at the Beverly Hills Presbyterian Church, where Stewart worshiped and sometimes sang in the choir, carried the theme of friendship.

His daughter continued: "Dad withdrew from the world after Mom died. He didn't know what to do with himself. But you, his friends, were never far away. Your support and your love gave him comfort."

The ceremony was conducted by the church's minister, the Rev. Jim Morrison, who commented: "He was a great star, but all of you here today knew him as a warm, caring, delightful human being."

The only other speaker was Lt. Gen. Roger DeKok, who represented the air force in which Stewart served during World War II and later in the reserves, rising to the rank of brigadier general.

DeKok related how, at the age of 33 in March 1941, Stewart enlisted in the Air Corps. At that time, an established star earning thousands of dollars per month, his new salary was $21 monthly.

The general cited the actor's 20 combat missions over Europe and the Distinguished Flying Cross presented to him by legendary Gen. Jimmy Doolittle.

Some of those attending represented periods of Stewart's life in Hollywood.

June Allyson, his co-star in "The Stratton Story" and "The Glenn Miller Story."

Carol Burnett, who began each of her seasons on television with her idol Stewart as her guest.

Bob Hope, who played a cameo in "The Greatest Show on Earth," in which Stewart appeared solely in clown makeup.

Lew Wasserman, the actor's agent and later his partner in groundmaking films like "Winchester '73" at Universal, for which Stewart received 50% of the profits.

Nancy Reagan, for whose husband (President Reagan) lifelong Republican Stewart campaigned.

Other notables attending included aquastar Esther Williams and Robert Stack.

The altar was decorated with 20 sprays of white roses and white gladiolas. The organ quietly played hymns and ended with the somber tunes of "Shenandoah," the title of one of Stewart's most successful frontier films.

At the end of the service, the sweet, pure sounds of a military bugle filled the church with "Taps."

The organ then played "Auld Lang Syne," the theme that ended director Frank Capra's classic "It's a Wonderful Life," a film about a man who recovers the meaning of life in the love of his friends.

Friends and relatives then attended a reception on a patio outside the church, where they had cookies and punch.

Outside the Santa Monica Boulevard church, about 2,000 media and fans watched quietly as the guests arrived and passed through an air force honor guard from Washington.

Bill Frye, a retired Hollywood producer-writer and Jimmy Stewart's friend of many years, was a pallbearer. He remembers that Henry Nicklas, Stewart's barber at the Bel-Air Country Club, was a guest at the memorial service. Frye told this story: "During Jimmy's last shave, the barber noticed that he had a bandage on the left side of his face. He asked Jimmy, 'Shall I take it off to shave your face?' Jimmy replied, 'Henry, don't worry about the left side of my face. God will take care of it.'"

THANKS

In the years that I have planned and worked on this book, many
people have come forward with ideas, stories, suggestions, background material, information, pictures, guidance, support, and,
above all, encouragement. Foremost among these friends and sup-
porters is Dr. Wesley "Wes" Phillips Newton, the distinguished air
power historian, university professor, author, combat infantryman,
World War II POW, dedicated friend, and confidant. I owe Wes
Newton my gratitude in the ultimate degree for his friendship and for
standing with me in the often dark times leading to the publication
of this book. Wes's Eighth Air Force book, *To Command the Sky*,
coauthored with Dr. Stephen McFarland, was absolutely invaluable in
recalling events and memories of my own days and nights in the
Eighth Air Force in England with Jimmy Stewart in World War II—
which is what this book is all about. And, above all, it was Wes's avid
interest in the book, standing with a hand on my shoulder, always
caring, always helpful.

Another friend and Eighth Air Force combat veteran who was of
monumental help on the book is John H. "Robbie" Robinson. Robbie
put his own Eighth Air Force memoir, *A Time To Live*, at my disposal
for generous quotes, reference points, and Stewart anecdotes. Robbie
is an artful and penetrating observer who knew and loved Jimmy
Stewart and wrote about him with personal knowledge and deep
affection. Robbie's friendship, the support he gave this book throughout

his own work, and his encouragement knew no limits. For all of this, I am extremely grateful.

The Air Force Historical Research Agency of the Air University at Maxwell Air Force Base in Montgomery, Alabama, was a constant and reliable source for many types of research assistance, checkpoints, pictures, and references. Anne Webb, Toni Petito, and Joe Caver were always standing by, only a phone call away, and I am thankful for their friendship and assistance. The Air University Library, with its bountiful stacks, immediate reference service, and a positive and highly professional staff headed by director Shirley Laseter, could always be counted on for just the right book or magazine and merits many thanks. The Air University History Office, directed by Jerome A. Ennels, and the Air University Press were research sources of great value.

Here are hearty thanks to my ETO friend and compatriot Walter Cronkite for his perceptive and well-remembered foreword for the book. Walter was there in England with us. He had a splendid career as a war correspondent for United Press, covered the Eighth Air Force, flew combat missions, and knew Jimmy Stewart. He wrote the foreword based on wartime experience and presence. Just as Ed Murrow defined broadcast news, Walter Cronkite was America's premier anchor at CBS for almost twenty years. After retirement he turned again to print journalism—writing a syndicated newspaper column, lecturing, and producing documentaries, some for public television. I am indeed thankful to Walter and his devoted, gracious, and multitalented chief of staff Marlene Adler.

Elizabeth Salome, director of the Jimmy Stewart Museum in Stewart's hometown of Indiana, Pennsylvania, was, from the beginning, a dependable and undistracted cheerleader. When I was in Indiana for hometown background color, Elizabeth, Jay Rubin, and other of Stewart's friends took me in hand with introductions, conversation, interviews, picture-taking, and hospitality. Elizabeth, with understanding, charm, and intelligence was the fountainhead of the visit and has been, over the years, a tremendous outlet for information and assistance. I shall always be grateful to Elizabeth and the Stewart Museum in his hometown.

Among my many Air Corps/Air Force friends who had a hand in the production of this book, the late Andy Low (Major General, Air Force Retired) was always in the forefront. Dating back to the early 1940s, at March Field in California, and moving through our times together with the Eighth Air Force in England with Stewart, Andy's knowledge in matters of this book was always constant, professional, and to the point. He never let me forget it, and throughout our friendship, that spanned more than half a century, Andy was a strong pillar of help and hope. He was Jimmy Stewart's best air force friend in war and peace and provided many up-close and personal vignettes of reminiscence and illustration. His book, *The Liberator Men Of Old Buc*, is a masterful chronicle of combat life in the Eighth Air Force with day-by-day focus on our own 453rd Liberator Bomb Group. Truly, it was a contributing factor in the production of this book. Fortunately, Andy was able to see the book to near completion before his death.

Like Jimmy Stewart and Jimmy Doolittle, Ramsay Potts was not a professional air corps officer before the war. All three were "citizen soldiers" who served brilliantly in the war and returned to civilian life when hostilities ceased but took up reserve commissions. Ramsay Potts (Major General, Air Force Reserve, Retired) was the epitome of an American citizen who for years successfully bridged the gap between military and civilian life, where he was a Harvard-trained attorney in Washington, D.C. In the war years, Potts was Stewart's commanding officer, mentor, role model, and friend. He served the same purpose for Andy Low, Starr Smith, Bob Bieck, and many others. For years, Ramsay Potts never left my side in the production of this book. And I'm very grateful to him.

General Jimmy Doolittle was not a personal friend of Jimmy Stewart. He knew Stewart only by reputation in civilian life and had an enormous respect for him as an air force officer, pilot, combat commander, and leader. As commander of the Eighth Air Force, Doolittle was Stewart's "big boss" for all the years he was on combat duty in England. General Doolittle was proud of Stewart's combat career, thought his story should be told, and encouraged me to tell it.

I am grateful to him for that. Heartfelt thanks to my longtime friend and mentor and Eighth Air Force commander General Ira Eaker, who, on our last visit, said, "Stick with the book, Starr."

General Harold "Hap" Arnold, wartime chief of the Army Air Corps/Army Air Force, made a timely phone call on my behalf early on that led to my combat intelligence assignment with the Eighth Air Force, and ultimately to the writing of this book. I will be eternally grateful to this great airman and perceptive and far-sighted military leader. In the evaluation of many historians, the two most significant American generals of World War II, above all others, were General Arnold and General George Marshall.

General "Tooey" Spaatz always asked about the book and had a pat on the back for me. I'm very grateful for his encouragement.

General Mike Ryan, immediate past Chief of Staff of the Air Force, is familiar with the Stewart book and offered words of enlightenment and help. The modern-day airman and Jimmy Stewart aficionado, retired Lieutenant General E. G. "Buck" Shuler, former commander of the Eighth Air Force and guiding light of the Mighty Eighth Air Force Heritage Museum in Savannah, Georgia, has been helpful beyond measure. Buck Shuler and his wife, Annette, have spent countless lovely hours talking with me about the book, always with a positive and upbeat pat on the back and heartening words. Above all, I am grateful

for their affection and friendship. Moreover, Buck Shuler is one of the most congenial, understanding, and thoughtful men I have ever known.

I owe lasting thanks to Kathleen Arnold, daughter of Colonel/General Walter "Pop" Arnold, who made the important phone call paving the way for Jimmy Stewart's combat

General Henry H. "Hap" Arnold and General Ira Eaker.

assignment. Kathleen provided cogent facts about her father's relationship with Stewart, including two significant and moving Stewart stories that are highlights of the book.

Kelly Stewart Harcourt of California has come forward with tender and memorable little sketches about her father that added a graceful and loving wellspring to those last melancholy times of his life. To Kelly, I say only, "Thanks for the talks and the memory."

My friends and wartime comrades of the 453rd Bomb Group were reassuring and supportive from the beginning, and their spirited support means a lot to me. Notably: Bob Bieck, Lloyd Prang, Don Olds, Francis Thomas, and Abe Wilen. I offer a snappy salute to Jordan Uttal and Evelyn Cohen of the Second Air Division, and to General "Ted" Timberlake, commander of the Second Combat Bomb Wing of the Eighth Air Force, and to his right-hand man, Captain Cal Stewart, the distinguished journalist and author.

Two Eighth Air Force warriors, F. C. "Hap" Chandler and Craig Harris, were steadfast in their support all the way and they have my devotion and thanks. The noted journalist and World War II veteran "Chuck" Glover drew on his long experience, knowledge, and insight to talk about the book and offer cogent suggestions and good words.

Ray Pytel is the editor of the Second Air Division Association *Journal*. Ray has been a strong supporter and endorser of the book for a long time. Several times, Ray has mentioned the upcoming book in the *Journal*. This has brought forth numerous little Stewart stories and anecdotes from men who served with him in the Second Air Division, many written on scraps of paper in longhand. Many of these stories were included in the book,

Abe Wilen, left, and Bob Bieck.

and I wish to thank all who sent them to me. And a hearty thanks to Ray Pytel for long and sustained confidence and support.

Two of the major architects of the air victory in the ETO knew about my plans to write this book, and they both offered inspiration and assistance before they died. They were Major General Fred Anderson and Congressional Medal of Honor recipient General Leon Johnson. Another Medal of Honor recipient, the late Colonel Bill Lawley, an Eighth Air Force warrior and friend, gave enheartened support.

I wish to give personal and professional thanks to two superb writers whose articles about Jimmy Stewart in the *Saturday Evening Post* furnished a strong and solid foundation for this book: The late Colonel Beirne Lay wrote about Stewart's wartime service in the SEP in 1945, and, in 1961, the brilliant reporter Pete Martin wrote a penetrating and embracing series in the magazine. I am ever so grateful to Bierne and Pete for invaluable help for *Jimmy Stewart: Bomber Pilot.*

Jackson Granholm was a captain in the ETO during the war. In 2002 he wrote a book, *The Day We Bombed Switzerland.* Two Eighth Air Force officers were involved. There was a court-martial. Colonel Jimmy Stewart presided at that trial. Jackson Granholm provided cogent information about Stewart's part in the court-martial which was included in the book. I am thankful to Jackson for that help.

Special thanks to family and longtime friends: My daughter, Sandra Starr Smith Miller and her husband Scott; my journalist sister Lois Smith Clover and her late husband Chandler Clover; my former wife, Virginia Seifert-Smith; my brother Jim Smith and his wife Verna; my brother, the late Colonel James W. Smith and his family; my granddaughter Trenton Miller Milam and her husband John Paul Milam; and the Yardbirds. Sara Jane Wade Kahn—my dear and departed, great and good friend—Algie Hill Neill, Judy Taunton, Richard and Beverly Amberg, Jack Kyle, Dixon Lovvorn, Bill and Linda Dunlap, Carolyn and Al Newman, Jim Davis, Dr. Merlin Newton, Janie and Brent Alexander, Ann Wade, Shearen and Tibby Elebash, Leon Loard, Joe D. and Bertie Smith, Chan and Ray Thompson, Ed Murrow, Lynn Jeter, Tom Scarritt, Rick and Maggie Harmon, Al Benn, Jake and Patty Saylor, Bonnie Warren, Dr. Paul

Hubbard and Ann, Carol Toulmin, Bob Capa, Charles Wertenbaker, Margaret Higgins, Wes Gallagher, Don Whitehead, Hal Boyle, Martha Gellhorn, Howard K. Smith, Judge Ira DeMent and Ruth, Bill Brown, Ellen Dossett, Willis Teel and Pam, Merrill "Red" Mueller (my boss at NBC Radio), Dr. John Wade and Kim Kirschenfeld, Suzanne Moon, Richard Howarth, Roy Nutt, Ila Flowers, Dr. Jack Kirschenfeld and Helen, Joe and Sandra McInnes, Bill Hardman, Colonel R. Ernest Dupuy (my boss at General Eisenhower's press headquarters in the ETO), Captain Harry Butcher (General Eisenhower's naval aide in the ETO), Mary Margaret van Diest, Linda and Millard Fuller, Howell Raines, Dr. David Bronner, Chrys and Ed Robins, Buford Boone, Wayne Greenhaw, Todd Clay, Senator Richard Shelby and Annette, Dr. Frank Rose and Tommye, Suzie Smith, Colonel Chauncey "Chuck" Whitehead, Don and Joanne Naman, Jim Boone, Colonel Barney Oldfield, Carolyn Hutchinson, Margie and Frank Hayes, and Eva and Haynes Thompson.

I also wish to thank: Winton "Red" and Carolyn Blount, William Bradford Huie, Alfred Asch, Marsha Wade, General Howard "Doc" Kreidler and Laverne, Colonel Clyde "Brad" Bradley and Liz, Jean and Larry Kloess, Reverend Freddie Carger, Colonel Warren Lacy, Catherine Arnold, B. J. "Jodie" Barry, Bill Frye, Dr. Hudson Strode, Mary Welsh Hemingway, Willie Morris, Bob Considine, Mirian Hill, Mike Kennedy, Nancy and Kenny Smith, Pat Ballard, Charles Collingwood, Bob Ward, Frank Mastin, Sandy Smith, Doris and Jimmy Thomas, Bonnie Nobles, C. J. Roberts, Alistair Cooke, Bern and Frankie Keating, Dr. Tom Geary, Carole Vandiver, Harry Shattuck, Bob Alden, Jack Scott, Vivian Holley, Eric Severeid, Kathy Kemp, Cornelius "Connie" Ryan, Jean Martin, Betty Callaway, Howard "Bo" Callaway, Charles Moore, Bill and Jean Jones, Dr. Wayne Flynt, Gay Talese, Millie Ball, Eric Friedheim, Prof. John Luskin, Deloris Boyle, John Bordsen, Oakley Melton, Priscilla Crommelin, John Scott, "Bubba" Trotman and Dora Haas, and Senator Larry Dixon and Gaynell. And, a high note of thanks and well-done to my agent, Alex Hoyt. And, to many, many others who, I hope, will forgive my oversight.

ꞅVꞅ

EPILOGUE

In putting this book together with Jimmy Stewart as the central figure, there were, nevertheless, other elements to the story—personal experiences of his associates and friends, historical accounts, background information, written material, oral interviews, vivid memories, and other recollections, opinions, and reactions. Along with these glimmerings from the past, there is a brief overview of the dramatic and revisional Tac School. All of this may perhaps expand the viewpoint, broaden the base of understanding, and enhance the history of one of the towering campaigns of World War II—the air war in Europe.

This collection was chosen at random. It ranges from the hearty commendation of Winston Churchill, and the post-war observations of the chief of the German air force, to Ramsay Potts' dedication of the American Air Museum in England—from a tribute to Jimmy Stewart by one of his combat crewmen, to Andy Low's story of a West Point class ring—from Stewart's fellow airman Abe Wilen's searing recollection of the horrors of being a German prisoner-of-war, to the ringing words of General Bob Burns describing the darkness and the danger of day-by-day combat in the Eighth Air Force in those crucial and consequential times in the ETO in World War II.

MAJOR GENERAL ANDREW S. LOW JR.

Andrew S. Low Jr., 83, a retired general and a teacher at the Institute of Flying Safety and System Management at the University of Southern California's graduate school for 16 years before retiring in 1987, died on Tuesday, August 1.

A retired Air Force major general, Mr. Low was a graduate of the U.S. Military Academy, where he was commissioned as a second lieutenant in 1942. He enlisted in the Rhode Island National Guard in 1936 and later became a squadron commander in the 2nd Division of the Eighth Air Force. A veteran of World War II, he was shot down over Germany in 1944 and spent the rest of the war in a prison camp.

Maj. Gen. Low was the director of aerospace programs for the Air Force before retiring in 1971, when he received the Distinguished Service Medal. He also received the Legion of Merit, Distinguished Flying Cross, Air Medal with one oak leaf cluster, Joint Service Commendation Medal with one oak leaf cluster, the Purple Heart, European-African Middle East Campaign Medal, National Defense Service Medal with one service star, and Air Force Longevity Service Award Ribbon with six oak leaf clusters, among other awards.

He was also authorized to wear the Missileman Badge and Wings of a command pilot in the Turkish Air Force, and was awarded the Former Prisoners of War Medal by Congress. In 1987, he was inducted into the Rhode Island Heritage Hall of Fame.

Besides his wife, Helen (Freeborn) Low, he leaves two sons, four daughters, a brother, a sister, ten grandchildren, and five great-grandchildren.

Burial was at the U.S. Military Academy Cemetery, West Point, NY.

IN MEMORIAM

Major General Andrew Low

Andy Low was the epitome of a brave, disciplined and patriotic airman.

When I arrived to take command of the 453rd Bomb Group in March 1944, Andy Low came to my attention immediately as one of the few officers in the Group who was a graduate of West Point. This marked him as an officer with special educational credentials who could be called upon to perform administrative duties with skill and devotion. Shortly after my arrival at the 453rd as Group Commander, Jimmy Stewart was assigned as the Operations Officer of our Group. This proved to be a most fortunate and opportune addition to the Group's leadership and, as we all know, Jimmy Stewart turned out to be one of the finest operations officers in the Eighth Air Force. But Stewart needed some expert help in planning and briefing the missions of the Group, and to assist him in this capacity, I appointed Andy Low as Assistant Group Operations Officer. In this capacity, Andy Low fulfilled all of my expectations and provided the most dedicated and faithful assistance to Jimmy Stewart.

Although he was carrying a heavy operational and administrative workload, Andy Low continued to fly on some of the most dangerous combat missions, and on some of these missions he served as the commander of the Group and even of the wing formation. On one of the most difficult penetrations of the Group, Andy's plane was shot down and he barely escaped with his life even though he suffered burn injuries. For the remainder of the War he was a prisoner of the Luftwaffe but did make a recovery from his burn injuries.

After the War ended and peace was declared, Andy was returned to duty in the United States. His later career as an air force officer fulfilled his early promise and he rose to the rank of Major General after serving in numerous difficult assignments.

We salute Andy Low—one of the finest officers ever to serve in the U.S. Air Force and, certainly, an officer who exemplified in the truest

sense of the word the dedication and fighting spirit of the 453rd
Bomb Group.

Ramsay D. Potts
Major General USAF
Reprint: 2nd AD. Journal

CHIVALRY IN ADVERSITY
By General Andy Low

Graduates of Service Academies have, for more than one hundred and fifty years, worn finger rings to commemorate their Alma Mater. In earlier years, before the advent of the gummed envelope, these commemorative rings served the useful purpose of imprinting the sealing wax on letters—even serving as an exterior identifier of the author. Many collegians of other institutions did a similar rite of passage. However, many of these collegians owed a closer allegiance to Greek-letter fraternities to which they belonged. Often their rings reflected this latter allegiance.

Since 1897, rings of West Point have reflected on the motto, "Duty, Honor, Country" and the Academy Crest, on one side of the ring, and a class adopted crest on the other. During the third year, great activity by each class member marks the arrival of class rings. Because of the closeness of the Academy experience—living in barracks, meals in a common mess, formations for all phases of daily life—the class ring is a ready manifestation of this closeness. Most graduates wear their rings much of the time—and certainly at activities associated with the Academy experience.

And thus, I was one who wore my class ring most of the time. In combat, in Europe, in early 1944, we were required to wear our issue name plates (dog tags) at all times, but we were discouraged from carrying other identification which might be "of aid and/or comfort to the enemy."

On 31 July 1944, there was some confusion on the assignment from our Group for the Combat Air Commander. He would command the Second Combat Wing, and the Second Air Division, which the Wing would lead. As Group Operations Officer, I had been up all night during mission preparations, and thus was most familiar with targeting, routes, communications, and the myriad of details to get over four hundred Liberator bombers to the target—Ludwigshafen, and the IG Farben Chemical Works. So, I took the assignment. In a last minute rush, I changed into my flying gear and proceeded by jeep to Wing Headquarters, some ten miles down the road.

Briefing, take-off, form-up, coast-out, tight formation—all went well until we began our bombing run. We were at 24,000 feet, the highest I had ever flown on an attack. We encountered heavy flak at our altitude, and took random hits with no personnel injuries up to "Bomb Doors Open." Just as the bombardier announced "Bombs Away" we took a burst just under our bomb-bay which set our hydraulic lines and reservoir on fire—a raging fire. The crew fought the fire but warned we were in serious condition, with a chance of an explosion of the gasoline tanks above the bomb-bay.

Quickly, the aircraft commander and I decided we had to leave the formation, dive to attempt to blow out the fire—and to clear the target area. I told the Deputy to take over the formation and we dove sharply in a sweeping arc away from the target. The Flight Engineer in the bomb-bay reported that the structure was catching fire. We knew we had to jump, and the aircraft commander sounded the "Stand-by to bail" on the alarm, and "Jump" almost immediately.

We were three on the flight deck, the Pathfinder Navigator, the Aircraft Commander, and me. The Navigator attempted to open our normal egress through the bomb-bay but the fire was just too much of a blazing inferno. I had shed my harness, and stood up as he was reclosing the door. Over my head was a hatch used on the ground during taxiing, but was not an authorized egress in the air. It was forward of the top turret, and could be blocked by guns. It was forward of the propellers—but both number two and number three engines had been feathered. There were two vertical stabilizers on the B-24J, but we found out we had already lost one in the dive. I bent down, grabbed the Navigator around the legs, and shoved him through the hatch. I followed quickly, and the Aircraft Commander was right behind me. We cleared the aircraft, pulled our ripcords—and the plane blew up.

I was alone as I floated out of the clouds close to the ground, and could see I was headed for farmland outside a village. As I neared the ground and prepared to land, I realized I was headed right at two military figures with rifles—and the longest fixed bayonets I had ever seen. I touched down, collapsed my chute, and the German soldiers were not twenty yards from me, rifles at ready.

"Haben sie pistole?" I did not understand what they said, but guessed. I shook my head and raised my arms, and then I realized I was really hurt. My flying suit was still smoldering. The Germans put down their guns and helped me beat out the embers. That done, they picked up their rifles, and began to search me. I was told to take off my watch by their motions. Then they emptied my pockets, found my dog tags, but did not take them, and then helped me pull off my burned gloves.

And there it was—my West Point 1942 Class Ring. They motioned me to take it off, and it was dropped into a pack one soldier carried. As they motioned me to march, I suddenly realized how scared I really was—and fearful of what was going to happen next.

We were taken to the village jail—all nine of us who made the jump. Two crewmen in the rear of the aircraft did not get out. We had all been quickly rounded up by the militia-type soldiers who had been turned out to look for downed men. From the civilian jail, we were taken to a German air force airfield. We were given some medical treatment, wrapped with paper bandages, and readied for a trip to the Interrogation Center. At the Interrogation Center, I was put in a plain, small solitary cell. I had told them my name, rank, and my serial number. I was bandaged so that I had to have someone feed me, and help me with trips to the personal facilities.

My first session with the Interrogator was brief. I repeated my name, rank, and serial number. He called me major, but said he needed to know more. As he remarked, they did not give medical treatment to spies. I hurt terribly, and was not sure what was happening under the bandages. But, I had endured West Point and I knew they were not going to be any tougher. The second morning was a repeat, giving only name, rank and serial number, and back I was sent to my cell, still hurting.

As I thought over my situation, and what was happening to the others whom I had not seen, I realized I had been riding with a 458th Bomb Group aircrew, transferred to the 389th as a lead crew. The aircraft wreckage would have 389th insignia. I deduced therefore that they were not too sure who I was. The third day session was another repeat. But the interrogator said I was foolish, as they would find me out. No medical treatment until they did. Back to my cell.

It was a warm August evening, but from my cell I could see nothing, and hear very little. Time dragged. Suddenly, the guard was opening my cell, and in came a German flying officer. His left arm was mangled, and heavily bandaged. The guard locked him in, and went away. In excellent English, with a British accent, he asked if I wanted a cigarette. I told him I did not smoke, so that ended that entrée. I really hurt and the bandage reeked, so I was angry enough to be rude. He asked if I would like something to read—*Life*, maybe. I replied I could not handle a book with my bandages.

He said he was sorry for me as an airplane pilot, for me the war was over. But he added, he would never fly again either. We warmed to each other—a little. He asked about my family. I told him I had a daughter I had never seen. He told me about his family. There was some more small talk, and then he arose to leave. He walked to the door, and then came back to me. His good hand was in his pocket. He pulled it out and dropped my Class Ring inside my clothes.

Simply he said, "I am sure this means something to you, and it means nothing to them. Hide, it, and do not wear it until you are free!" With that he turned quickly and left me alone—with my thoughts.

Can there be such chivalry among such obvious adversity? For me, there was.

Reprint: 2nd AD. Journal

ADDRESS BY MAJOR GENERAL RAMSAY POTTS
at the American Air Museum in Britain

Major General Ramsay D. Potts, USAF Ret., was invited to speak on behalf of the veterans at the impressive new American Air Museum in Britain, at Duxford Airfield near Cambridge, which opened on 1 August 1997. The dedication by Queen Elizabeth was a happy occasion for the 4,000 attendees, including about 1,500 American veterans. Potts was an original pilot of the 93rd Bomb Group and served in various positions within the Eighth Air Force throughout World War II. He is active in both the 93rd Bomb Group and the 2nd Air Division Association, and has served on the Board of Directors of the Mighty Eighth Air Force Heritage Museum since its beginning. Following is the speech he delivered at the dedication at Duxford:

Your Majesty, Your Royal Highnesses, Your Excellencies, My Lords, Ladies, and Gentlemen:

It is indeed a *signal* honor for me to have been invited to speak on behalf of all the veterans here today, especially those who served in England.

In 1942 I came to England as a pilot with the 93rd Bomb Group, the first B-24 Liberator Group based in England with the Eighth Air Force. Later, in 1944, I commanded bomber groups at bases in Norfolk not far from here, and then later still became Director of Bomber Operations for the Eighth Air Force, commanded by General Jimmy Doolittle.

We thank you, Your Majesty, for opening the American Air Museum in Britain, and we thank our British friends, especially those who brought this museum to fruition.

Throughout World War II, American airmen received warm and generous support from the English people in the towns and villages near our bases.

More importantly, Your Majesty, your father and mother, King George and Queen Elizabeth, took a particular interest in us and visited many of our bases, including my own, thereby enhancing the morale of all ranks.

We Americans seem to have center stage here today, but I should like to pay a special tribute to the Royal Air Force. The American air forces could not have accomplished what they did without *unstinting* support from the RAF. The RAF gave us our bases and protected them; provided us with communications; furnished us with intelligence about the enemy; and even fished us out of the North Sea when we were forced to *crash land in the water*.

This was a wartime manifestation of that special relationship between our two countries, which we veterans are determined to *strengthen* and *preserve*.

As Secretary Widnall said: This American Air Museum has attracted widespread support in the United States and especially among those who served in Britain in World War II.

On behalf of all those veterans, those who are here today, and those who could not join us *but wish they were here*, I predict a long and flourishing life for our magnificent museum.

Thank you, and God bless you, each and every one.

Reprint: 2nd AD. Journal

EPILOGUE

POST-WAR COMMENTS ON THE ALLIED VICTORY IN EUROPE

Words from Winston Churchill as reprinted in "Air Power," newsletter of the General Doolittle Chapter, 8 AFHS

We need to pay our tribute of respect and admiration to the officers and men who fought and died in this fearful battle of the air, the like of which had never been known or even with any precision imagined. The moral test to which the crew of a bomber were subjected reached the limits of human valor and sacrifice. Here chance was carried to its most extreme and violent degree above all else.

There was a rule that no one should go on more than thirty raids without a break. But many who entered on their last dozen wild adventures felt that the odds against them were increasing. How can one be lucky thirty times running in a world of averages and machinery?

Detective-Constable McSweeney, one of the Scotland Yard officers who looked after me in the early days of the war, was determined to fight in a bomber. I saw him several times during his training and his fighting. One day, gay and jaunty as ever, but with a meaningful look, he said, "My next will be my twenty-ninth." It was his last.

Not only our hearts and admiration but our minds in strong comprehension of those ordeals must go to those heroic men whose duty to their country and their cause sustained them in super human trials. I have remembered facts like "The Americans had sixty of their large Bomber aircraft destroyed out of 291," and on another occasion "out of 795 aircraft dispatched by the British Bomber command against Nuremberg, ninety-four did not return."

The American Bombers carried a crew of ten men, and the British night bombers seven. Here we have each time six or seven hundred of these skilled, highly trained warriors lost in an hour. This was indeed ordeal by fire.

In the British and American bombing of Germany and Italy during the War, the casualties were over a hundred and forty thousand, and in the period with which this chapter deals, there were more British and

American casualties than were killed and wounded in the great operation of crossing the Channel. Those heroes never flinched or failed. It is to their devotion that in no small measure we owe our victory. Let us give them our salute.

Note: Mr. Churchill used an early version of the B-24 Liberator as his personal transportation.

*   *   *

In his Wartime Diaries, *the Reich Minister for Armaments and War Production, Albert Speer, second only to Adolph Hitler, Chancellor of the Third Reich, writes:*

The real importance of the air war consisted in the fact that it opened a second front long before the invasion of Europe. That front was the skies over Germany. The fleets of bombers might appear at any time over any large German city or important factory. The unpredictability of the attacks made this front gigantic; every square meter of the territory we controlled was a kind of front line. Defense against air attacks required the production of thousands of antiaircraft guns. The stockpiling of tremendous quantities of ammunition all over the country, and holding in readiness hundreds of thousands of soldiers, who in addition had to stay in position by their guns, often totally inactive, for months at a time.

As far as I can judge from the accounts I have read, no one has yet seen that this was the greatest lost battle on the German side. The losses from the retreats in Russia or from the surrender of Stalingrad were considerably less. Moreover, the nearly 20,000 antiaircraft guns stationed in the Homeland could almost have doubled the antitank defenses on the Eastern Front. In the territory of the Reich these guns were virtually useless. Over the attacked cities they did little more than provide a kind of reassuring fireworks display for the population. By that time bombers were operating from such high altitudes that the shells of the 8.8-centimeter flak guns reached the planes at too slow a speed.

In his book *The War in the Air: A Pictorial History of WWII Air Forces in Combat,* Major Gene Gurney (USAF) quotes German Marshal Hermann Goering:

I knew first that the Luftwaffe was losing control of the air when the American long-range fighters were able to escort the bombers as far as Hanover. It was not long before they were getting to Berlin. We then knew we must develop the jet planes. Our plan for their early development was unsuccessful only because of your bombing attacks.

Allied attacks greatly affected our training program, too. For instance, the attacks on oil retarded the training because our pilots couldn't get sufficient training before they were put into the air.

I am convinced that the jet planes would have won the war for us if we had had only four or five months' more time. Our underground installations were all ready. The factory at Kahla had a capacity of 1,000 to 1,200 jet airplanes a month. Now with 5,000 to 6,000 jets, the outcome would have been quite different.

We would have trained sufficient pilots for the jet planes despite oil shortage, because we would have had underground factories for oil, producing a sufficient quantity for the jets. The transition to jets was very easy in training. The jet-pilot output was always ahead of the jet-aircraft production.

Germany could not have been defeated by air power alone, using England as a base, without invasion—because German industry was going underground, and our countermeasures would have kept pace with your bombing. But the point is, that if Germany were attacked in her weakened condition as now, then the air could do it alone. That is, the land invasion meant that so many workers had to be withdrawn from factory production and even from the Luftwaffe.

We bombed cities in England instead of concentrating on aircraft and engine factories despite my original intention to attack only military targets and factories, because after the British attacked Hamburg our people were angry and I was ordered to attack indiscriminately.

Allied precision bombing had a greater effect on the defeat of Germany than area bombing, because destroyed cities could be evacuated but destroyed industry was difficult to replace.

Allied selection of targets was good, particularly in regard to oil. As soon as we started to repair an oil installation, you bombed it again!

We didn't concentrate on the four-engine Focke-Wulf planes as heavy bombers after the Battle of Britain, because we were developing the HE-177 and trying to develop the ME-264, which was designed to go to America and return. Because our production capacity was not so great as America's, we could not produce quickly everything we needed. Moreover, our planes were subject to constant bombing.

If I had to design the Luftwaffe again, the first airplane I would develop would be the jet fighter—then the jet bomber. It is now a question of fuel. The jet fighter takes too much. The ME-264 awaited only the final solution of the fuel-consumption problem. According to my view the future airplane is one without fuselage (flying wing) equipped with turbine in combination with the jet and propeller.

Before D-Day, the Allied attacks in northern France hurt us the most because we were not able to rebuild in France as quickly as at home. The attacks on marshalling yards were most effective, next came low-level attacks on troops, then attacks on bridges. The low-flying planes had a terror effect and caused great damage to our communications. Also demoralizing were the umbrella fighters, which after escorting the bombers would swoop down and hit everything, including the jet planes in the process of landing.

The Allies owe the success of the invasion to the air forces. They prepared the invasion; they made it possible; they carried it through.

Without the U.S. Air Force the war would still be going on elsewhere, but certainly not on German soil.

THE TAC SCHOOL

In the 1930s, an annually changing group of bright and innovative Army Air Corps officers gathered every day in classrooms. They were instructors and students at the Air Corps Tactical School (ACTS) at Maxwell Field near Montgomery, Alabama. These were the elite of the air corps, the best and the brightest, with hundreds of hours of flying time in the air corps aircraft of the 1930s—the Boeing B-9, Martin B-10, B-12, and the pursuit planes—P-26, P-35, P-36, and, later, the Bell P-39 Aircobra and Curtiss P-40 Warhawk. The B-9 and B-10 were transitional bombers, from wood-and-fabric to all-metal, retractable landing gear design. The great four-engine bomber, the Boeing B-17 Flying Fortress was yet to come, and, the B-24 Liberator, still later.

On July 23, 1934, a *New York Times* headline stated "2,320 Planes for Army." Momentous times were at hand. And the keen and curious men there in the classrooms at Maxwell's Austin Hall—huddling over maps, aircraft models, charts, books, slide rules, relying on their own flying experience, and seeking a new battle doctrine for the defense of America—knew it.

Many of these ACTS men, instructors and students, were West Pointers, most were college trained. Their average age was early forties. Ranks varied: lieutenants, captains, a sprinkling of majors, and a rare lieutenant colonel. Indeed, these were the men who, as generals, led the air force to victory in World War II—Carl "Tooey" Spaatz, Ira Eaker, Muir Fairchild, Nathan Twining, Barney Giles, Joe Cannon, Fred and Orvil Anderson, Pete Quesada, Hoyt Vandenberg, Larry Kuter, Curt LeMay, Don Wilson, George Kenney, Kenneth Walker, who received the Medal of Honor, Earle Partridge, Pat Timberlake, Larry Norstad, Lewis Brereton, and another Congressional Medal of Honor winner, Leon Johnson. There were others—including the passionate and fiery Claire Chennault—the Air Corps' most active advocate, champion, and promoter of pursuit/fighter aviation. Many graduates stayed on as instructors, notably Captain/Major Harold George and Lieutenant Haywood "Possum" Hansell, two of the premier bombardment strategists of World War II.

But the instructors and students did not confine themselves only to air power as it applied to traditional wartime techniques and practices of the past. Indeed, it was the school's raison d'etre to explore the whole theory of warfare in an attempt to discover if this new and truly untried weapon of the air had changed the very nature of modern war. In these terms, Major George spoke to the incoming class in 1935:

> From today on much that we shall study will require us to start with nothing more than an acknowledged truth and then attempt, by the utilization of common sense and logic, to evolve a formula which we believe will stand up under the crucial test of actual conditions. We shall attempt to develop logically, the role of air power in future war, in the next war. We are not concerned with fighting the past war—that was done eighteen years ago. We are concerned, however, in determining how air power shall be employed in the next war and what constitutes the principles governing its employment, not by journeying into the hinterlands of wild imaginings but by traveling the highway of common sense and logic.
>
> The question for you to consider from today on war, to have constantly before you as you continue your careers, is substantially this:
>
> Has the advent of air power brought into existence a method for the prosecution of war which has revolutionized that art and given to air forces a strategical objective of their own, independent of either land or naval forces.

General "Hap" Arnold, the air corps' top commander, did not attend ACTS, known as the Tac School, but kept a close and constant eye on the school, its instructors and graduates. The astute commander-in-chief was well aware of the fact that the Air Corps Tactical School in its dual mission of providing advance professional military education for promising and likely Air Corps officers, and, serving as a think tank for air power strategy and doctrine—was unique among all air forces in those times. Arnold obviously came to believe strongly in the Maxwell school. It has been reported that at the time of Pearl Harbor, Arnold had nine ACTS graduates on his staff.

During the war years when the theories of the Tactical School were being hammered into established doctrine—the interesting fact is: that of 320 general officers on duty with the U.S. Army Air Force at the end of World War II, 261 were Tac School graduates, including three four-star generals—McNarney, Kenney and Spaatz. During the Clinton Administration, by act of Congress, Doolittle and Ira Eaker, another Tactical School graduate, were promoted to four-star rank. Both Eaker and Doolittle were former Eighth Air Force commanders.

The multi-talented, dedicated and all-seeking air warriors of the "Tac School," were not only instructors and students—they were thinkers, theorists, transformers, pioneers, and, above all, explorers and essayists—searching for the ultimate doctrine in the planning and development of air power, and the most profitable utilization of bombardment aircraft in future American wars. A lecturer, Major Donald Wilson, stressed the importance of attacking the "industrial fabric" of an enemy nation since industrial production was essential in the successful prosecution of a modern war. Harold George, at the end of World War II, was a lieutenant general, and one of the architects of the separate air force. He was also known as a "prophet of air power." Hansell retired as a major general, after service as a bomber commander in both Europe and the Pacific. In his post-war memoir, *The Quest*, General Hansell reflected:

> The instructors at ACTS did not restrict them-
> selves to the expressed military doctrine of the War
> Department. If they had, the students would have
> limited themselves to studies in coastal defense and

consequently would have been unprepared for the
realities of military aviation in World War II.

World War I, the "Great War" ended before strategic bombing received
any real test, and the peacetime years between 1918 and 1939 offered
little opportunity for air combat bombardment action. The Spanish Civil
War and Japanese aggression in China were, if limited, exceptions.

In Alabama, at Maxwell Field, the theory-minded instructors and
students at the Tactical School found much to investigate and study
in the activities of three military airmen who emerged from the
"Great War" as leaders and theorists: the Italian Giulio Douhet, the
Englishman Hugh Trenchard, and, more importantly, the American
William "Billy" Mitchell.

The thinking, writing, theories, and wartime experiences of the
pioneering, exploring—and, one might say—air bombardment
revolutionaries of Douhet, Trenchard, and Mitchell made considerable impact on the like-minded American air officers at the Tac
School. In some ways and in varying degrees—the collective
thoughts, viewpoints, experiences and influence of the greatest of
these "prophets of air power" became a sort of "playbook" for the
future leaders of the United States Army Air arm in the looming
second world war.

*   *   *

Trenchard, Mitchell, and Douhet were not the only prophets of
air power in the era of its coming of age between the world wars.
They were the ones whom historians have identified persistently as
the figures whose ideas most influenced the development of long-
range strategic air forces by the only two nations possessing them in
World War II. Their legacies continue in the modern era.

With the war raging in Europe and the Army Air Corps in a rapid
expansion mode in this country, in mid-summer of 1941—the Tac
School was closed. By this time a doctrine of air bombardment—

notably with the Eighth Air Force—was in place. Earlier, the Air Corps' most active proponent of the pursuit/fighter doctrine, Major Claire Chennault, had left the Tactical School and resigned from the United States Army and departed for China where he headed air operations for the Chinese government against the Japanese. Later, he formed the Flying Tigers and ultimately commanded the U.S. Fourteenth Air Force with the rank of major general. In his book *The Quest*, General Hansell concluded: "Independent strategic air action against a hostile industrial nation would achieve the ultimate aim of destroying the will of an enemy to resist."

EXCERPT OF ORAL HISTORY OF
MAJOR GENERAL ROBERT W. BURNS USAF, MARCH 1979
(Group Commander, Eighth Air Force)

"I could talk about the ETO and the lessons you learn and the exposures you had, the sights, the sounds, the emotions. The emotion is a thing that is awfully hard to describe but the emotions of that particular combat situation, I suspect, are fairly unique. The Germans were pretty efficient as a fighting force. And while living conditions in England were not the world's worst by any manner or means, the weather was. And to get up at 2:30 or 3 o'clock on a cold, dreary, foggy, or rainy English morning, stumbling around in the dark, eating the rations we had, you know, powdered eggs, spam, all this sort of stuff, in preparation to going down and getting in the airplane and hauling off through that miserable weather into combat over Germany took its toll. . . ."

"The fact that we had so many who didn't throw in the towel, who were able to weather it and retain their emotional stability, I think speaks pretty well of the general stability of the American population we were dealing with in those days. There was no reluctance to do the hard chores; there was no reluctance or outward reluctance to expose yourself to this sort of combat. There was never a question in anybody's mind that, I don't want to do it. None of us wanted to do it, but we did it."

MEMORIES OF GERMAN PRISONER-OF-WAR CAMP

By A. Edward "Abe" Wilen
453rd Bomb Group, Eighth Air Force, Ex-POW

Andy Low led our 453rd Bomb Group and we in turn led the entire Eighth Air Force on a mission to Brunswick, Germany on May 8, 1944. We were badly hit by fighters and our plane went down. Four of us from original crew #8, pilot Dick Witton, copilot Buck Croxford, bombardier Walt Conneely and myself, navigator Abe Wilen, wound up in Stalag Luft III, where the "Great Escape" took place. Seventy-six men tunneled out of our camp. Seventy-three were captured and fifty of them were executed on Hitler's orders. They were cremated, ashes put in urns and returned to us with the warning that this would be the fate of anyone trying to escape.

Andy went down July 29 and after sixteen days in the hospital, joined us at Stalag Luft III, but in another compound. We experienced numbing cold while waiting hours in soup lines, pelted by sleet, feet numb and fingers nearly frozen.

We suffered through loss of freedom, loss of dignity, loss of hope, fear of never being free again, of never again seeing our families. Our guards stated that if they won the war we would spend the rest of our lives as slave labor rebuilding the cities we bombed out and if they lost, they had orders to execute us all.

On January 27, 1945 at a staff meeting, Adolph Hitler issued the order to evacuate Stalag Luft III. He was fearful that 10,000 Allied airmen would be liberated by the Russians who were only twenty kilometers from our camp. The order triggered an ordeal that would be frozen for life into the psyches of every POW who survived it—blizzard conditions, bitter cold (at times going down as low as sixteen degrees below zero). Icy winds penetrated our clothes and froze our shoes stiff on our feet. We started out with the warning that anyone trying to escape would be shot.

We covered 35 miles in 27 hours, then stumbled into a tile factory to thaw out for 30 hours. We continued on for 15.5 miles to a railroad yard where we were jammed into cattle cars—at least sixty men into a car that at best could hold forty. Here we split. Croxford and Conneely went on to Stalag 7A in Moosburg. Andy, Witton and I went on to 13D which was a mile outside the railroad yards in Nuremberg.

On the ride we sweated out bombings and strafing from our own planes. The only air in the cars was through cracks in the wall planks. We had to alternate sitting and standing. Men were sick with dysentery and nausea and with no toilet facilities and with the doors locked, the stench became horrendous.

In Nuremberg, the barracks crawled with all types of vermin. It was cold and damp. No indoor toilets, only an open pot at the end of the hall. We existed through the worst winter with little food, minimal clothes, no medical supplies or facilities. We were fighting dampness, chill, nausea, dysentery and fearful of getting a critical illness with no strength or medicine to fight back.

Being beside the railroad yards, our own planes bombed us day and night. The night bombing by the British kept us in constant fear. They dropped on flares and the enemy put other flares around to create confusion. Bombs were dropping all around us and in our midst. One barracks was hit and suffered casualties.

At the beginning of April as Gen. Patton's Third Army headed our way, the Germans evacuated us and headed us on a march south to rejoin our crew members in Stalag 7A in Moosburg, near Munich and the infamous concentration death camp Dachau. We marched 90 miles in 10 days. En route we were strafed by our own planes who thought we were enemy troops. We dove for the ditches many times until we tore up white fabrics and spelled out POW beside the road.

At Moosburg we were jammed with 130,000 other Allied prisoners in a camp built for 14,000. As we were the last ones in, Andy, Witton and myself were in tents next to the perimeter and were in a great position to see the Third Army tanks come in to liberate us April 29, 1945. We all cheered wildly when the Nazi flag came down and "Old Glory" went up in place and when Gen. Patton came in and gave us a welcome back speech.

Reprint: Lib. Men of Old Buc.

JIMMY: THE QUINTESSENTIAL AIRMAN

Remarks of Colonel Starr Smith (Air Force Reserve, Retired) at Brigadier General James Maitland Stewart's Memorial Dedication on October 1, 1999, at the Mighty Eighth Air Force Heritage Museum, Savannah, Georgia:

In September of 1945, Colonel Jimmy Stewart came home to America aboard the Queen Elizabeth. The war in Europe had been over since May of that year, and, now, the majestic British luxury liner, converted into a troop ship early in the war, was bringing the boys home. Jimmy's mother and father, Alex and Bessie, had come to New York from their Indiana, Pennsylvania family home to welcome their son. But they had to wait for a while at the St. Regis Hotel—because Colonel Stewart shook the hand and said farewell to all of his men as they stepped off the Queen Elizabeth.

Almost two years earlier, Captain Jimmy Stewart—flying a B-24 Liberator bomber—had led his squadron of the 445th Bomb Group from Sioux City, Iowa to England—by way of Florida, Puerto Rico, the islands of the Caribbean, and on to Brazil. There, they flew across the South Atlantic to Senegal in Africa, and on to Marrakesh in Morocco. From there, Captain Stewart and his crew flew out over the Atlantic—in order to avoid the German fighter planes based in that dangerous zone.

After the long over-water flight, they landed in England. The 445th's new home was at Tibenham, in East Anglia, on the North Sea, not far from London. It was then that Captain Stewart joined the Eighth Air Force. It was a fortuitous encounter—with far-reaching implications—for the Eighth was then emerging as the most powerful aerial war machine the world had ever known. Thus, this mighty organization became Stewart's military home for almost two years. And, actually, the Eighth Air Force was Stewart's emotional home for the rest of his life. Years later, he would tell an interviewer that World War II was the greatest experience of his life. The interviewer said, "Greater than the movies?" And Stewart said, "Much greater."

In the space of time—that the Liberator landed at Tibenham, and the arrival of the Queen Elizabeth in New York—Jimmy Stewart had been in the uniform of his country, on constant combat duty with the Eighth Air Force for almost two years. He had entered military service in March of 1941 as a private.

In March, 1945, he was promoted to full colonel—thus becoming one of the few men in American history to rise from private to full colonel in little more than four years time.

The road from an induction station in California to a bomber base in England was not easy for Jimmy Stewart. In 1940, he was 32 years old. He had been turned down by the draft: "Underweight." Still, Stewart was determined. The war was not going well for England. Ed Murrow told that bleak story in his dramatic "This Is London" broadcasts, and Stewart's British friends were leaving Hollywood to go home to enlist. Stewart stood resolute and firm. He was determined to join the fight. He gained the necessary weight, and was accepted by the army—almost a year before Pearl Harbor. Stewart was already a pilot, owned an airplane, and had over 300 flying hours in his log book. Now, at 33, he was too old for the army's flying schools for younger students. But, as a private, he embarked on an intensive schedule of the old Air Corps flying instruction and ground school work. Stewart won his silver pilot's wings and second lieutenant's commission in late January of 1942.

After Stewart's commission came through, the long, hard months of training began—checking out on twin-engine aircraft, flying bombardier students, graduating from the B-17 transitional school, and serving as an instructor pilot in B-17s. All the while, Stewart desperately wanted an overseas combat assignment. But there was a roadblock: It seemed that nobody wanted to take the responsibility of sending a famous American movie star into combat. Finally, after months of instructor flying, in dangerous weather in Idaho, he found a friend. His commanding officer, Colonel Walter "Pop" Arnold, recommended him to Colonel Bob Terrill, who had his 445th group of B-24 Liberators in third phase training in Sioux City, Iowa. Terrill took Stewart, a captain, as a squadron operations officer, and within a month promoted him to squadron commander. At long last, Stewart was headed for the fighting, and after months of training and training others, he felt that he was ready.

Shortly after Stewart came to the 445th, this notation appeared in the group history: "When Captain Jimmy Stewart came to the group, we didn't know what to think about this movie star in our midst. But he turned out to be a regular guy."

Jimmy Stewart flew twenty combat missions against the enemy in Europe. He ended a distinguished career with over 2,000 flying hours. His wartime record reads like this: Squadron Commander in 445th Bomb Group—Group Operations Officer, 453rd Bomb Group—Operations Officer, 2nd Bomb Wing—Chief of Staff, 2nd Bomb Wing, and, finally, as World War II ended, Commander of the 2nd Bomb Wing.

Stewart spent his entire time overseas in World War II flying the B-24 Liberator in combat with units of the 2nd Bomb Wing of the Eighth Air Force, promoted up the ladder from squadron commander to wing commander, and flying on many missions as command pilot. Stewart served in the Air Force Reserve as a colonel from 1945 until President Eisenhower appointed him to Brigadier General in 1959 in the Air Force Reserve. He retired in 1968. Jimmy Stewart was awarded the Presidential Medal of Freedom in 1985.

Colonel James M. Stewart wore the ribbons of valor in wartime—the Distinguished Flying Cross with two Oak Leaf Clusters, the Air Medal with three Oak Leaf Clusters, and the Croix

Stewart is decorated by the French government with the Croix de Guerre, January 29, 1945.

de Guerre from the French government. Stewart's first Distinguished Flying Cross was presented by Eighth Air Force Commander General Jimmy Doolittle, himself the holder of the Medal of Honor for his historic Tokyo Raid, earlier in the war. Stewart's citation read, in part:

"For extraordinary achievement while serving as Deputy Leader of a Combat Wing formation on a bombing mission over Germany . . . In spite of aggressive fighter attacks and, later, heavy, accurate, antiaircraft fire, Major Stewart was able to hold the formation together and direct a bombing run over the target. . . . The courage, leadership, and skillful airmanship displayed by Major Stewart were, in large measure, responsible for the success of the mission."

As I stand before you here today, I believe Jimmy Stewart would be very proud of this magnificent museum—this historic repository—a lasting tribute to his thousands of comrades-in-arms, men and women, who served in the Eighth Air Force in World War II. Three years ago, the museum created an annual award for outstanding airmanship, and named it in Jimmy Stewart's honor. It is proper and fitting that this building will stand forever as a memorial for the warriors of the air who fought for America in World War II. To paraphrase a great American newspaper, *The Denver Post*: "Ah, love of country, devotion to duty, honor and courage—when expelled from all other haunts—make the Mighty Eighth Air Force Heritage Museum—thy Dwelling Place."

So today, as we are gathered at this time and in this place, only a few miles from the birthplace of the Eighth Air Force—Jimmy Stewart's military and emotional home—I have the unforgettable pleasure—in the name of human decency, patriotism, and, above all, honor, love of country, and courage under fire—to dedicate this memorial to the memory of a brave and a remarkable American, Brig. Gen. James Maitland Stewart.

THE QUIET AMERICAN HERO FLEW B-24s!
By John Harold Robinson (445th)

We have witnessed the passing of one of America's really great citizens, Jimmy Stewart. He wasn't an actor as most people saw him, he was just himself, "Jimmy Stewart."

"The Quiet American Hero" is what the Queen of England called James Stewart in the fiftieth anniversary Battle of Britain Queen's Ball Brochure in London in 1990.

Jimmy Stewart was as much a success in war with the United States Army Air Force as he became on the silver screen. Jimmy Stewart rose from the ranks of private to colonel during the war years to 1945 and later to Brigadier General in 1959.

Jimmy Stewart never spoke openly or in depth about his wartime service. He once said, "Uh!, I just did what everybody else did."

Yes! Stewart trained for heavy bomber service on B-17 heavy bombers at Hobbs Field with thirty others who graduated. One of those thirty was my pilot, George Wright, who was in the class with him. Stewart went on to Salt Lake City and Boise, Idaho and then became Squadron Commander on B-24 heavy bombers of the 703rd Squadron, 445th Bomb Group in Sioux City, Iowa.

Now those of us of the original B-24 703rd Squadron of 1943/44 knew of his deeds, his sincerity to win the war. He was our leader, our commander; his dedication to God and his country just rubbed off on you. Stewart felt that everyone must do his part to bring down the tyranny in this world. At the same time, the compassion and feeling that Stewart carried for each of the 120 combat air crewmen under his command made each one of us feel that he really was our big brother and at times like a mother hen looking over us, making us all feel that we would follow him through anything in this war.

My personal experience with Captain Stewart began in Sioux City, Iowa when my crew (Lt. George Wright, pilot) was transferred from Pocatello, Idaho to Sioux City, 703rd Squadron, on very short notice. We were to replace a crew that had crashed. I was the aerial engineer.

Arriving in the evening of 1 September 1943 all ten of us entered and crowded into a small office on the flight line. There sat behind a small desk a long, lanky officer in flight fatigues with lieutenant bars on his collar. (Later I understood he was a captain.) After a few words of welcoming us to the 703rd, this officer stood up halfway from his chair, rubbed his chin and stated, "Well uh! See that water tank up there? Uh! you are replacing a crew that hit it last week; please kind-Uh! be careful and don't hit it. We just can't lose another B-24." The next statement was, "How would you fellows like to have about five days at home?" Well, that question didn't need an answer. "You can pick up your travel orders and Uh! papers at Headquarters." Then he said, "Well Uh! Fellows be sure and get back here in five days." With a quick salute, out the door we went. Stewart returned the salute but his hand didn't quite make it to his head. Maybe it was just because it was just too far up.

From that day on, being associated with Jimmy Stewart until 31 March 1944, as I look back on all the events of that time, it was really like living with Jimmy Stewart on the silver screen in one big movie.

James Stewart was one person that if his life ever touched yours, you could never forget him. Well, maybe some of the feelings that Stewart had for our crew had something to do with George Wright's father and James Stewart's father growing up together as good friends. James Stewart was always giving George Wright a fatherly talking to and flight checks to see if we knew our job and would fly as a crew. Stewart wanted and personally saw to it that each individual under his command knew how to do his job, and he expected it to be done well. That was James "Jimmy" Stewart.

There were so many events and quotes during the period that I was associated with Jimmy Stewart from 1 September 1943 to 31 March 1944 when Stewart was transferred to the 453rd as an Operation Officer. While Stewart was Squadron Commander of the 703rd, you didn't know until the last minute if Jimmy Stewart was going to fly the mission. He would just come out in combat clothes and get in one of the trucks.

After our arrival at Tibenham, England on 25 November 1943, we prepared for the group's first mission on 13 December 1943. The target was Kiel, Germany. Jimmy Stewart flew his first mission as copilot on Lt. Cook's aircraft 42-75559. Jimmy Stewart had to fly the first mission that the 703rd Squadron flew. That was Jimmy Stewart!

The missions my crew, with Lt. George Wright, flew in a position either under and behind Jimmy Stewart's aircraft tail or on his left wing. George was usually lead of the second echelon with his nose within ten feet of the first echelon lead aircraft tail. Stewart would tell Wright to stay out of his tail. (Wright had the ability to put an aircraft within inches of another and stay there in flight.)

James Stewart was made a major, and was transferred over to the 453rd Bomb Group as Operations Officer on March 31, 1944. At that time in the 703rd there were 71 officers and 433 enlisted men, fifteen aircraft under Jimmy Stewart's command.

All of us in the 703rd felt that we had lost a part of us with the loss of our commander Jimmy Stewart. The empty void that it left made you feel that now you were really on your own to get through this conflict.

I flew many other missions that Jimmy Stewart did not fly. One can see by the above list of enemy targets that Stewart had selected to fly missions that Headquarters was not very happy about.

They were concerned for his safety. Eventually he was transferred to an Operations Officer position in another group. But he continued to fly combat.

In 1988 I wrote a manuscript and put it into a book, *A Reason to Live*, in which many of my encounters with Jimmy Stewart are told. I received several letters from Stewart during this time, and afterward he autographed a photo of himself that I had taken with a box Brownie camera in 1943. I sent him six copies and he autographed five of the copies with a note, one for each of my three daughters and one for my son. He also autographed one for me, and he kept the other.

No book can relate all the feelings and sayings that James "Jimmy" Stewart expressed for the men he went to war with. As he said, "I was only doing the job that everyone else was doing."

Yes! James "Jimmy" Stewart was "The Quiet American Hero," and he did fly B-24s in combat—for I was there!

Author's Note: John Harold "Robbie" Robinson, author of A Reason to Live, *flew thirty missions officially, and four others over enemy territory that didn't count. Nine missions were missions that Stewart flew.*

THE FALCON FOUNDATION

3116 Academy Drive
Suite 200
USAF Academy, CO 80840-4480

February 24, 2003

Colonel Starr Smith
Montgomery, AL 36101

Dear Colonel Smith:

I have searched our old files regarding contributions James "Jimmy" Stewart made to the Falcon Foundation. It appears he donated his U.S. Air Force retired pay starting in July 1968 through November 1992. In 1983, the Falcon Foundation established a scholarship funded in perpetuity in Jimmy Stewart's honor—brochure attached. This scholarship is awarded to a young person each year to help them compete for an appointment to the U.S. Air Force Academy.

The formal dedication of the James "Jimmy" Stewart Falcon Foundation Scholarship was held on October 28, 1983 at the Officers' Club, United States Air Force Academy. The Secretary of the Air Force, the Chief of Staff of the Air Force and the cadets in all four classes who were Falcon Foundation Scholarship recipients were among those in attendance. A portrait of Jimmy Stewart was presented to the Superintendent of the Air Force Academy to hang in the Hall of Great Airmen in Fairchild Hall.

Sincerely,
Pearl L. Swofford

Pearl L. Swofford
Executive Assistant to the President

BRIEF SKETCH OF JIMMY STEWART'S
WARTIME CAREER

After Stewart's commission in January 1942, he completed basic and advanced flight training and was flying instructor in AT-9s, Advanced Trainers—Mather Field. Second Lieutenant—Instructor—until August 1942.

Flew bombardiers at Bombardier Training School, Kirtland Field, Albuquerque, New Mexico. First Lieutenant—Pilot—from August–December 1942.

Attended Four-Engine Training School at Hobbs, New Mexico.—First Lieutenant—Pilot—from December 1942–February 1943.

From Hobbs, he went to Gowen Field in Boise, Idaho, as a B-17 instructor and became Operations Officer during a nine-month period at that station. Captain—Flying instructor—February–August 1943.

Major Jimmy Stewart, operations officer, awaits the returning mission at the control tower at Old Buc in 1944.

He then was transferred to Sioux City, Iowa to the 445th Bomb Group (H), commanded by Colonel Robert Terrill. Captain—Squadron Commander 703rd Bomb Squadron—August 1943–November 1943.

He took his squadron to England on November 10, 1943, across the South Atlantic to the 445th Station at Tibenham. He arrived in England on November 23, 1943. Major—Squadron Commander—November 1943–March 1944.

Transferred to the 453rd Bomb Group (H)—Old Buckenham—Group Operations Officer—March 31–June 30, 1944.

Headquarters 2nd Combat Wing (H), 2nd Division, Eighth Air Force—Major–Lieutenant Colonel, Chief of Staff at Hethel—July 1 to December 1944.

Lieutenant Colonel—Operations Officer—Headquarters 2nd Combat Bomb Wing (H)—Hethel—December 1944–January 1945.

Colonel—Chief of Staff—Headquarters 2nd Combat Bomb Wing (H)—Hethel—January–May 1945.

Colonel—Commander—Headquarters 2nd Combat Bomb Wing (H) Hethel—May–June 1945.

Colonel—Commander—2nd Combat Bomb Wing (H) at Hethel—June–August 1945.

Appointed Colonel in Air Force Reserve—September, 1945.

DECORATIONS

Distinguished Flying Cross with one Oak Leaf Cluster
    April 1944 for bombing mission over Germany 2-20-44
    April 1944—OLC

Air Medal with three Oak Leaf Clusters
 February 1944
 March 1944—OLC
 March 1945—OLC

Army Commendation Ribbon
American Campaign Medal

European, African, Middle-Eastern Campaign Medal with
six Bronze Service Stars

Croix de Guerre with Palm
 January 29, 1945

Distinguished Service Medal
 June 1, 1968

Promotions
 Commissioned Second Lieutenant—January 19, 1942
 First Lieutenant—July 7, 1942
 Captain—July 9, 1943
 Major—January 20, 1944
 Lieutenant Colonel—June 3, 1944
 Colonel—March 29, 1945
 Colonel (AC Res)—September 28, 1945
 Colonel USAFR—January 30, 1953
 Brigadier General—July 23, 1959

Retired June 1, 1968

Served a total of 27 years, 2 months, 9 days
 (57 months, active duty)
 (22 months in ETO)

WHERE THEY ARE NOW

General H. H. "Hap" Arnold, Chief of Staff of the Army Air Force, wearing the five-star insignia of General of the Air Force, retired from active duty in 1946. He died in 1950 at 64.

General Carl "Tooey" Spaatz, first Chief of Staff of the United States Air Force, and commander of the Army Air Force (AAF) in Europe in World War II, retired from active duty in 1950 as a four-star general and died in 1974 at 82.

General Ira Eaker, "Father of the Eighth Air Force" and former commander of the Eighth and Fifteenth in Europe in World War II, retired from active duty in 1947 and died in 1987 at 91 as a four-star general.

General Jimmy Doolittle, former commander of the Eighth Air Force, retired from active duty in 1946 and died in 1992 at 97 as a four-star general.

Major General Frederick L. "Fred" Anderson, former deputy for operations at USSTAF (Spaatz headquarters in Europe in World War II) and former chief of personnel for the Army Air Force in Washington after World War II, retired from active duty in 1947 to embark on a civilian business career, and died in 1969.

Brigadier General Edward "Ted" Timberlake, former commander of the 2nd Combat Bomb Wing in the ETO, retired from the USAF in 1964 with the rank of Lieutenant General. He died in 1992.

Colonel Robert "Bob" Terrill, former commander of the 445th Bomb Group in the ETO and Jimmy Stewart's first commander in the Eighth Air Force retired from active duty in 1964 and died in 1992. He retired as lieutenant general.

Colonel Ramsay Potts, former commander of the 453rd Bomb Group in the ETO, and former director of bomber operations for the Eighth Air Force (a reserve officer) returned to civilian life after World War II, attended Harvard Law School and became an attorney in Washington, D.C., where he is now in semi-retirement. He was inducted into the prestigious "Gathering Of Eagles" at Maxwell Air Force Base in 2000.

Colonel Walter "Pop" Arnold, former commander of 29th Training Group in Boise, Idaho, and former commander of 485th Bomb Group in Italy, retired in 1968 with rank of major general and died in February of 2002.

Major Andrew S. "Andy" Low, Jimmy Stewart's assistant operations officer (and later operations officer) at 453rd Bomb Group at Old Buc (former POW) and author of *The Liberator Men of Old Buc*, retired from the USAF as a major general in 1971 and embarked on a successful career in the academic world, and remained until his death a close friend of Jimmy Stewart and constant supporter of the Eighth Air Force and especially the "liberator men of Old Buc." He died in 2001.

S/Sergeant John Harold "Robbie" Robinson, gunner on the Wright crew of 445th Bomb Group in ETO and friend of Jimmy Stewart during and after World War II. Flew 30 bombing missions with 445th, returned home

Robbie Robinson wearing his flight jacket in Colliersville, Tennessee, many years after the war.

and civilian life in Memphis, Tennessee, resumed his career as an engineer, and wrote his wartime book, *A Reason to Live.* "Robbie" maintained his friendship with Jimmy Stewart until Stewart's death in 1997. He is now retired, active in air force affairs, and lives with wife, Elizabeth, in Collierville, Tennessee—near Memphis.

Note: Of the five AAF officers of World War II who guided and directed Jimmy Stewart's wartime career and who, also, became his friends— "Pop" Arnold, Terrill, Potts, Low, and Timberlake—only Ramsay Potts is still alive. During and after the war, Andy Low was closest to Stewart, and Potts saw him frequently in Washington before his death. Potts, Low, and Starr Smith had a weekend together at the Jimmy Stewart Museum in his hometown shortly after his death.

BIBLIOGRAPHY

Arnold, Elliott. *Blood Brother*. Duell, Sloan & Pearce, 1947.

Arnold, H. H. *Global Mission*. Harper & Brothers, New York, 1949.

Bach, Steven. *Marlene Dietrich: Life and Legend*. William Morrow, 1992.

Bacon, James. *Made in Hollywood*. Contemporary Books, 1977.

———. *It's A Wonderful Life Book*. Alfred A. Knopf, 1986.

Bliss, Edward, Jr. *In Search of Light: The Broadcasts of Edward R. Murrow 1938–1961*.

Bradley, Omar and Clay Blair. *A General's Life*. Simon and Schuster, 1983.

Burns, James MacGregor. *Roosevelt: Soldier of Freedom 1940–1945*. (1970).

Butcher, Harry. *My Three Years with Eisenhower*. Simon and Schuster, 1946.

Butler, Lord. *The Churchill Years*. Viking Press, 1965.

Butterfield, Roger. *FDR*. Harper & Row, 1948.

Caidin, Martin. *Black Thursday: The Story of the Schweinfurt Raid*. Ballantine, 1960.

Carter, Violet Bonham. *Winston Churchill: An Intimate Portrait*. Harcourt, Brace, 1965.

Catledge, Turner. *My Life and The Times*. Harper & Row, 1971.

Chisholm, Anne and Michael Davie. *Lord Beaverbrook*. Alfred A. Knopf, 1993.

Churchill, Winston. *The Second World War*. Volumes: 1–6. Houghton Mifflin, 1949.

Cloud, Stanley and Lynne Olson. *The Murrow Boys*. Houghton Mifflin, 1996.

Collier, Peter. *The Fondas: A Hollywood Dynasty*. G.P. Putnam's Sons, 1991.

———. *Margaret Sullavan: Child of Fate*. St. Martin's, 1986.

Colville, John. *Winston Churchill*. Wyndham Books, 1981.

Davis, Richard G. *Carl A. Spaatz and the Air War in Europe.* Smithsonian Press, 1992.

De Havilland, Olivia. *Every Frenchman Has One.* Random House, 1961.

The Development of Air Doctrine in the Army Air Arm 1917–1941. Office of Air Force History, USAF, Washington, 1985.

Doolittle, Jimmy. *I Could Never Be So Lucky Again* with Carroll V. Glines. Bantam Books, 1991.

Editors. *Page One*: Major Events 1920–1975 Presented in the *New York Times.*

Eisenhower, Dwight D. *Crusade in Europe.* Doubleday, 1948.

Eyles, Allen. *Jimmy Stewart.* Stein & Day, 1984.

Fairbanks, Douglas, Jr. *A Hell of a War.* St. Martin's Press, 1993.

Finney, Robert T. *History of the Air Corps Tactical School 1920–1940.* (1992.)

Fitzgerald, F. Scott. *The Great Gatsby.* Charles Scribner's Sons, 1925.

Fonda, Henry (Howard Teichmann). *My Life.* New American Library, 1981.

Freeman, Roger A. *The Mighty Eighth: A History of the Eighth Air Force.* Doubleday, 1970.

Frost, David and Antony Jay. *The English.* Stern and Day, 1967.

Fussell, Paul. *Wartime: Understanding and Behavior in the Second World War.* Oxford University Press, 1989.

Gingold, Hermione. *How to Grow Old Disgracefully.* St. Martin's Press, 1988.

Glines, Carroll V. *I Could Never Be So Lucky Again: General James H. Doolittle.* Bantam Books, 1991.

————. *The Compact History of the United States Air Force.* Hawthorn Books, New York, 1963.

Granholm, Jackson. *The Day We Bombed Switzerland.* Airlife Publishising, 2002.

Griffith, Charles. *The Quest: Haywood Hansell and American Strategic Bombing in World War II.* Air University Press, 1999.

Grunwald, Henry. *One Man's America.* Doubleday, 1997.

Hall, Grover C., Jr. *1000 Destroyed: The Life and Times of the 4th Fighter Group*. Hero Publishing, 1978.

Hall, R. Cargill. *Case Studies in Strategic Bombardment*. Air Force History & Museum Program, 1998.

Harris, Sir Arthur "Bomber". *Bomber Offensive*. Collins, London, 1947.

Hayward, Brooke. *Haywire*. Alfred A. Knopf, New York, 1977.

Heston, Charlton. *In the Arena*. Simon & Schuster, 1995.

Higham, Charles. *The Life of Marlene Dietrich*. Norton, 1977.

Houston, John W. *American Air Power Comes of Age: Gen. H. H. Arnold's World War II Diaries*. Volumes: I and II. Air University Press, 2002.

Jenkins, Roy. *Churchill: A Biography*. Farrar, Straus & Giroux, 2001.

Johnson, Pamela Hansford. *Hungry Gulliver: A Critical Appraisal of Thomas Wolfe*. Charles Scribner's, New York, 1948.

The Journal of Military History. Vol. 66, #4, 2002. Bruce Vandervort, Editor.

Kaltenborn, H. V. *Fifty Fabulous Years: 1900–1950*. G. P. Putnam Sons, 1950.

Keegan, John. *The Second World War*. Viking Penguin, 1990.

Kendrick, Alexander. *Prime Time: The Life of Edward R. Murrow*. Little Brown, 1969.

Kennedy, David M. *Freedom from Fear*. Oxford University Press, 1999.

LeMay, Curtis and McKinley Cantor. *Mission with LeMay: My Story*. Doubleday, 1965.

Liebling, A. J. (Joe). *The Road Back to Paris*. Modern Library (Random House), 1939.

Logan, Joshua. *Josh: My Ups and Downs, In and Out of Life*. Delacorte Press, New York, 1976.

Low, Andy. *The Liberator Men of Old Buc: The Story of the 453rd Bombardment Group*. 1979.

Luskin, John. *Lippman, Liberty, and the Press*. University of Alabama Press, 1972.

Maurer, Maurer. *Air Force Combat Units of World War II*. Air University–Franklin Watts, New York. USAF Historical Division.

McBrien, William. *Cole Porter: A Biography*. Alfred A. Knopf, 1998.

McFarland, Stephen and Wesley P. Newton. *To Command the Sky*. Smithsonian Press, 1991.

Meredith, Burgess. *So Far, So Good: A Memoir*. Little Brown, Boston, 1994.

Mets, David R. *Master of Airpower: Gen. Carl A. Spaatz*. Presidio Press, 1988.

Mosher, Leonard. *Marshall: Hero of Our Times*. Hearst Books, New York, 1982.

Newton, Wesley P. (with Stephen McFarland). *To Command the Sky*. Smithsonian Press, 1991.

The Official Pictorial History of the AAF. Duell, Sloan & Pearce, New York, 1947.

Overy, R. J. *The Air War—1939–1945*. Stern & Day, 1980.

Parton, James. *Air Force Spoken Here: Gen. Ira Eaker and the Command of the Air*. Adler & Adler, 1986.

Persico, Joseph E. *Edward R. Murrow: An American Original*. McGraw Hill, 1988.

————. *Roosevelt's Secret War*. Random House, New York, 2001.

Pickard, Roy. *Jimmy Stewart*. St. Martin's Press, 1992.

Rauch, Basil. *The Roosevelt Reader*. Rinehart & Co. 1957.

Reston, James (Scotty). *Deadline: A Memoir*. Random House, 1991.

Robbins, Jhan. *A Biography of Jimmy Stewart: Everybody's Man*. Paperback, Putnam & Sons, New York, 1985.

Robinson, John Harold "Robbie." *A Reason to Live: Moments of Love, Happiness and Sorrow*. Castle Books, Memphis, Tennessee, 1988.

Rogers, Ginger. *My Story*. Harper Collins, 1991.

Schlesinger, Arthur M., Jr. *The Age of Roosevelt*. Volumes: 1–3.

Smith, Margaret Chase. *Declaration of Conscience*. Doubleday, 1972.

Smith, Starr. *Only the Days Are Long: Reports of a Journalist and World Traveler*. Yoknapatawpha Press, 1986.

Sperber, A. M. *Murrow*. Freundlich Books, 1986.

Stafford, Jean. *The Press—A. J. Liebling.* Ballantine Books, 1961–64–75.

Stewart, Carroll and James Dugan. *Ploesti.* Random House, 1962.

Stewart, Carroll. *Ted's Traveling Circus.* Sun World Communications, Lincoln, Nebraska, 1996.

Sulzberger, Cyrus L. *A Long Row of Candles.* Macmillan, New York, 1969.

————. *American Heritage Pictorial History of World War II.* Simon & Schuster.

Thompson, Inspector Walter Henry. *Assignment Churchill.* Farrar, Straus and Young, 1955.

Toye, Donald C. *Flight from Munich.* Northwest Publishing, Salt Lake City, Utah, 1993.

Vidal, Gore. *Palimpsest: A Memoir.* Random House, 1995.

Weiner, Ed. *Let's Go To Press: A Biography of Walter Winchell.* G.P. Putnam's Sons, 1955.

White, Theodore H. *In Search of History: A Personal Adventure.* Warner Books, 1978.

Winchell, Walter. *Winchell Exclusive.* Prentice-Hall, 1975.

Wolfe, Thomas. *You Can't Go Home Again.* Perennial Library, 1973

Woodward, Bob. *The Commanders.* Pocket Books, Simon & Schuster, 1991.

Ziegler, Philip. *London at War.* Alfred A. Knopf, 1995.

PERIODICALS AND NEWS SOURCES

Albuquerque Journal
Associated Press
Boise Statesman
Chicago Sun-Times
Chicago Tribune
Columbia Broadcasting System
  (CBS)
Sheila Graham Syndicated
  Newspaper Column
Hedda Hopper Syndicated
  Newspaper Column
Hollywood Reporter
Houston Chronicle
Indiana Gazette
Jackson Daily News
LIFE—Sept. 24, 1945
London Daily Telegraph
Los Angeles Times
Louella Parsons Syndicated
  Newspaper Column
Magnolia Gazette
McCalls—May 1964
Montgomery Advertiser
New Orleans Times-Picayune
New York Daily Mirror
New York Herald-Tribune
New York Post
New York Times
Newsweek—Sept. 2, 1957
North American Newspaper
  Association

Parade Magazine
Pittsburgh Post-Gazette
Salt Lake City Desert News
San Francisco Chronicle
San Francisco Examiner
Saturday Evening Post
  Colonel Beirne Lay, Jr.
    September 8, 15—1945
Saturday Evening Post
  Pete Martin (5-part series)
    in Feb. and March, 1961
Second Air Division Journal
  Ray Pytel, Editor
Time
Times of London
United Press
Washington Post
Washington Star

INDEX

Starr Smith is an international journalist and author who has chronicled his adventures to more than one hundred countries. Smith was a combat intelligence officer with the Eighth Air Force in England during World War II, and later served on General Eisenhower's press staff at his London and Paris headquarters.

After the war, Smith worked with the military's top brass, including Anderson, Arnold, Doolittle, Eaker, Kenney, Spaatz, and other great World War II leaders and generals. He has been a correspondent for NBC Radio, a reporter for *Newsweek*, and his byline has appeared in newspapers and magazines from six continents.

Smith's other books include *Only the Days are Long* and *Starr Smith's Southern Scenes*. He lives in Montgomery, Alabama.